WHERE DOES MONEY COME FR...

A GUIDE TO THE UK MONETARY A...

JOSH RYAN-COLLINS
TONY GREENHAM
RICHARD WERNER
ANDREW JACKSON

FOREWORD BY
CHARLES A.E. GOODHART

NEW
ECONOMICS
FOUNDATION

Where Does Money Come From?
Second edition published in Great Britain in 2012 by
the New Economics Foundation.

Reprinted 2011

The moral right of Josh Ryan-Collins, Tony Greenham, Richard Werner
and Andrew Jackson to be identified as the authors of this work has been
asserted by them in accordance with the Copyright, Designs and Patents
Acts of 1988.

Every effort has been made to trace or contact all copyright holders.
The publishers will be pleased to make good any omissions or rectify
any mistakes brought to their attention at the earliest opportunity.

British Library Cataloguing in Publication Data. A catalogue record
for this book is available from the British Library.

ISBN: 9781521043899

New Economics Foundation
10 Salamanca Place
London
SE1 7HB
www.neweconomics.org

Acknowledgements

The authors would like to thank Ben Dyson for his valuable contributions to the writing of this book.

We are also most grateful to Professor Victoria Chick, Jon Relleen, James Meadway, Professor Charles Goodhart, Mark Burton and Sue Charman for their helpful insights and comments.

Our thanks go to Angie Greenham for invaluable assistance with editing, proofing and production control and to Peter Greenwood at The Departure Lounge for design and layout.

Finally, we would like to express our gratitude to James Bruges and Marion Wells, without whom the book would not have been written.

CONTENTS

LIST OF EXPLANATORY BOXES

Appendices

LIST OF FIGURES, CHARTS AND GRAPHS

LIST OF T-CHARTS

Foreword

Far from money being 'the root of all evil', our economic system cannot cope without it. Hence the shock-horror when the Lehman failure raised the spectre of an implosion of our banking system. It is far nearer the truth to claim that 'Evil is the root of all money', a witty phrase coined by Nobu Kiyotaki and John Moore.

If we all always paid our bills in full with absolute certainty, then everyone could buy anything on his/her own credit, by issuing an IOU on him/herself. Since that happy state of affairs is impossible, (though assumed to their detriment in most standard macro-models), we use – as money – the short-term ('sight') claim on the most reliable (powerful) debtor. Initially, of course, this powerful debtor was the Government; note how the value of State money collapses when the sovereign power is overthrown. Coins are rarely full-bodied and even then need guaranteeing by the stamp of the ruler seigniorage. However, there were severe disadvantages in relying solely on the Government to provide sufficient money for everyone to use; perhaps most importantly, people could not generally borrow from the Government. So, over time, we turned to a set of financial intermediaries: the banks, to provide us both with an essential source of credit and a reliable, generally safe and acceptable monetary asset.

Such deposit money was reliable and safe because all depositors reckoned that they could always exchange their sight deposits with banks on demand into legal tender. This depended on the banks themselves having full access to legal tender, and again, over time, central banks came to have monopoly control over such base money. So, the early analysis of the supply of money focused on the relationship between the supply of base money created by the central bank and the provision by commercial banks of both bank credit and bank deposits: the bank multiplier analysis.

In practice however, the central bank has always sought to control the level of interest rates, rather than the monetary base. Hence, as Richard Werner and his co-authors Josh Ryan-Collins, Tony Greenham and Andrew Jackson document so clearly in this book, the supply of money is actually determined primarily by the demand of borrowers to take out bank loans. Moreover, when such demand is low, because the economy is weak and hence interest rates are also driven down to zero, the relationship between available bank reserves (deposits at the central bank) and commercial bank lending/deposits can break down entirely. Flooding banks with additional liquidity, as central banks have done recently via Quantitative Easing (QE), has not led to much commensurate increase in bank lending or broad money.

All this is set out in nice detail in this book, which will provide the reader with a clear path through the complex thickets of misunderstandings of this important issue. In addition the authors provide many further insights into current practices of money and banking. At a time when we face up to massive challenges in financial reform and regulation, it is essential to have a proper, good understanding of how the monetary system works, in order to reach better alternatives. This book is an excellent guide and will be suitable for a wide range of audiences, including not only those new to the field, but also to policy-makers and academics.

Charles A. E. Goodhart,
Professor Emeritus of Banking and Finance,
London School of Economics

19 September 2011

INTRODUCTION

The importance of money and banking to the modern economy has increasingly come under the global spotlight since the North Atlantic financial crisis of 2008. Yet there remains widespread misunderstanding of how new money is created, both amongst the general public and many economists, bankers, financial journalists and policymakers.

This is a problem for two main reasons. First, in the absence of a shared and accurate understanding, attempts at banking reform are more likely to fail. Secondly, the creation of new money and the allocation of purchasing power are a vital economic function and highly profitable. This is therefore a matter of significant public interest and not an obscure technocratic debate. Greater clarity and transparency about this key issue could improve both the democratic legitimacy of the banking system, our economic prospects and, perhaps even more importantly, improve the chances of preventing future crises.

By keeping explanations simple, using non-technical language and clear diagrams, *Where Does Money Come From?* reveals how it is possible to describe the role of money and banking in simpler terms than has generally been the case. The focus of our efforts is a factual, objective review of how the system works in the United Kingdom, but it would be brave indeed of us to claim this as the complete and definitive account. Reaching a good understanding requires us to interpret the nature and history of money and banking, as set out in Chapter 3, both of which contain subjective elements by their very nature.

Drawing on research and consultation with experts, including staff from the Bank of England and ex-commercial bank staff, we forge a comprehensive and accurate conception of money and banking through careful and precise analysis. We demonstrate throughout *Where Does Money Come From?* how our account represents the best fit with the empirical observations of the workings of the system as it operates in the UK today.

1.1.
Key questions

The financial crisis of 2008 raised many more questions about our national system of banking and money than it answered. Along with questions around the crisis itself – Why did it happen? How can we prevent it happening again? – there has been broad basic questioning of the nature of banks and money including:

- Where did all that money come from? – in reference to the 'credit bubble' that led up to the crisis.
- Where did all that money go?   in reference to the 'credit crunch'.
- How can the Bank of England create £375 billion of new money through 'quantitative easing'? And why has the injection of such a significant sum of money not helped the economy recover more quickly?
- Surely there are cheaper and more efficient ways to manage a banking crisis than to burden taxpayers and precipitate cutbacks in public expenditure?

These questions are very important. They allude to a bigger question which is the main subject of this book: 'How is money created and allocated in the UK?' This seems like a question that should have a simple answer, but clear and easily accessible answers are hard to find in the public domain.

1.2.
Overview of key findings

1.2.1.
The money supply and how it is created

Defining money is surprisingly difficult. In *Where Does Money Come From?* we cut through the tangled historical and theoretical debate to identify that anything widely accepted as payment, particularly by the Government as payment of tax, is money. This includes bank credit because although an IOU from a friend is not acceptable at the tax office or in the local shop, an IOU from a bank most definitely is.

New money is principally created by commercial banks when they extend or create credit, either through making loans, including overdrafts, or buying existing assets. In creating credit, banks simultaneously create brand new deposits in our bank accounts, which, to all intents and purposes, is money. This basic analysis is neither radical nor new. In fact, central banks around the world support the same description of where new money comes from – albeit usually in their less prominent publications.

We identify that the UK's national currency exists in three main forms, of which the second two exist in electronic form:
1. **Cash** – banknotes and coins.
2. **Central bank reserves** – reserves held by commercial banks at the Bank of England.
3. **Commercial bank money** – bank deposits created mainly either when commercial banks create credit as loans, overdrafts or for purchasing assets.

Only the Bank of England or the Government can create the first two forms of money, which is referred to in this book as 'central bank money' or 'base money'. Since central bank reserves do not actually circulate in the economy, we can further narrow down the money supply that is actually circulating as consisting of cash and commercial bank money.

Physical cash accounts for less than 3 per cent of the total stock of circulating money in the economy. Commercial bank money – credit and coexistent deposits – makes up the remaining 97 per cent.

1.2.2.
Popular misconceptions of banking

There are several conflicting ways to describe what banks do. The simplest version is that banks take in money from savers and lend this money out to borrowers. However, this is not actually how the process works. Banks do not need to wait for a customer to deposit money before they can make a new loan to someone else. In fact, it is exactly the opposite: the making of a loan creates a new deposit in the borrower's account.

More sophisticated versions bring in the concept of 'fractional reserve banking'. This description recognises that the banking system can lend out amounts that are many times greater than the cash and reserves held at the Bank of England. This is a more accurate picture, but it is still incomplete and misleading, since each bank is still considered a mere 'financial intermediary' passing on deposits as loans. It also implies a strong link between the amount of money that banks create and the amount held at the central bank. In this version it is also commonly assumed that the central bank has significant control over the amount of reserves that banks hold with it.

In fact, the ability of banks to create new money is only very weakly linked to the amount of reserves they hold at the central bank. At the time of the financial crisis, for example, banks held just £1.25 in reserves for every £100 issued as credit. Banks operate within an electronic clearing system that nets out multilateral payments at the end of each day, requiring them to hold only a tiny proportion of central bank money to meet their payment requirements.

Furthermore, we argue that rather than the central bank controlling the amount of credit that commercial banks can issue, it is the commercial banks that determine the quantity of central bank reserves that the Bank of England must lend to them to be sure of keeping the system functioning.

1.2.3.
Implications of commercial bank money creation

The power of commercial banks to create new money has many important implications for economic prosperity and financial stability. We highlight four that are relevant to proposals to reform the banking system:
1. Although possibly useful in other ways, capital adequacy requirements have not and do not constrain money creation and therefore do not necessarily serve to restrict the expansion of banks' balance sheets in aggregate. In other words, they are mainly ineffective in preventing credit booms and their associated asset price bubbles.
2. In a world of imperfect information, credit is rationed by banks and the primary determinant of how much they lend is not interest rates, but confidence that the loan will be repaid and confidence in the liquidity and

solvency of other banks and the system as a whole.

3. Banks decide where to allocate credit in the economy. The incentives that they face often lead them to favour lending against collateral, or existing assets, rather than lending for investment in production. As a result, new money is often more likely to be channelled into property and financial speculation than to small businesses and manufacturing, with associated profound economic consequences for society.

4. Fiscal policy does not in itself result in an expansion of the money supply. Indeed, in practice the Government has no direct involvement in the money creation and allocation process. This is little known but has an important impact on the effectiveness of fiscal policy and the role of the Government in the economy.

1.3.
How the book is structured

Where Does Money Come From? is divided into seven chapters. Chapter 2 reviews the popular conception of banks as financial intermediaries and custodians, examines and critiques the textbook 'money multiplier' model of credit creation and then provides a more accurate description of the money creation process.

Chapter 3 examines what we mean by 'money'. Without a proper understanding of money, we cannot attempt to understand banking. We criticise the view, often presented in mainstream economics, that money is a commodity and show instead that money is a social relationship of credit and debt. The latter half of the chapter reviews the emergence of modern credit money in the UK, from fractional reserve banking, bond-issuance, creation of the central bank, the Gold Standard and deregulation to the emergence of digital money in the late twentieth century.

Chapter 4 outlines in simple steps how today's monetary system operates. We define modern money through the notion of purchasing power and liquidity and then set out how the payment system works: the role of central bank reserves, interbank settlement and clearing, cash, deposit insurance and the role of the central bank in influencing the money supply through monetary policy. This chapter includes a section on the recent adoption, by the Bank of England and other central banks, of 'Quantitative Easing' as an additional policy tool. We also examine the concepts of bank 'solvency' and 'capital' and examine how a commercial bank's balance sheet is structured.

Chapter 5 examines the extent to which commercial bank money is effectively regulated. We analyse how the Bank of England attempts to conduct monetary policy through interventions in the money markets designed to move the price of money (the interest rate) and through its direct dealings with banks. This section also includes a review of the financial crisis and how neither liquidity nor capital adequacy regulatory frameworks were effective in preventing asset bubbles and ultimately the crisis itself. Building on the theoretical analysis in Chapter 3, we examine examples, including international examples, of more direct intervention in credit markets.

Chapter 6 considers the role of government spending, borrowing and taxation, collectively referred to as fiscal policy, alongside international dimensions of the monetary system, including the constraints on money creation imposed by the European Union and how foreign exchange affects the monetary system. More detail is provided in Appendix 3.

Finally, the conclusion in Chapter 7 summarises the arguments and sets out a range of questions which seek to explore how reform of the current money and banking system might look. The authors summarise some alternative approaches which have been discussed in the book and provide references for further research.

Our intention in publishing *Where Does Money Come From?* is to facilitate improved understanding of how money and banking works in today's economy, stimulating further analysis and debate around how policy and decision makers can create a monetary system which supports a more stable and productive economy.

References

1   McKenna, R., (1928). *Postwar Banking Policy*, p.93. London: W. Heinemann

2   Keynes, J. M., (1930). *Preface to A Treatise on Money*, 3 Volumes, pp. vi-vii

2

WHAT DO BANKS DO?

Our bankers are indeed nothing but Goldsmiths' shops where, if you lay money on demand, they allow you nothing; if at time, three per cent.'
Daniel Defoe, Essay on Projects, 1690[1]

It proved extraordinarily difficult for economists to recognise that bank loans and bank investments do create deposits.
Joseph Schumpeter, 1954[2]

2.1.
The confusion around banking

There is significant confusion about banks. Much of the public is unclear about what banks actually do with their money. Economics graduates are slightly better informed, yet many textbooks used in university economics courses teach a model of banking that has not applied in the UK for a few decades, and unfortunately many policymakers and economists still work on this outdated model.

The confusion arises because the reality of modern banking is partially obscured from public view and may appear complex. In researching *Where Does Money Come From?*, the authors have pieced together information spread across more than 500 documents, guides and manuals as well as papers from central banks, regulators and other authorities. Few economists have time to do this research first-hand and most individuals in the financial sector only have expertise in a small area of the system, meaning that there is a shortage of people who have a truly accurate and comprehensive understanding of the modern banking and monetary system as a whole. This section gives a brief overview of the common misconceptions about what banks do, and then gives an initial overview of what they actually do. A more detailed explanation is provided in Chapter 4.

2.2.
Popular perceptions of banking 1: *the safe-deposit box*

Most people will have had a piggy bank at some point in their childhood. The idea is simple: keep putting small amounts of money into your piggy bank, and the money will just sit there safely until you need to spend it.

For many people, this idea of keeping money safe in some kind of box ready for a 'rainy day' persists into adult life. A poll conducted by ICM Research on behalf of the Cobden Centre[3] found that 33 per cent of people were under the impression that a bank does not make use of the money in customers' current accounts. When told the reality – that banks don't just keep the money safe in the bank's vault, but use it for other purposes – this group answered "This is wrong – I have not given them my permission to do so."

2.2.1.
We do not own the money we have put in the bank

The custodial role that one third of the public assume banks play is something of an illusion. Similar confusion is found over the ownership of the money that we put into our bank accounts. The ICB/Cobden Centre poll found that 77 per cent of people believed that the money they deposited in banks legally belonged to them.[4] In fact, the money that they deposited legally belongs to the bank. When a member of the public makes a deposit of £1,000 in the bank, the bank does not hold that money in a safe box with the customer's name on it (or any digital equivalent). Whilst banks do have cash vaults, the cash they keep there is not customers' money. Instead, the bank takes legal ownership of the cash deposited and records that they owe the customer £1,000. In the bank's accounting, this is recorded as a liability of the bank to the customer. It is a liability because at some point in the future, it may have to be repaid.

The concept of a 'liability' is essential to understanding modern banking and is actually very simple. If you were to borrow £50 from a friend, you might make a note in your diary to remind you to repay the £50 a couple of weeks later. In the language of accounting, this £50 is a liability of you to your friend.

The balance of your bank account, and indeed the bank account of all members of the public and all businesses, is the bank's IOU, and shows that they have a legal obligation (i.e. liability) to pay the money at some point in the future. Whether they will actually have that money at the time you need it is a different issue, as we explain later.

2.3.
Popular perceptions of banking 2: *taking money from savers and lending it to borrowers*

The ICM/Cobden Centre poll also found that around 61 per cent of the public share a slightly more accurate understanding of banking: the idea that banks take money from savers and lend it to borrowers. When asked if they were concerned about this process, this group answered "I don't mind as long as the banks pay interest and aren't too reckless."

This view sees banks as financial intermediaries, recycling and allocating our savings into (we hope) profitable investments that provide us with a financial return in the form of interest. The interest we receive on savings accounts is an incentive to save and a form of compensation for not spending the money immediately. Banks give lower interest to savers than they charge to borrowers in order to make a profit and cover their losses in case of default. The difference between the interest rate banks pay to savers and the interest they charge to borrowers is called the 'interest rate spread' or 'margin'.

Banks intermediate money across space (savings in London may fund loans in Newcastle); and time (my savings are pooled with those of others and loaned over a longer-term period to enable a borrower to buy a house). Shifting money and capital around the economy, and transforming short-term savings into long-term loans, a process known as 'maturity transformation', is very important for the broader economy: it ensures that savings are actively being put to use by the rest of the economy rather than lying dormant under our mattresses. We can also invest our money directly with companies by purchasing shares or bonds issued by them. The process of saving and investment indirectly through banks, and directly to companies, is summarised in Figure 1.[5]

2. WHAT DO BANKS DO?

Figure 1: Banks as financial intermediaries

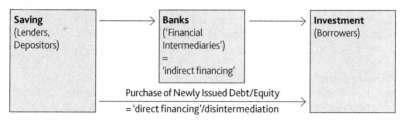

Banks, according to this viewpoint, are important, but relatively neutral, players in our financial system, almost like the lubricant that enables the cogs of consumption, saving and production to turn smoothly. So it is perhaps understandable that orthodox economists do not put banks or money at the heart of their models of the economy. Maybe sometimes things go wrong – banks allocate too many savings, for example, to a particular industry sector that is prone to default – but in the long run, so the theory states, it is not the banks themselves that are really determining economic outcomes.

Box 1: Retail, commercial, wholesale and investment banking

Banking is commonly categorised according to the type of activities and the type of customers. In this book we use the generic term 'commercial banks' to refer to all non-state deposit-taking institutions, and to distinguish them from the central bank. However, commercial banking can also be used to describe the provision of services to larger companies. The Independent Commission on Banking sets out the following different categories of banking:[6]

Retail and commercial banking
The provision of deposit-taking, payment and lending services to retail customers and small and medium-sized enterprises (SMEs), (retail, or 'high-street' banking) and to larger companies (commercial banking).

Wholesale and investment banking
'Wholesale retailing' generally refers to the sale of goods to anyone other than the individual customer. Similarly, 'Wholesale banking' involves the provision of lending and assistance (including underwriting) to institutions such as governments and corporations rather than lending to individual customers. Wholesale banking can include assistance in raising equity and debt finance, providing advice in relation to mergers and acquisitions, acting as counterparty to client trades and 'market-making' (investment banking). An investment bank may also undertake trading on its own account (proprietary trading) in a variety of financial products such as derivatives, fixed income instruments, currencies and commodities.

Note that investment banks need not necessarily hold a licence to accept deposits from customers to carry out some of these trading and advisory activities.

This theory is incorrect, for reasons that will be covered below. It also leads to assumptions about the economy that do not hold true in reality, such as the idea that high levels of savings by the public will lead to high investment in productive businesses, and conversely, that a lack of savings by the public will choke off investment in productive businesses.

Most importantly, this understanding of banking completely overlooks the question: Where does money come from? Money is implicitly assumed to come from the Bank of England (after all, that's what it says on every £5 or £10 note); the Royal Mint or some other part of the state. The reality is quite different, as the rest of this chapter explains.

2.4.
Three forms of money

At this point we must clarify the different forms of money that we use in our economy.

The simplest form is **cash** – the £5, £10, £20, and £50 bank notes and the metal coins that most of us have in our wallets at any point in time. Paper notes are created under the authority of the Bank of England and printed by specialist printer De La Rue. Although cash is being used for fewer and fewer transactions, the fact that prices tend to rise and the population is growing means that the Bank of England expects the total amount of cash in circulation in the economy to keep growing over time.

Of course, we do not like having to ferry around huge sums of cash when making payments, as this is expensive and also runs the risk of theft or robbery. So instead, most payments for larger sums are made electronically. This raises the question of who creates and allocates electronic money or computer money. Not surprisingly, the Bank of England can create electronic money. It may do so when granting a loan to its customers, allowing them to use a kind of 'overdraft' facility or when making payments to purchase assets or pay the salaries of its staff. The most important customers are the Government and the commercial banks.

While many assume that only the Bank of England has the right to create computer money, in actual fact this accounts for only a tiny fraction of the money supply. The majority of the money supply is electronic money created by commercial banks. How these mostly private sector banks create and allocate the money supply remains little known to both the public and many trained economists, as it is not covered in most textbooks.

These first two types of money – cash and reserves – are collectively referred to as **central bank money**. Transactions between banks can either be settled bilaterally between themselves or via their accounts with the central bank – where they hold what is known as **central bank reserves**. These central bank reserves, created by the Bank of England, are electronic money and are risk-free. However, unlike cash, members of the public cannot access or use central bank reserves. Only high-street and commercial banks that have accounts with the Bank of England are able to use this type of money. Central bank reserves are used by banks for the settlement of interbank payments and liquidity management, further explained in Chapter 4.*

The third type of money, however, is not created by the Bank of England, the Royal Mint, or any other part of government. This third type of money is what is in your bank account. In banking terminology, it's referred to as bank deposits or demand deposits. In technical terms, it is simply a number in a computer system; in accounting terms, it is a liability of the bank to you. The terminology is somewhat misleading, as we shall see. A bank deposit is not a deposit in the sense that you might store a valuable item in a safety deposit box. Instead, it is merely a record of what the bank owes you.

In fact, not all deposits with banks were actually deposited by the public. When banks do what is commonly, and somewhat incorrectly, called 'lend money' or 'extend loans', they simply credit the borrower's deposit account, thus creating the illusion that the borrowers have made deposits. This focus on bank deposits, including deposits with the central bank, distract from the money creation process. We can learn more about credit creation – when banks lend or make payments – from other parts of their balance sheet.

Bank deposits are not legal tender in the strict definition of the term – only coins and notes under certain conditions meet this test[†] – but as we will discuss, they function as money and most members of the public would consider them to be as good as cash. The term 'money supply', usually refers to cash and bank deposits taken together, with the latter being by far the most significant. On the Bank of England's standard definition of the money supply, known as M4, **this type of money now makes up 97.4 per cent of all the money used in the economy.**[‡] In this book we refer to the money created by banks as **commercial bank money**.

---

[*] *'Central bank money in the UK economy takes two forms: banknotes and banks' balances with the Bank of England (reserves). As a risk-free asset, reserves are used by banks for settlement of interbank payments and liquidity management'.* **Bank of England, Red Book, p.4.**

[†] *'Legal tender has a very narrow and technical meaning in the settlement of debts. It means that a debtor cannot successfully be sued for non-payment if he pays into court in legal tender. It does not mean that any ordinary transaction has to take place in legal tender or only within the amount denominated by the legislation. Both parties are free to agree to accept any form of payment whether legal tender or otherwise according to their wishes.'* Extract from the Royal Mint website.[7]

[‡] Bank of England statistics for the M4 measure of broad money supply. Calculated by removing Notes & Coins from M4 and calculating the ratio.

2.5.
How banks create money by extending credit

The vast majority of money in our economy was created by commercial banks. In effect what the UK and most other countries currently use as their primary form of money is not physical cash created by the state, but the liabilities of banks. These liabilities were created through the accounting process that banks use when they make loans (Section 2.8). An efficient electronic payments system then ensures that these liabilities can function as money: most payments can be settled electronically, without any physical transfer of cash, reducing the balance of one account and increasing the balance of another. As we shall see in Chapter 3, this form of 'clearing' has been a function of banks as far back as historical records go. The vast majority of payments, by value, are made in this way.

We might object that the commercial banks are not really creating money – they are extending credit – and this is not the same thing. The next chapter examines the nature and history of money in greater depth and concludes that in fact money is always best thought of as credit. But for now let us just consider whether it is really meaningful to describe the balance in your bank account as anything other than money. You can use it to pay for things, including your tax bill, and the Government even guarantees that you will not lose it if the bank gets into trouble.*

Box 2: Building societies, credit unions and money creation

Building societies and credit unions also have the right to create money through issuing credit. Credit unions, however, have a range of strict controls on their credit creation power in the UK, more so than in many other countries.[8] Prior to 2012, credit unions could only make loans to individuals, not to businesses or third sector organisations, and only to individuals living in a defined geographical area. In addition, they can only make loans up to £15,000. A Legislative Reform Order (LRO) which came in to force on 8th January 2012, means that credit unions can now lend to businesses and organisations but only up to a small percentage of their total assets.[9] Partially as a result of these restrictions, the credit union sector remains very small in terms of retail lending compared to many other industrialised countries. For the remainder of the book when we use the terms 'bank' or 'commercial/private bank' we also include building societies, which, like banks but unlike credit unions, have no specific legislative restrictions on their credit creation powers.

While the idea that most new money is created by the likes of Barclays, HSBC, Lloyds, and the RBS rather than the Bank of England will be a surprise for most members of the public (although not as much of a shock as if you tried to convince them that their bank deposits were not really money at all), it is well

---

* Balances up to £85,000 per person per banking group are guaranteed by the Government under the Financial Services Compensation Scheme. Prior to October 2007 only the first £2,000 was fully covered, with 90 per cent of the next £33,000 covered. The guarantee was progressively raised during the financial crisis to try to maintain depositors' confidence and prevent any further bank runs after the run on Northern Rock.

known to those working in central banks. The following quotes testify to this and also confirm the point that bank deposits are, in essence, money:

> *In the United Kingdom, money is endogenous – the Bank supplies base money on demand at its prevailing interest rate, and broad money is created by the banking system.*
> **Bank of England (1994)**[10]

> *By far the largest role in creating broad money is played by the banking sector... When banks make loans they create additional deposits for those that have borrowed.*
> **Bank of England (2007)**[11]

> *Money-creating organisations issue liabilities that are treated as media of exchange by others. The rest of the economy can be referred to as money holders.**
> **Bank of England (2007)**[12]

> *...changes in the money stock primarily reflect developments in bank lending as new deposits are created.*
> **Bank of England (2007)**[13]

> *Given the near identity of deposits and bank lending, Money and Credit are often used almost inseparably, even interchangeably...*
> **Bank of England (2008)**[14]

> *Each and every time a bank makes a loan, new bank credit is created – new deposits – brand new money.*
> **Graham Towers (1939), former Governor of the central bank of Canada**[15]

> *Over time... Banknotes and commercial bank money became fully interchangeable payment media that customers could use according to their needs.*
> **European Central Bank (2000)**[16]

> *The actual process of money creation takes place primarily in banks.*
> **Federal Reserve Bank of Chicago (1961)**[17]

> *In the Eurosystem, money is primarily created through the extension of bank credit... The commercial banks can create money themselves, the so-called giro money.*
> **Bundesbank (2009)**[18]

There are two main ways of describing the process by which banks create money. The textbook model is given below, and we explain why we consider this model to be inaccurate. A more accurate model of the modern UK banking system, based on primary research, is described in Chapter 4.

2.6.
Textbook descriptions: the multiplier model

Many economics textbooks use a 'multiplier'* model of banking to explain how the 2.6 per cent of money that is cash is 'multiplied' up to create the 97.4 per cent that is simply liabilities of banks i.e. numbers in bank accounts. The model is quite simple and runs as follows:

A member of the public deposits his salary of £1,000 into Bank A. The bank knows that, on average, the customer will not need the whole of his £1,000 returned at the same time – it is more likely that he will spend an average of £30 a day over the course of a month. Consequently, the bank assumes that much of the money deposited is 'idle' or spare and will not be needed on any particular day. It keeps, or is mandated to keep by the central bank, back a small 'reserve' of say 10 per cent of the money deposited with it (in this case £100), and lends out the other £900 to somebody who needs a loan.

Now both the original depositor and the new borrower think they have money in their bank accounts. The original deposit of £1,000 has turned into total bank 'deposits' of £1,900 comprising £1,000 from the original deposit plus £900 lent to the borrower.

This £900 is then spent in the economy, and the shop or business that receives that money deposits it back into Bank B. Bank B then keeps £90 of this as its own reserve, while lending out the remaining £810. Again the process continues, with the £810 being spent and re-deposited in Bank C, who this time keeps a reserve of £81 while re-lending £729. At each point in the re-lending process, the sum balance of all the public's bank accounts increases, and in effect, new money, or purchasing power, has been created.

This process continues, with the amount being lent getting smaller at each stage, until after 204 cycles of this process the total balance of the public's bank deposits has grown to £10,000. Figure 2 shows this step-by-step process, with the additional lending (and the new money created as a result) shown in black.

---

* For a classic account of the money multiplier, see Phillips (1920)[19]. For an explanation of how the system used to work in the United States, see: Nicols. (1992/1961)[20]

Figure 2: The money multiplier model

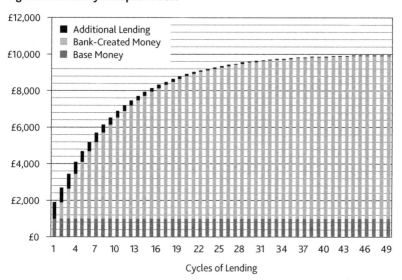

This model implies three important things. First, it implies that banks cannot start lending without first having money deposited with them. In an economy with just a single bank, it would have to wait until someone deposited money (the amount shown in black in Figure 2), before it could lend anything, whatever the reserve ratio. So this model supports the concept of banks being primarily intermediaries of money. The banks in this example can be thought of as intermediating in succession, the outcome being 'credit creation' – the creation of new purchasing power in the bank accounts of the public.[21]

Secondly, this money multiplier model suggests that by altering the reserve ratio or the monetary base (cash plus central bank reserves), the central bank or the Government can closely control bank reserves and, through this, the amount of credit issued into the economy. If the reserve ratio is raised to 20 per cent by the Government or central bank, for example, Bank A will only be able to lend out £800 instead of £900, Bank B £720 instead of £810, etc. Alternatively, if the amount of money at the base of the pyramid (Figure 3) is doubled, but the reserve ratio stays at 10 per cent, then the total amount of money in the economy will also double.

Figure 3: The money multiplier pyramid

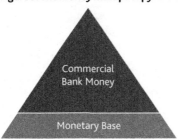

Thirdly, it implies that the growth in the money supply within the economy is mathematically limited – as shown by the flattening of Figure 2. With a 10 per cent reserve ratio, there is an increase in the money supply for the first approximately 200 cycles, but after this point there is no discernible increase, because the amounts being effectively re-lent are infinitesimal. Even with a tiny – but more realistic – reserve ratio of 2 per cent, the multiplier stops having an effect after around 1,140 cycles and, in an economy of 61 million people, this number of cycles of re-lending would take a few weeks at most.

This model of money creation can therefore be envisaged as a pyramid (Figure 3), where the central bank can control the total money supply by altering the size of the base, by controlling the amount of base money and the steepness of the sides by changing the reserve ratio.

Consequently, economists and policymakers following a simple textbook model of banking will assume that:

1. Banks are merely intermediaries and have no real control over the money supply of the economy.
2. Central banks can control the amount of money in the economy.
3. There is no possibility that growth in the money supply can get out of control because it is mathematically limited by the reserve ratio and the amount of base money.

Unfortunately this textbook model of banking is outdated and inaccurate and, as a result, these assumptions will be untrue.

2.7.
Problems with the textbook model

The textbook model of banking implies that banks need depositors to start the money creation process. The reality, however, is that when a bank makes a loan it does not require anyone else's money to do so. **Banks do not wait for deposits in order to make loans**. Bank deposits are created by banks purely on the basis of their own confidence in the capacity of the borrower to repay the loan.

As a Deputy Governor of the Bank England puts it:

> *Subject only (but crucially) to confidence in their soundness, banks extend*
> *credit by simply increasing the borrowing customer's current account, which*
> *can be paid away to wherever the borrower wants by the bank 'writing a*
> *cheque on itself'. That is, banks extend credit by creating money.*
>
> **Paul Tucker, Deputy Governor at the Bank of England and member of the**
> **Monetary Policy Committee, 2007**[22]

In the UK, there are currently no direct compulsory cash-reserve requirements placed on banks or building societies to restrict their lending (Section 6.3).* The main constraint on UK commercial banks and building societies is the need to hold enough liquidity reserves and cash to meet their everyday demand for payments.†

This means that the Bank of England cannot control bank money creation through adjusting the amount of central bank reserves that banks must hold, as in the multiplier model. In reality, rather than the Bank of England determining how much credit banks can issue, we could argue that it is the banks that determine how much central bank reserves and cash the Bank of England must lend to them. This is particular obvious in the case of countries where compulsory reserve requirements have been reduced to zero – such as the UK. This will be explained in more detail in Chapter 4.

2.8.
How money is actually created

Rather than the pyramid implied by the textbook model of money creation, the reality is closer to a 'balloon' of bank-created money wrapped around a core of base money (Figure 4).[23]

The Bank of England, given its own current choice of monetary policy tools and instruments, has relatively little direct control over the total amount of the balloon of commercial bank money, and therefore over the amount of money in the economy as a whole.

---

* The Financial Services Authority is currently bringing in legislation that will require Banks to hold an amount determined by 'stress testing' the potential for 100 per cent outflows of liabilities over a two-week period.[24]

† In the United States, for example, there is still a 10 per cent liquidity reserve ratio on certain deposits and in China the Government actively changes its liquidity reserve ratio in an attempt to restrain credit creation in order to fight inflation – at the time of writing it stood at 20.5 per cent (having been raised for the fourth time in 2011. See *Financial Times* (17 April 2011). 'China raises bank reserve requirements'. The reserve requirement tool notwithstanding, the most important monetary policy tool in China remains its direct quota system for the quantity of credit creation, known as 'window guidance'.[25]

Figure 4: 'Balloon' of commercial bank money

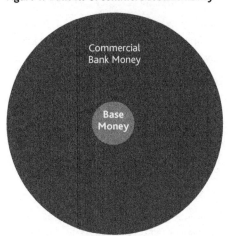

This lack of control can be seen empirically over the last few decades. Prior to the crisis, the ratio between commercial bank money and base money increased so much that in 2006 there was £80 of commercial bank money for every £1 of base money.* This creation of money fuelled much of the unsustainable credit boom running up to 2007 (Figure 4).

Conversely, during the crisis, the Bank of England's 'Quantitative Easing' (QE) scheme (see section 4.7.3) pumped hundreds of billions of new base money into the system (Figure 6), yet this had no noticeable impact on lending, as shown by credit measure M4L, which continued to contract in 2010, 2011 and 2012 (figure 5). The only significant impact was a decrease in the ratio between commercial bank money and base money. This illustrates that banks' reserves with the central bank are not a very meaningful measure of money supply: they may indicate that the amount of money could potentially rise, but at any moment in time they do not measure money that is used for transactions or necessarily affecting the economy in any positive way (see also Figure 7 in section 3.6.3 showing the historical UK money supply). For instance, if the central bank creates more reserve money, as happened in Japan under the Bank of Japan's QE, then everything else being equal this does not in any way stimulate the economy. However, an increase in bank credit creation will have a positive impact on the value of economic transactions.

---

* Bank of England statistics, 2006, ratio of M4 (broad money) to M0 (base money – notes and coins plus Bank of England reserves).

Figure 5: Growth rate of commercial bank lending excluding securitisations, 2000-12

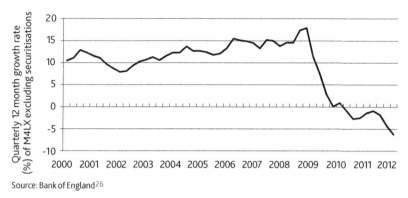

Source: Bank of England[26]

Figure 6: Change in stock of central bank reserves, 2000-12

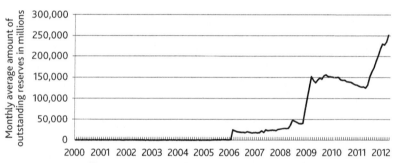

Source: Bank of England[27]

Our research finds that the amount of money created by commercial banks is currently not actively determined by regulation, reserve ratios, the Government or the Bank of England, but largely by the confidence of the banks at any particular period in time. The current arrangements are not inevitable, however. The Bank of England or the Government could intervene in order to influence or control money created by commercial banks, as they did in the past and as we explore in chapter 3. In other words, the authorities are not free of responsibility for results produced by the largely unchecked behaviour of the banking sector.

When banks are confident, they will create new money by creating credit and new bank deposits for borrowers. When they are fearful, they rein in lending, limiting the creation of new commercial bank money. If more loans are repaid than issued, the money supply will shrink. The size of the commercial bank credit balloon, and therefore the money supply of the nation, depends mainly on the confidence and incentives of the banks.

This pattern appears to be the case despite the Bank of England's implicit guaranteeing of the commercial banking system in terms of its function as 'Lender of Last Resort', promising to provide credit at times of crisis when no-one else will – see Section 3.5, and deposit insurance (see Section 4.6.1), policies that apply singularly to the banking sector.

One reason that banks' confidence may be volatile is the fact that, despite their ability to create money, they can nevertheless go bust. Banks can create deposits for their customers, but they cannot create capital directly for themselves. Banks must ensure at all times that the value of their assets are greater than or at least match their liabilities. If the value of their assets falls, and they do not have enough of their own capital to absorb the losses, they will become insolvent. Once a bank is insolvent, it is illegal for them to continue trading. Equally, while banks can create deposits for their customers, they cannot create central bank reserves. Therefore, they can still suffer a liquidity crisis if they run out of central bank reserves and other banks are unwilling to lend to them. We explore solvency, liquidity and banks going bust in greater depth in Section 4.8.

The historical evidence explored in Chapter 3 suggests that the most important external factor in determining the quantity of money created by banks is the central bank's attitude to the regulation of credit itself. When a central bank chooses to adopt a laissez-faire policy concerning bank credit, as now in the UK, boom-bust credit cycles are likely to result, with all their implications for economic analysis and policy. This is obvious if we think about the link between credit creation and economic activity. When banks create credit, and hence expand the money supply, whether the money is used for GDP or non-GDP transactions is crucial for determining the impact on the economy. Unproductive credit creation (for non-GDP transactions) will result in asset price inflation, bursting bubbles and banking crises as well as resource misallocation and dislocation. In contrast credit used for the production of new goods and services, or to enhance productivity, is productive credit creation that will deliver non-inflationary growth. This 'Quantity Theory of Credit' has been developed by one of *Where Does Money Come From?'s* authors, Richard Werner, and is discussed in more detail in section 5.6.[*]

Historical evidence suggests that left unregulated, banks will prefer to create credit for non-productive financial or speculative credit, which often maximises short-term profits (see section 4.6.3). This may explain why the Bank of England, like most central banks, used to impose credit growth quotas on banks, as we show in Chapter 3. However, such credit controls were abolished in the early 1970s.

---

[*] A document entitled 'The Quantity Theory of Credit' was first issued by Richard Werner in 1992[28] and presented to the Royal Economic Society Annual Conference in York in April 1993[29]. Subsequent work has added a substantial body of empirical evidence and practical applications of the theory, for instance for monetary policy advice or forecasting in asset management. See Richard A. Werner (1997, 2005, 2011, 2012).

2. WHAT DO BANKS DO?

If you are keen to understand in more depth exactly how money is created by the banking system today, then you may wish to skip ahead to Chapter 4. However, it is important to see how money and banking have developed over time to give us the current system. In the next chapter we shall see that political and economic developments, coupled with financial innovations, led to a situation where bank-created credit-money (henceforth 'commercial bank money') came to be accepted by the state and eventually came to dominate the monetary system.

References

1   Defoe, D. (1690). Essay on Projects (London), quoted in Davies, G. (2002). *A History of Money.* Wales: University of Wales Press, p. 251

2   Schumpeter, J. (1994/1954.) *History of Economic Analysis.* London: Allen & Union, p. 1114. Quoted in Werner, R. (2005). *New Paradigm in Macroeconomics.* Basingstoke: Palgrave Macmillan, p.189

3   ESCP Europe/Cobden Centre. (June 2010). *Public attitudes to banking.* Retrievable from http://www.cobdencentre.org

4   *Ibid.*

5   Adapted from Werner, R.A. (2005). *New Paradigm in Macroeconomics.* Basingstoke: Palgrave Macmillan, p. 150

6   Independent Commission on Banking. (2010). *Issues Paper: Call for Evidence,* pp.144–145, Retrievable from http://bankingcommission.independent.gov.uk/wp-content/uploads/2010/07/Issues-Paper-24-September-2010.pdf

7   Extract from the Royal Mint website. Retrievable from http://www.royalmint.com/corporate/policies/legal_tender_guidelines.aspx [accessed 9 August 2011].

8   Werner, R.A. (2009). *Can credit unions create credit? An Analytical Evaluation of a Potential Obstacle to the Growth of Credit Unions.* Southampton: Centre for Banking, Finance and Sustainable Development, Discussion Paper Series, No. 2/09, pg. 5

9   See Association of British Credit Unions Limited, *Legislative Reform Order re-laid in Parliament,* retrievable from http://www.abcul.org/media-and-research/news/view/151

10 King, M. (1994). The transition mechanism of monetary policy. *Bank of England Quarterly Bulletin,* August 1994, p. 264. Retrievable from http://www.bankofengland.co.uk/publications/quarterlybulletin/qb940301.pdf

11 Berry, S., Harrison, R., Thomas, R., de Weymarn, I. (2007). Interpreting movements in Broad Money. *Bank of England Quarterly Bulletin 2007* Q3, p. 377. Retrievable from http://www.bankofengland.co.uk/publications/quarterlybulletin/qb070302.pdf

12 Burgess, S., Janssen, N. (2007). Proposals to modify the measurement of broad money in the United Kingdom: A user-consultation. *Bank of England Quarterly Bulletin 2007* Q3, p. 402. Retrievable from http://www.bankofengland.co.uk/publications/quarterlybulletin/qb070304.pdf

13 Berry *et al.* (2007) *op. cit.* p. 378

14 Tucker, P. (2008). Money and Credit: Banking and the macroeconomy, speech given at the monetary policy and markets conference, 13 December 2007, *Bank of England Quarterly Bulletin 2008,* Q1, pp. 96–106. Retrievable from http://www.bankofengland.co.uk/publications/speeches/2007/speech331.pdf

15 Towers, G. (1939). *Minutes of Proceedings and Evidence Respecting the Bank of Canada (1939).* Committee on Banking and Commerce, Ottawa. Government Printing Bureau, quoted in Rowbotham, M. (1998). *The Grip of Death.* Oxford: John Carpenter Publishing, p. 12

16 ECB. (2000). *Domestic payments in Euroland: commercial and central bank money.* Speech by Tommaso Padoa-Schioppa, Member of the Executive Board of the European central bank, at the European Commission Round-Table *Establishing a Single Payment Area: State of Play and Next Steps, Brussels,* 9 November 2000, quoted in Werner, R., (2009). *op. cit.,* p. 5

17 Nichols, D. M. (1992/1961). *Modern Money Mechanics: A workbook on Bank Reserves and Deposit Expansion.* Chicago: Federal Reserve Bank of Chicago. Retrievable from http://www.archive.org/stream/ModernMoneyMechanics/MMM - page/n1/mode/2up

18 Bundesbank. (2009). *Geld und Geldpolitik,* as cited and translated by Werner, R.A. (2009). Topics in Monetary Economics, Lecture Slides for Masters in Money and Finance. Frankfurt: Goethe University

19 Phillips, C.A., (1920). *Bank Credit.* New York: Macmillan

20 Nicols. (1992/1961). *Modern Money Mechanics: A workbook on Bank Reserves and Deposit Expansion.* Chicago: Federal Reserve Bank of Chicago. Retrievable from http://www.archive.org/stream/ModernMoneyMechanics/MMM#page/n1/mode/2up [accessed 29 April 2011]

21 Werner, R. A. (2005). *op. cit.,* p. 175

22 Tucker (2008). *op. cit.*

23 For a similar visual approach to describing money see: Credit Suisse (5 May 2009). *Market Focus - Long Shadows: Collateral Money, Asset Bubbles and Inflation*, p. 7

24 Financial Services Authority, October 2009, PS09/16: Strengthening liquidity standards including feedback on CP08/22, CP09/13, CP09/14. Retrievable from http://www.fsa.gov.uk/pages/Library/Policy/Policy/2009/09_16.shtml [accessed 14 May 2011]

25 Werner, R.A. (2005). *op. cit.*

26 Bank of England interactive database: 'Quarterly 12 month growth rate of M4 lending excluding securitisations (monetary financial institutions' sterling net lending excluding securitisations to the private sector), seasonally adjusted', code LPQVWVP; retrievable from http://www.bankofengland.co.uk/boeapps/iadb/FromShowColumns.asp?Travel=NIxSSx&SearchText=LPQVWVP&POINT.x=12&POINT.y=9 [accessed 28th September 2012]

27 Bank of England interactive database: 'Monthly average amounts of outstanding (on Wednesdays) of Bank of England Banking Department sterling reserve balance liabilities (in sterling millions), not seasonally adjusted', code LPMBL22, available online at http://www.bankofengland.co.uk/boeapps/iadb/FromShowColumns.asp?Travel=NIxSSx&SearchText=LPMBL22&POINT.x=8&POINT.y=12 [accessed 28th September 2012]

28 Werner, R. A. (1992), *A Quantity Theory of Credit*. University of Oxford, Institute of Economics and Statistics, mimeo

29 Werner, R. A. (1993), Japanese Capital Flows: Did the World Suffer from Yen Illusion? Towards a Quantity Theory of Disaggregated Credit. Paper presented at the *Annual Conference of the Royal Economic Society*, London

3

THE NATURE AND HISTORY
OF MONEY AND BANKING

The significance of money as expressing the relative value of commodities is ... quite independent of any intrinsic value. Just as it is irrelevant whether a [physical measuring instrument] consists of iron, wood or glass, since only the relation of its parts to each other or to another measure concerns us, so the scale that money provides for the determination of values has nothing to do with the nature of its substance. This ideal significance of money as a standard and an expression of the value of goods has remained completely unchanged, whereas its character as an intermediary, as a means to store and to transport values, has changed in some degree and is still in the process of changing.
Georg Simmel (1907), Sociologist and Philosopher[1]

Money is not metal. It is trust inscribed. And it does not seem to matter much where it is inscribed: on silver, on clay, on paper, on a liquid crystal display.
Niall Ferguson (2009), Historian[2]

3.1.
The functions of money

Money is clearly fundamental to capitalist systems. It is hard to envisage a modern economy without it. While the medium of money may change with technological developments – from coins to notes to cheques to credit and debit cards and online e-payments – the activity of exchanging, storing, and accumulating units of value called money has been with us for centuries and shows no sign of going away.

Yet money and banking, as subjects for serious examination in their own right, have been largely neglected by orthodox economics over the past 60–70 years. This seems strange, since, with the exception of a brief period of stability from the end of WWII to 1970, we have seen an increase in the frequency and severity of both currency and banking crises, culminating in the North Atlantic financial crisis of 2008, the most severe since the Great Depression of the 1930s*

Let us start with trying to understand what money is for. Money is generally described by economists in terms of its functions rather than any kind of overarching property or essence. It is generally viewed as having four key functions:[4]

1. **Store of value** – holding on to money gives us confidence in our future ability to access goods and services – it gives us future 'purchasing power'.
2. **Medium of exchange** – enables us to conduct efficient transactions and trade with each other. Money enables us to move beyond barter relations which require both parties to have exactly the right quality and quantity of a commodity to make an exchange – a 'double coincidence of wants'.[5]
3. **Unit of account** – without a widely agreed upon unit of measurement we cannot settle debts or establish effective price systems, both key elements of capitalist economies.
4. Means of making final payment or **settlement**†.

Whilst there is some consensus that these four functions are all important in constituting money, there is less agreement about their relative importance and their role in the origins of money and relationship to banking. We explore two major theories of money‡ to elaborate this issue as it lies at the heart of our challenge of understanding money and banking properly.

---

* Prior to 2003, there had been 96 currency crises since 1970, the year before the US dollar was de-coupled from Gold.[3]

† This fourth function is closely related to the function of unit of account and not always identified as a separate function. Other functions commonly ascribed to money include a 'standard for deferred payments' and 'common measure of value'.

‡ There are many other theories and 'schools' of money than the two described here, not least Austrian, Post-Keynesian, 'Circuitist', Marxist, Feminist and Green but these are the two that have come to greatest prominence in academic literature. See Goodhart (1998)[6] and Smithin (2000)[7]. Useful guides to different schools of thought on money include Smithin (2000). *op. cit.* and Ingham (ed) (2005)[8].

3.2.
Commodity theory of money: money as natural and neutral

3.2.1.
Classical economics and money

Classical economists, Adam Smith, John Stuart Mill, David Ricardo, and Karl Marx argued that real economic value lay not in money but in land, labour, and the process of production. Money is simply a symbol representing that value. Mill, for example, stated that money's existence 'does not interfere with the operation of any laws of value' and that:

> *There cannot, in short, be intrinsically a more insignificant thing, in the economy of society, than money; except in the character of a contrivance for sparing time and labour. It is a machine for doing quickly and commodiously what would be done, though less quickly and commodiously, without it; and, like many other kinds of machinery, it only exerts a distinct and independent influence of its own when it gets out of order.*[9]

The classical economics account of money is as a way of optimising the efficiency of exchange. Money 'naturally' emerges from barter relations as people find certain commodities to be widely acceptable and begin to use them as media of exchange rather than keeping or consuming them.[10]

Commodities with the most money-like properties (intrinsic value, portability, divisibility, homogeneity) naturally become adopted as money over time. Hence, gold and silver coins, possessing all these properties, became the dominant medium for money, according to the classical account.[11] In the orthodox story, where optimal money-like commodities are not available, alternatives will naturally appear. The classic example is the prisoner-of-war camp where cigarettes became a substitute for money.[12] Cigarettes were widely available as prisoners were usually given an equal amount along with other rations. They are fairly homogenous, reasonably durable, portable and of a convenient size for the smallest or, in packets, for the largest transactions (divisible). The centrality of the commodity itself in determining the nature of money led to this theory being called the 'commodity theory of money' or the 'metallist theory of money'.

As the economist Joseph Schumpeter describes it, the logic of this argument leads to a conception of money as a neutral, imaginary 'veil' lying over the 'real' economy:[13]

> *'Real analysis' proceeds from the principle that all essential phenomena of economic life are capable of being described in terms of goods and services, of decisions about them and of relations between them. Money enters the picture only in the modest role of a technical device that has been adopted in order to facilitate transactions... so long as it functions normally, it does not*

affect the economic process, which behaves in the same way as it would in a
barter economy: this is essentially what the concept of Neutral Money implies.

3.2.2.
Neo-classical economics and money

Modern neoclassical economics built on this conception of neutral exchange-optimising money as it developed 'scientific' models of the economy in the late nineteenth and twentieth century based on mathematical rules of supply and demand.[14] In these 'general equilibrium' models, which still dominate the economics profession today, 'real' transactions – those involving goods and services – are facilitated by the existence of money, but money itself has no significant role.

Under the conditions of 'perfect information' that are assumed for markets to 'clear', where the quantity supplied meets the quantity demanded, people 'automatically' exchange goods and services, without delay or friction, according to the production costs of the commodity and people's 'marginal utility' – that is, the balance between the convenience obtained and the risk avoided from its possession.[15]

This approach posed a question for how to include money. French economist Leon Walras created a hypothetical numeraire, a symbolic representation of existing commodity values, to enable him to model an exchange economy in which the market 'clears' under conditions of equilibrium. To do so, Walras had to postulate the existence of an omnipotent 'auctioneer' capable of knowing all exchange and utility values at all times. This deity enabled Walras to happily ignore money.

But other economists were not happy with the 'imaginary auctioneer'. Since money was a commodity, it must also have a production function and, since everyone wants it, also a utility function. What was special about money was that it had unique properties of durability and very high velocity (speed at which it circulates through the economy in transactions), both of which reduced its relative production costs to near zero.[16] Hence, in orthodox economic theory, the demand for money can be understood almost entirely through its marginal utility.[17] And this was presumed to be relatively constant, in the long run at least, since money was simply representative of the value of other 'real' commodities.* Hence money was built in to models of general equilibrium with the concept of its neutrality effectively maintained. Mainstream macro-economic models today

---

* Fisher formulated this approach with the equation of exchange which states that under any given conditions of industry and civilisation, deposits tend to hold a fixed or normal ratio to money in circulation. The equation of exchange is $MV = PT$, where M is Money (including bank deposits), V is the velocity of money, P is the general price level and T, the volume of transactions. This equation eventually gave rise to the 'Quantity Theory of Money' which has dominated macro-economics for much of the last century.[19]

treat money this way, by including a 'money-in-utility' function that attempts to show why people desire money, whilst preserving its neutrality.[18]

3.2.3.
Problems with the orthodox story

If this description of the role of money in the economy seems a little strange to you, you will be pleased to know you are not alone in questioning it. Any economic model requires generalisations, assumptions, and simplifications in order to tell us something interesting about how things work. But in the case of orthodox economics' description of the relationship between human beings and money, the assumptions are so far-fetched that they fatally undermine the model.

The most obvious failure is that the theory is internally inconsistent. If you take the assumption of perfect information to its logical conclusion, there would be no need for money or indeed any other kind of intermediating financial service (including banking) in the economy at all.* For if everyone did indeed have perfect information at all times about everything, as with Walras's auctioneer, they really would exchange goods and services in barter-like fashion without the need for any commodity like money to provide them with information about the value of those goods and services. So, paradoxically, under conditions of perfect information and certainty, money becomes redundant, which of course undermines neoclassical explanations of the origins of money in commodity-exchange in the first place.† This circularity has been grappled with by proponents of general equilibrium models ever since.[20,21,22]

But it is not necessary to conduct these kinds of thought experiments to realise the logical inconsistency of the orthodox story. Think about any of the successful entrepreneurs you know. You will probably find that most of them started out with very little money and had to get loans from the bank, friends, or family before they could begin selling their services or products on the market. As Marx pointed out, in the capitalist system, money (or capital/financing) is required prior to production,[26] rather than naturally arising after production as a way of making exchange more convenient. This is why it is called 'capital-ism'. So building a model that starts with market clearing and allocation and then tries to fit in money as a veil on top of this makes little sense.

---

* For a comprehensive and amusing list of the activities and organisations that would not exist under conditions of perfect information see Werner (2005)[23]; they include insurance, advertising, consultancy, legal advice, estate agents, economic forecasting, meetings, stockbroking, fund management and securitisation.

† The historical evidence of 'pure barter' economies is also lacking. Anthropologists argue that there has never been such a thing as a 'pure bartering economy' as hypothesised by classical economists and hence call into question the emergence of money from barter.[24] Humphrey maintains that 'The search for coincidence of wants is not necessary, since the time and place of barter for common items was established long in the past' and that barter 'has been misconstrued largely because of the persistence of the creation-myth in classical and neoclassical economics that in barter lie the origins of money and hence of modern capitalism.'[25]

As American economist Hyman Minsky argues:

> *...we cannot understand how our economy works by first solving allocation problems and then adding financing relations; in a capitalist economy resource allocation and price determination are integrated with the financing of outputs, positions in capital assets, and the validating of liabilities. This means that nominal values (money prices) matter: money is not neutral.*[27]

Besides this, there is no explanation of how money is injected into the economy in the first place and in what quantity. Money is simply called forth by individual demand – but there is no account for how and why individuals handle money or why the demand for or supply of money is at a certain level, at a particular point of time.[28]

In addition, the notion that money might be used as a store of value and hence not immediately put back into circulation cannot easily be incorporated into general equilibrium models as the velocity of money is assumed to be stable in the long run. Keynes, writing during the 1930s at the time of the Great Depression, argued that the demand for money was much more complex than the orthodox story allows: in a 'monetary economy' people choose to hoard or save money under certain conditions, as well as using it as a means of exchange.[29]

Neither does the orthodox story provide a satisfactory explanation of the existence of modern 'fiat' money – that is, money backed only by the authority of a sovereign (previously the King, now the state or central bank) rather than any commodity. The £10 banknote in your wallet or the £400 of digital money deposited in your bank account does not appear to be backed by any commodity. You cannot change it into gold or silver.

3.3.
Credit theory of money: money as a social relationship

Have a look in your wallet to see if you have any sterling notes. Notice that on a £10 note it states that 'I promise to pay the bearer on demand the sum of ten pounds'. It appears this money is a future claim upon others – a social relationship of credit and debt between two agents. This relationship is between the issuer of the note, in this case the state, and the individual. It does not appear to have anything to do with relations of production, between an agent and an object, or with the exchange of commodities (object-object relations).

The orthodox economics narrative rests upon deductive* assumptions about

---

* Deductive reasoning is concerned with whether conclusions logically follow from a set of assumptions. We can have an argument that is sound, but its usefulness is questionable if the assumptions do not fit well with our experience of the real world. This approach contrasts with inductive reasoning which attempts to draw conclusions from empirical observations. These conclusions are more grounded in evidence, but provide less certainty in the argument because they are always vulnerable to being refuted by new observations that contradict our previous experience.

reality that enable the construction of abstract models.[30] In contrast, researchers who have chosen a more inductive approach, investigating empirically how money and banking actually works, have been more likely to favour the view that money is fundamentally a social relation of credit and debt. These researchers of money come from various academic disciplines. They include: heterodox economists (including some early twentieth-century economists), anthropologists, monetary and financial historians, economic sociologists and geographers and political economists.[31,32,33,34,35,36] In fact, the only thing they have in common in terms of their academic discipline is that they are *not* neo-classical economists.

3.3.1.
Money as credit: historical evidence

From an historical perspective, the earliest detailed written evidence of monetary relations is to be found in the financial system of Babylon and ancient Egypt. These civilisations used banking systems thousands of years before the first evidence of commodity money or coinage.[37] Much as banks do today, they operated accounting-entry payment systems, in other words lists or tallies of credits and debts. As the monetary historian Glynn Davies puts it:

> *Literally hundreds of thousands of cuneiform blocks have been unearthed by archaeologists in the various city sites along the Tigris and Euphrates, many of which were deposit receipts and monetary contracts, confirming the existence of simple banking operations as everyday affairs, common and widespread throughout Babylonia. The code of Hammurabi, law-giver of Babylon, who ruled from about 1792 to 1750 BC, gives us categorical evidence, available for our inspection in the shape of inscriptions on a block of solid diorite standing over 7ft high, now in the Paris Louvre, showing that by this period 'Bank Operations by temples and great landowners had become so numerous and so important' that it was thought 'necessary to lay down standard rules of procedure'.[38]*

The historical record suggests that banking preceded coined money by thousands of years. Indeed, historical evidence points to the written word having its origins in the keeping of accounts. The earliest Sumerian numerical accounts consisted of a stroke for units and simple circular depression for tens.[39]

These banks conducted 'clearing' or 'book-keeping' activities, also often described as 'giro-banking' – giro from the Greek 'circle'. If enough people recorded their debts with a single bank, that bank would be in a position to cancel out different debts through making adjustments to different accounts without requiring the individuals to be present. Modern banks still undertake this clearing activity by entering numbers into computers as we shall see in Chapter 4.

Whilst clay tablets were used in Babylon, tally sticks were used in Europe for many centuries to record debts.[40] Tally sticks were sticks of hazel-wood created when the buyer became a debtor by accepting goods or services from the seller who automatically became the creditor. The sticks were notched to indicate the amount of the purchase or debt and then split in two to ensure that they matched in a way that could not be forged. They were used in England until 1826 and can still be seen in the British Museum today.[41]

Another historical argument is that the practice of measuring value came from elaborate compensation schedules – Wergeld – developed to prevent blood feuds in primitive societies.[42] These required measuring the debt one owed for injuries, actual and imagined, inflicted on others. These became increasingly formalised and determined in public assemblies as societies developed. In contrast to the orthodox story, they were not the result of individual negotiation or exchange.[43] The nature and value of these items was determined by the relative severity of the injury and the ease of access to the item (they would be commonly available) and had nothing to do with their exchange or use value. 'Geld' or 'Jeld' was the Old English and Old Frisian term for money and is still used in Dutch and German.[44]

Both these examples of tallies and compensation show money as tokens, not necessarily having any intrinsic value, which record a social relationship between credit and debtor.

3.3.2.
The role of the state in defining money

Another important part of the story has been the role of the state in ensuring the acceptability of such tokens. Standardisation occurred with the development of upper classes and temple, and later palaces and communities. Evidence points to the common origins of money, debts and writing in the tax levies of the palaces.[45]

One strand of monetary theory, known as Chartalism, argues that as palaces expanded their domains, tax payments became standardised in terms of quantities or weights of widely used commodities, such as wheat or barley. These formed the basis for all the early 'money of account' units, such as the mina, shekel, lira and pound. Money originated then, not as a cost-minimising medium of exchange as in the orthodox story, but as the unit of account in which debts to the palace, specifically tax liabilities, were measured.[46,47]

It is the state's coercive power to tax its citizens that defines the unit of account as the primary function of money, as Mitchell Innes stated in 1913:

> *The Government by law obliges certain selected persons to become its debtors*
> *This procedure is called levying a tax, and the persons thus forced into this*
> *position of debtors to the Government must in theory seek out the holders of the*
> *tallies and acquire from them the tallies by selling to them some commodity*
> *in exchange for which they may be induced to part with their tallies.*
> *When these are returned to the Government treasury, the taxes are paid.*[48]

Financier and heterodox economist Warren Mosler uses the metaphor of a household currency to try to make clear the relationship between the state and citizens:

> *The story begins with parents creating coupons they then use to pay their children for doing various household chores. Additionally, to 'drive the model,' the parents require the children to pay them a tax of 10 coupons a week to avoid punishment. This closely replicates taxation in the real economy, where we have to pay our taxes or face penalties. The coupons are now the new household currency. Think of the parents as 'spending' these coupons to purchase 'services' (chores) from their children. With this new household currency, the parents, like the federal government, are now the issuer of their own currency.[49]*

The state then defines the unit of account as that which it 'accepts at public pay offices, mainly in payment of taxes'.[50] The Government's acceptance underpins the broader acceptability of these tokens.[*]

As we have seen, the means of payment varied over time, but for many centuries the instrument used was not coins. When coins did come into common usage, rarely was the nominal value of coins the same as the value of the metal of which they were made.[52] Instead, the state determined the value of the coin and was free to change it whenever it felt like it.[†] In England, Queen Elizabeth I established in 1560-61 a setting of four ounces of sterling silver as the invariant standard for the pound unit of account. Incredibly, this setting lasted until World War I, the longest historically recorded period for an unchanging unit of account in any state.[53]

However, the use of metal coins through the ages does not unsettle the central conception of money as being created through credit/debt relationships rather than depending on, or even deriving from, the intrinsic value of an underlying commodity to give it its 'money-ness'.[‡] As historian Niall Ferguson says, 'Money is not metal. It is trust inscribed.'[57] The long period of the use of gold and silver coins as the tokens of choice to represent money may be one explanation for

---

[*] Some have criticised the Chartalist school of thought for overstating the extent to which money and credit creation is a creature of the state rather than the private sector. They argue the usefulness of bank deposits lies just as much in the ability to use them to repay liabilities to others as to the state. See Eladio (2009).[51] A further criticism of Chartalism is that the theory does not take sufficient account of the differences between the US and EU systems, as is explored in more detail in chapter 5.

[†] The state has, historically, used violent coercion to enforce the use of and taxation in national currencies, including execution, imprisonment and branding with the coin. In nineteenth-century colonial Africa, for example, taxation backed by severe punishment for non-payment was used to coerce subjugated populations into wage labour and tax would be pitched at a level that elicited the required amount of work.[54] On the link between money and violence see also Tolstoy (1904).[55] Central banks also have a long record of banning or taxing out of existence private or local currency systems, not least the 5000 currencies that were estimated to circulate in the United States at the beginning of the twentieth century.[56]

[‡] Whether it might be *sensible* or *desirable* to pin the value of money to a commodity such as gold is a different question entirely.

the powerful grip that the commodity theory of money has on the imagination. Another may be the history of the development of modern banking and the role of the goldsmiths of London in the story.

3.4.
Key historical developments: promissory notes, fractional reserves and bonds

The origins of modern banking in Europe and the UK are a complex mixture of constitutional, fiscal, and monetary developments and there is not room for an in-depth historical account in this book.[58] Instead, we will review briefly three key financial innovations that have given rise to the modern monetary system:

1. The emergence of private media of exchange (Bills of Exchange) in the form of **promissory notes** that circulated independently of state money, which at the time was mainly gold and silver coinage.
2. The practice, by the custodians and exchangers of precious metals and coinage, of issuing deposit receipts to a value greater than the value of deposits the custodians actually possessed – a practice that would later be described as **fractional reserve banking**.
3. The perceived need for a stable source of long-term borrowing by governments from the custodians and exchangers of precious metals – a practice that would come to be known as **bond issuance**.

All three of these innovations came fatefully together in Britain in the seventeenth century, a time of almost continual warfare.* At the time, silver coinage was the state currency. Crown and Parliament were in a constant struggle to raise enough taxes and mint enough silver coinage to meet the resulting debts.[59]

This also meant that there was not much demand for luxury goods at the time, including jewellery. As their name suggests, goldsmiths' original task was fashioning jewellery from precious metals. But goldsmiths also played a useful custodial and exchange role – their vaults were secure places to keep gold and silver coin, bullion and jewels. And as London grew in prominence, attracting traders from across Europe, the goldsmiths, along with other professions such as pawnbrokers and scriveners (someone who could read and write), became important holders and exchangers of domestic and foreign coinage.[60] The 'seizure of the mint' by King Charles I in 1640 coupled with the outbreak of civil war in 1642 led to a significant increase in demand for their custodial services in particular.[61]

---

* These included the Civil War (1642–52) and colonial wars with Spain, Holland and France.

3.4.1.
Promissory notes

Goldsmiths would issue 'deposit receipts' to people who left gold and silver coins with them. These were simple acknowledgements of a personalised debt relationship between the goldsmith and the owner of the gold placed in their care; the earliest known such receipt, issued to Laurence Hoare, dates back to 1633.[62] Goldsmiths also began to carry out clearing and bookkeeping activities.* Everyone soon found that it was a lot easier simply to use the deposit receipts directly as a means of payment. The bankers' deposit receipts effectively became a medium of exchange, much as had the Bills of Exchange that began circulating through Europe considerably earlier.†

3.4.2.
Fractional reserve banking

Goldsmiths also soon realised that they could lend out a proportion of the metallic coins they kept safe since it was inconceivable that all of their customers would choose to withdraw all of their deposits at exactly the same time. By charging interest on these loans (the rules on usury had been considerably liberalised in England to a 5 per cent interest rate maximum), goldsmiths were able to make a good and exponentially growing return on this service for very little effort.[65]

Soon goldsmiths further realised that as the real deposit receipts were being used as a means of exchange as opposed to the metal itself, they could equally issue deposit receipts instead of actual metal for their loans. And this meant they could issue more gold deposit receipts than they had actual gold deposited with them. Goldsmiths chose to keep just a fraction of their total loan value in the form of gold in their vaults.‡ Thus they created new money and **fractional reserve banking** was born.

---

* The first regular banker was reputed to be Mr Francis Child, a goldsmith who kept a shop on Fleet Street, London, who was followed in the practice by Messrs Snow and Dunne on the same street[63]. Child & Co is still operating as a private bank today and is owned by the Royal Bank of Scotland.

† In sixteenth century Latin Christian Europe, Central Europe and Italy in particular, early forms of privately issued credit money called 'Bills of Exchange' or 'Bills of Trade' came in to being. Networks of traders, integrated through regular interactions on established trade routes and cities, began to accept these Bills in lieu of payment in the coinage of the period, determined by city-states of the time. In the German lands, these Bills were traded and settled in regular intervals at the major trade fairs (Messe). If one merchant owed another a sum of money which could not be paid in cash until the conclusion of a transaction some months hence, the creditor could draw a bill on the debtor and either use the bill as a means of payment in its own right or obtain cash for it at a discount from a banker willing to act as a broker.[64]

‡ Accounts of fractional reserve type activities outside the UK go back much earlier than the goldsmiths however. For a thorough ranging review see Huerta de Soto (2006/1998)[67]. For a user-friendly and colourful introduction to the origins of fractional reserve banking, download Paul Grignon's animated film *Money as Debt*[68].

In the words of financial journalist Hartley Withers:

... some ingenious goldsmith conceived of the epoch making notion of giving notes not only to those who had deposited metal, but also to those who came to borrow it, and so founded banking.[66]

As has been pointed out by a range of different scholars, from a legal perspective, the goldsmiths were committing fraud.[69] Their deposit receipts, when issued to those borrowing (as opposed to depositing) gold from them, stated that the goldsmith actually held in reserve the gold that they were borrowing. This was simply not true – no deposit had been made and the gold was not there. The receipts were fictitious – they were pure credit and had nothing to do with gold. But no-one could tell the difference between a real deposit receipt and a fictitious one. As Karl Marx describes the process in Das Kapital:

With the development of interest-bearing capital and the credit system, all capital seems to double itself, and sometimes treble itself, by the various modes in which the same capital, or perhaps even the same claim on a debt, appears in different forms in different hands. The greater portion of this 'money-capital' is purely fictitious. All the deposits, with the exception of the reserve fund, are merely claims on the banker, which, however, never exist as deposits.[70]

Aside from its questionable legality, fractional reserve banking was and remains a business model quite different from normal market-based activities.[71] For most businesses, there is a direct relationship between revenues and the provision of goods and services and hence costs, usually at a declining rate. And in true intermediary banking activity, for example, the loaning of time deposits as described at the start of this chapter, profits are limited by the interest-rate differential between what the bank has to pay to the saver and demand from the borrower.

But by lending at interest through fractional reserve banking, the revenue stream can rise exponentially, without the provision of any new goods or services to anyone, and hence without further costs (see also Box 8, Section 4.4). A bank can charge compound interest, for example, on its loan, whereby interest incurred is added to the principal loan and further interest charged upon both the principal and the additional interest on an ongoing basis.[72] The bank has not paid any equivalent interest to any saver in order to create the loan – it has simply created a highly profitable stream of income backed by nothing more than the perceived ability of the borrower to repay the loan or the collateral owned by the borrower (for example their home).* This is not to say that the bank has not provided a

---

* There is some confusion in the various debates around the role of interest and fractional reserve banking literature about which is more important. We would argue that there is not a problem with non-compounding interest when it genuinely represents the lost opportunity cost of not having a resource (in this case money). But in the case of fractional reserve banking, as we have seen, there is no loss of resource by the bank when it makes a loan – no money is being taken from anywhere else. For a useful guide to the historical use of interest see Pettifor (2006)[73]

valuable service to the borrower by extending credit, and so therefore some profit is justified by the increased liquidity risk that the bank runs as a result of the additional credit. If the bank needs to obtain additional central bank reserves to maintain liquidity it will incur additional funding costs. However, it should be noted that such liquidity risk may in the end be directly or indirectly underwritten by the community.

3.4.3.
Bond issuance and the creation of the Bank of England

With their ability to create new credit seemingly from nowhere, it was not surprising that goldsmiths were popular. Soon the King and Parliament, unable to raise enough taxes or mint silver coinage quickly enough to meet the demands of the Civil War and French wars of the period, began to borrow from goldsmiths, too. The demand for goldsmiths' lending services, from both private individuals and government grew to be so profitable that in order to boost their deposits they began to offer to pay interest on 'time deposits' – that is, deposits left for a guaranteed period of time. Any remaining doubts about the negotiability and status of goldsmiths' notes was removed in the Promissory Notes Act of 1704 which confirmed the legality of the common practices that goldsmiths had being employing since the 1640s.[74]

The state's informal and eventually legal acceptance of goldsmiths' fictitious deposit receipts increased the state's spending power and allowed the creation of modern commercial bank money. Commercial bank money was already in use in seventeenth-century Holland and Sweden and it was now developed in England. These countries were engaged in wars at the time and were short of money. As a result, they took to issuing bonds (Box 3) to the rich merchants and goldsmiths of their respective countries. The practice of bond issuance had begun much earlier in the city states of northern Italy and was another transformative financial innovation – a way for the state and later companies to fund expansionary trade through long-term borrowing without the need for additional metal coinage.[75]

Box 3: Bonds, securities and gilts

A bond is a debt instrument which enables companies or states to access cash through issuing an IOU to an investor. The investor, who could be an individual, but these days is more often an institutional investor (e.g. a pension fund) loans a certain amount of money, for a certain amount of time, with a certain interest rate, to the company or country. In return, the investor receives a certificate which they can use to redeem the bond when it matures (i.e. the date at which it expires). Meanwhile, a fixed payment is usually made by the issuer to the holder (the coupon). This is why bonds are also called fixed income securities. Furthermore, when market interest rates rise, the value of bonds falls, and vice versa, as the value of the expected future income stream from the fixed coupon payment changes. Bonds are an example of debt based securities or tradable securities (stocks are equity based securities).   ➔

Bonds issued by companies are generally termed commercial bonds, commercial paper (which are for a shorter term than bonds) or commercial securities.

Bonds issued by states have a variety of names, including government bonds, government securities, Treasury bills (which refer to short-term government bonds) and in the UK they are referred to as gilts. The term gilt or gilt-edged security originated from the gilded edges of the certificates themselves and has come to represent the primary characteristic of gilts as an investment: that they have proved safe investments over time. The British government has never (yet) failed to make interest or principal payments on gilts as they fall due.

Bonds can be issued by a government in foreign currencies; these are often referred to as sovereign bonds.

Because most governments do not default, government bonds are an attractive form of investment, in particular for risk-averse investors such as pension funds. For the same reason, government bonds can be highly 'liquid' or 'tradable'. So-called benchmark bonds, with high issuance volumes, can often be sold very rapidly in exchange for cash or bank money, which are the final means of payment in modern societies.

The Dutch brought the concept to England following the successful invasion by the Dutch Prince William III of Orange in the 'Glorious Revolution' of 1688, who displaced the reigning monarch. Under the reign of William III (and Mary), the charging of interest (usury) was soon allowed and bank-friendly laws were introduced. Given the previous repeated defaults by indebted kings and a raid on the national mint; Parliament and creditors of the state (namely the merchants and goldsmiths of the Corporation of London) lobbied for the creation of a privately owned Bank with public privileges – the Bank of England – and the secession of one square mile of central London as a quasi-sovereign state within the state.*

The merchants loaned £1.2 million to the state at 8 per cent interest, which was funded by hypothecated customs and excise revenues.[77] The English state had begun to issue bonds and borrow at interest and for the first time, the state committed a proportion of its tax revenues towards the interest payments on long term debts.[78] This system of private credit creation superseded the former system of public money issuance in the form of tallies issued by the Treasury. To symbolise this, tally sticks were buried in the Bank of England's foundations. This was the first time taxation became a tool for the state to repay debts to wealthy private sector creditors.

---

* The City of London Corporation, the municipal authority for London's financial district, has unusual powers to this day, often expressed in ceremonial oddities such as the granting of 'permission' from the Lord Mayor for the Queen to cross the City boundaries, as well as unique features of more practical importance such as the ability of corporations and partnerships to vote in elections; its own police and the power to amend its own constitution. For fascinating detail about the 'offshore tax haven' in the middle of London, see Chapter 12 of Shaxson (2010)[76].

The Bank of England was created in 1694 and three years later was granted a royal charter and the right to take deposits, issue bank notes, and discount promissory notes. The promissory notes that had previously circulated only amongst the goldsmiths and trader networks, could now be traded at the Bank of England at a discounted rate for state money.

The two major monetary innovations of the period – public debt in the form of state bond issuance and promissory notes – were now integrated for the first time in history in a single institution: the newly created, privately owned Bank of England. In this new arrangement, the state now raised taxes at least partially to fund interest payments on its debts to the creditor class. And at the same time, the previously private deposit receipts now became accepted, at a discounted rate, by the Bank of England; the Promissory Notes Act of 1704 made all notes, whether payable to 'X', to 'X or order', or to 'X or bearer', legally transferable, giving credit money a public monetary sphere[79]. They were now just one small step from being equivalent to state money, which at the time was coinage, and hence accepted as payment of tax.

3.5.
Early monetary policy: the Bullionist debates and 1844 Act

The new integration of the state and its creditor class proved to be successful for England and is often held up as one of the key reasons for its defeat of France in the war that followed and for the expansion of English commercial, trade and military power.[80,81] It was a model that was eventually imitated over much of the rest of the Western world. Yet, the Bank was less successful at preventing volatility in the issuance of paper money and coinage. Whilst private banks in London were gradually absorbed into the Bank of England, elsewhere in the UK industrialists were forming regional commercial banks – or 'country banks' – which played an important role in the industrial revolution.[82] These did not have access to the backing of the central bank as lender of last resort and relied on working through accounts at London clearing banks. The country banks issued paper notes of various types and qualities which were discounted (i.e. exchanged for Bank of England notes or credit entries in banks' accounts with the Bank of England) at relatively low rates of interest.[83]

Despite the Bank of England's notes being linked to gold, currency and banking crises remained frequent and inflation rampant. A great debate began between two schools of thought over how best to solve the problem, a debate which continues to this day in modern monetary theory.* The Bullionist (later 'Currency') school claimed that rising prices were the fault of the Bank of England

---

* See Galbraith (1975)[85] for a brief review of the debate. The Banking versus Currency school debate was later continued in the main dividing line in twentieth-century monetary theory between the Monetarist school who believed the Government could determine the money supply exogenously through changing the base rate and the neo- or post-Keynesian school which viewed credit creation as 'endogenously' determined by the economy itself.

for discounting too great a volume of bills issued by private banks. Convinced of the intrinsic value and stability of gold (the commodity theory of money – Section 2.2), they called for the return of full convertibility of bank-note issuance to gold reserves. In contrast, the anti-Bullionist (later 'Banking') school claimed that rising prices were a natural result of increased economic activity and trade, resulting in a natural increase in the price of gold and the demand for loans.[84]

As financial crises continued into the first half of the nineteenth century, the Government eventually acted. First, the Bank Charter Act 1833 made Bank of England notes legal tender for the first time in England and Wales. In addition, the act abandoned the 5 per cent usury laws for the Bank of England's discounting facility. The hope was that by increasing the discount rate, the Bank could suppress the issuance of notes by private banks by driving up the cost of converting them into legal tender. As Davies suggests, 'in this quiet way, what was to become the famed 'Bank Rate' instrument of policy for the next 150 years was born'.[86]

But these measures proved to be insufficient for creating financial stability. Further banking failures in 1836 and 1839 led to massive drains on the Bank of England's gold reserves as customers feared that their privately issued bank-notes would become inconvertible. Finally, the 1844 Bank Charter Act banned the creation of any new banks with note-issuing powers (including amalgamations of existing banks) and limited the issue of new notes by the Bank of England.[87] What English economist and journalist Walter Bagehot described as the 'cast iron' system limited the issue of new notes to the existing £14 million in circulation that were backed by government securities.[88] Beyond that, any new notes issued would have to be backed by additional gold and silver reserves. The result was the gradual dying out of private bank-note issuance by the country banks and an effective monopoly for the Bank of England on the printing of new notes.*

However, importantly, the Act exempted demand deposits – the accounting entries that banks made either when people deposited money with them or, more likely, were created as a result of borrowing – from the legal requirement of the 100 per cent gold reserve backing. We have seen how fractional reserve banking allowed banks to lend multiples of the amount of gold in their vaults. Similarly, they could create new bank deposits through lending or purchasing assets, which were multiples of the amount of now restricted banknotes. Because these account balances were technically a promise by the bank to pay the depositor, they were not restricted by the Act in the same way that banknotes were. This meant that the country banks were able to create them without breaking counterfeiting laws. Furthermore the 1844 Act did not incorporate demand deposits as part of its legislation as it would be very difficult for any customer or state regulator to be able to tell the difference between a fictitious demand deposit, created by the

---

* Davies records that country bank note issues ceased in 1921 when Lloyds absorbed Fox, Fowler and Co. of Wellington, Somerset with its 55 branches.

banks when they issue a loan, and a 'real' demand deposit placed at a bank by a customer who, for example, has just received their salary. Both types of money will look exactly the same in the banks accounting reports. As Werner suggests:

As banks work as the accountants of record – while the rest of the economy assumes they are honest accountants – it is possible for the banks to increase the money in the accounts of some of us (those who receive a loan), by simply altering the figures. Nobody else will notice, because agents cannot distinguish between money that had actually been saved and deposited and money that has been created 'out of nothing' by the bank.[89]

No doubt the failure to include demand deposits in the 1844 Act was also related to the strength of the commodity theory of money (Section 3.2) at the time, manifest in the rhetoric of the Bullionist school. The paper notes issued by the country banks were much more tangible than their demand deposits and more obviously competitors with commodity money (gold and silver). Railing against paper money, Bullionist William Cobbett argues:

We see the country abounding with paper money; we see every man's hand full of it; we frequently talk of it as a strange thing, and a great evil; but never do we inquire into the cause of it. There are few of you who cannot remember the time when there was scarcely ever seen a bank note among Tradesman and Farmers … If you look back, and take a little time to think, you will trace the gradual increase of paper money and the like decrease of gold and silver money…[90]

It was not long before the country banks, no longer able to issue their own private banknotes, began to specialise in deposit taking and the issuing of cheques or account statements.[91] These cheques and statements could be redeemed for Bank of England notes or gold in just the same way as the old banknotes had been. As the Federal Reserve Bank of Chicago puts it:

Transaction deposits are the modern counterpart of banknotes. It was a small step from printing notes to making book-entries crediting deposits of borrowers, which the borrowers in turn could 'spend' by writing checks, thereby 'printing' their own money.[92]

The result was that the 1844 Act failed to stop fractional reserve banking – the creation of new money by private banks. It merely led to a financial innovation in the medium of exchange. At the same time it made the ability of banks to create money out of nothing far less visible: while it is more obvious in Scotland and Northern Ireland, where banks continue to issue paper money carrying their own branding, the general public in England and Wales has no daily reminder of the banks' role as the creators of the money supply. This has served to perpetuate the myth – widespread even today – that only the central bank or possibly the Government can create money.

Whilst the 1844 Act is widely considered to be a key ingredient of the Golden Period of UK financial history over the next 70 years, it was not very effective in preventing banking crises in the remainder of the nineteenth century. Indeed, the act was repeatedly repealed – in 1847, 1857, and 1866 – to allow the Bank of England to print new notes in excess of its gold reserves to prevent massive financial collapses following bank failures (for it is far cheaper for central banks to step in and bail out banks than it is for the tax payer to do the same).

Many historians attribute the Golden Period not so much to the 1844 Act as to Britain becoming the dominant world power. This underpinned the credibility of the Bank of England's governance of the whole international monetary system through Sterling as the world's reserve currency. It had the additional feature that the British state increasingly came to rely on issuing bonds at interest, just as the United States has been able to do through most of the twentieth century.

3.6.
Twentieth century: the decline of gold, deregulation, and the rise of digital money

3.6.1.
A brief history of exchange rate regimes (see also Section 5.6.1)

Historically, during the long phase of 'commodity-money', the exchange rate would depend upon the amount of gold, silver or copper contained in the coins of each country. A coin containing ten grams of gold would exchange for two coins containing five grams of gold and so on.

Similarly, after the advent of paper money and the gold standard, the exchange rate depended upon the amount of gold a government promised to pay the holder of bank notes. These amounts did not vary greatly in the short-term and as such, exchange rates between currencies were relatively stable. Consequently those who traded across currencies faced little risk that movements in exchange rates would affect their profits, meaning that there was less opportunity for currency speculation and less requirement for 'hedging' against the risk of an exchange rate changing.

3.6.2.
WWI, the abandonment of the gold standard and the regulation of credit

The Golden Period came to an abrupt end with the onset of WWI. The Government once again became in desperate need of funds and the 1844 Act was again abandoned with little hesitation. Britain left the gold standard in 1914 by unofficially ceasing specie payments: meaning that one could no longer redeem banknotes for gold coins. Following the successful US example, the Government instead issued its own money (Bradbury bills, named after the then Secretary to the Treasury, John Bradbury) to raise finance for the war. This direct government money was not borrowed from any bank or investor through bond issuance and it proved successful in combating the acute banking crisis that followed Britain's declaration of war on Germany in August 1914 and contributed to the war economy. As Davies observes,

The cessation of internal gold circulation, then conceived simply as an urgent temporary expedient, thereafter became permanent. Thus ended without fuss or fanfare nearly 700 years of intermittent gold coinage circulation, including a century of the full gold standard, ousted ignominiously by bits of scrappy paper.[93]

After the war, countries attempted to reinstate the gold standard, believing this would restore stability to the international financial system. The UK fixed the value of sterling to gold at its pre-war level under the Gold Standard Act of 1925, but the public could no longer exchange bank notes for gold coins, only gold bullion.

However, the inter-war gold standard did not last for long. In 1931, following a period of financial upheaval, concerns began to surface about Britain's investments in Europe. By September that year, speculators increasingly presented pounds to the Bank of England in order to convert them into gold. In response to this, with the Bank of England unable to support the pound at its official value, on 19 September 1931 Britain abandoned the gold standard. The pound floated freely once again.[94] Other countries had either already left the gold standard or would do so soon after.[95]

The rigid adherence to the standard, the consequent inability for exchange rates to adjust to reflect changes in international competitiveness and the high interest rates required to defend currencies from speculative attacks have been blamed for deepening the Great Depression, with some studies finding a correlation between the length of countries' adherence to the standard and the severity of the depression in that country.[96,97] It has also been suggested that inter-war instability was in part a result of the shift of power from the pre-war dominance of sterling to the new global reserve currency – the US dollar – and hence the de facto governance of the global financial system passing to the US Federal Reserve, which was unaccustomed to and ill-prepared for such an undertaking. Following WWII, a 20-year period of relative financial stability ensued in much of the Western world, with the Bretton Woods agreement providing a fixed exchange rate against the US dollar, which in turn was convertible into gold at a fixed price. The system lasted into the 1970s until, just like Britain in 1931, the USA found itself unable to live up to the promise to convert dollars into gold. European commentators accused the USA of abusing the system by simply creating too many dollars, with which US firms then bought European companies and assets. The French government responded by demanding the conversion of its dollar balances into gold. As with the British gold standard, it turned out that the promise to convert into gold worked only as long as it was not acted on. In response to the French 'raid on Fort Knox', US President Nixon cancelled the dollar convertibility into gold. By 1976 all the world's major currencies were allowed to float freely against each other.

As with the earlier Golden Period, where the UK's well-established currency and institutions were associated with international stability, it was the institutional structures and macro-economic context of the immediate post-war period that underpinned the stability of currencies rather than the US retention of a gold standard of $35 an ounce. Importantly during this period there were strict credit controls placed on banks in many Western states. Britain was no different. Banks were required to hold 8 per cent of their assets in the form of cash and a more general liquidity reserve ratio of 28–32 per cent was imposed.[98]

But even this was not seen as enough control at the time. Britain's central bank developed its own qualitative and quantitative credit controls. Known as 'moral suasion', this informal guidance of bank credit by the central bank limited the total amount of credit banks could create and set quotas for specific sectors. As reported in a review of monetary policy in the 1960s:

> For much of the ten-year period [the 1960s] the circumstances required more severe restraint on credit than could be achieved by acting on liquidity and ratios. It was therefore necessary to have recourse to direct forms of control – the imposition of lending ceilings. Direct requests to the deposit banks to restrict the level of their advances had been made at times in the 1950s … [T]he terms of the request were fairly general (… that the recent rate of increase in advances should be greatly reduced). Lending ceilings were re-imposed in 1965 when all banks and hire purchase finance houses were asked to restrict their lending to an annual rate of increase of 5 per cent in the twelve months to March 1966. Specific ceilings of this general kind have been in force for most of the time since then. The quantitative ceilings have been accompanied by qualitative guidance – again not a new development – on the direction of lending. This guidance has always accorded priority to export finance.[99]

As we can see from Figure 7, during this period there was something of a balance between the amount of money in circulation issued by the state in the form of notes, coins and bank-money (it was about 50/50). Such 'window guidance' bank credit controls were abandoned in the early 1970s. As Figure 7 shows, that is when bank credit began to increase rapidly.

Figure 7: UK money supply, 1964-2011: Broad money (M4) and Base money

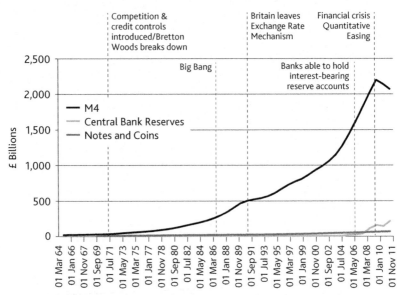

Notes: Total stock of M4, Central Bank Reserves and Notes and Coins adjusted for inflation (the Retail Price Index), and shown in 2012 prices .

Source: Bank of England[100] and authors' calculations

3.6.3.
Deregulation of the banking sector in the 1970s and 1980s

The period from the late 1960s until the present day saw the gradual deregulation of banking and credit both on an international and national scale. Much of the theoretical support for such deregulation was based on an analysis that thought of banks as mere financial intermediaries, as described in Chapter 2, Section 2.3 and which neglected their crucial function as creators of the money supply.

A range of new actors, in particular foreign banks, 'fringe' or 'secondary' banks* and hire purchase houses entered the UK financial markets and began lending aggressively. Hire purchase houses, which were not regulated as banks by the Bank of England, provided enormous amounts of credit for the purchase of consumer durables, in particular motor vehicles, which were thought to be highly inflationary.[101] These institutions were not classified as banks and as such were not subject to the credit controls that were only applied to the big clearing banks of the day.

---

* Fringe banks – or secondary banks – were individual small lenders who were not subject to banking regulations.[102]

Figure 8: Decline in UK liquidity reserve ratios [103]

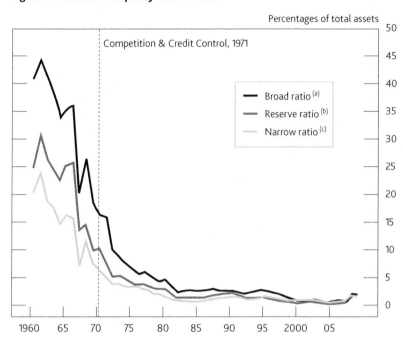

Sources: Bank of England, Bankers Magazine (1960-68) and Bank calculations. Data before 1967 cover only the London clearing banks.

(a) Cash + Bank of England balances + money at call + eligible bills + UK gifts

(b) Bank of England balances + money at call + eligible bills

(c) Cash + Bank of England balances + eligible bills

In response, in 1971, the Government introduced the Competition and Credit Control (CCC) reforms, which replaced the 8 per cent cash reserve ratio and 28 per cent liquidity reserve ratio with a new 12.5 per cent liquidity reserve ratio (see figure 8).[†] At the same time, however, the Bank brought a much wider range of financial institutions into the remit of banking regulation – previously only the large clearing banks had been included. It also permitted clearing banks to engage freely in the fast-growing 'wholesale' money markets (Box 4) where financial instruments such as government and commercial bonds were traded; previously they had only been able to trade in this through finance house subsidiaries or 'discount houses'. This also meant that banks could now access central bank money and cash from the money market rather than being dependent on the central bank itself to access central bank reserves and sterling. Most of all, despite its name, the Act marked the abolition of credit controls. A credit boom followed,

---

[†] 12.5 per cent of banks deposits would have to be held in the form of 'eligible reserve assets', which included balances in the Bank of England, Treasury bills and money at call with the discount markets.[104]

fuelling a housing boom, which led to the inevitable banking crisis (see Box on the Quantity Theory of Credit in Section 5.6), known as the secondary banking crisis of 1974. Property prices collapsed as bank credit became tight, and banks had to be rescued by the Bank of England.

Box 4: Wholesale money markets

The term 'money market' covers the vast network of deals involving the lending and borrowing of liquid assets in a range of currencies, generally between financial institutions such as banks, as well as non-financial companies and the Government. These assets include tradable securities, such as government securities, Treasury bills or corporate IOUs (commercial paper, or 'CPs'), bank debt (certificates of deposit, 'CDs') usually maturing within a year or less.

'Wholesale' means funds borrowed or lent by those financial institutions in large quantities, rather than the smaller amounts dealt in by private individuals.

As Davies suggests, the Competition and Control reforms saw a fundamental shift in emphasis from the central bank which:

> ....changed from rationing bank credit through quantitative ceilings on bank advances and qualitative or selective guidance... to rely on the more generally pervasive influence of the price mechanism, with variation in the rate of interest becoming the main weapon.[105]

The Bank abandoned its age-old Bank Rate and replaced it with a Minimum Lending Rate (MLR), now described as the Policy Rate or short-term interest rate, which determined the rate at which banks and other financial institutions could access cash and Bank of England reserves.[106] These organisations could then lend reserves to other banks at whatever rate they wanted. Hence monetary regulation became more subject to market forces and the goal of the bank turned to attempting to ensure the market rate of interest was reasonably close to the policy rate.[107]

In 1979, exchange controls which prevented any but authorised UK banks engaging in foreign exchange were lifted and, with the Bretton Woods fixed exchange rate system having been abandoned, as a result there was an explosion in international capital flows in and out of the UK. The UK became an international centre for foreign exchange with a flood of foreign banks opening up in London and the growth of the 'euro-dollar' market* which had begun to develop in the 1960s.[108]

---

* Eurodollars is the generic name for US dollar deposits held by non-US banks outside the USA and therefore outside the jurisdiction of the US Federal Reserve. This market developed from the combination of the status of the US dollar as the global reserve currency after WWII, and the desire of the Soviet Union to move its holdings out of the USA during the Cold War, as well as the build-up of dollar revenues from oil exporting countries that they preferred to hold outside the US.

The oil crises of the 1970s and rapid inflation helped usher into power the free-market-oriented governments of Margaret Thatcher and Ronald Reagan in the UK and USA, respectively, who, influenced by neoclassical free-market economics, began to further dismantle state controls on bank credit, including interest-rate caps. UK Conservative finance ministers Geoffrey Howe and Nigel Lawson oversaw the abolition of all controls over consumer credit together with the deregulation of housing finance in the 'Big Bang' reforms of 1986.[109] Compulsory liquidity reserve ratios were gradually reduced from the 12.5 per cent set in 1971, until eventually they were made voluntary (Figure 8). The next credit boom ensued, resulting in banking problems by the end of the 1980s.

A review of the arguments at the time makes clear that the theoretical support for such deregulation was based on the unrealistic assumptions of neoclassical theoretical economics, in which banks also perform no unique function and are classified as mere financial intermediaries just like stockbrokers. This does not recognise their pivotal role in the economy as the creators of the money supply. As a consequence, no regulator has since explicitly monitored the quantity of credit created by banks, and the qualitative allocation and direction of these new money injections. There is no monitoring of whether newly created credit is used for transactions that contribute directly to GDP or not. As figure 9 (overleaf) demonstrates, since the 1980s, bank credit creation has decoupled from the real economy, expanding at a considerably faster rate than GDP. According to the Quantity Theory of Credit (see Section 5.6) this is evidence that an increasing amount of bank credit creation has been channelled into financial transactions. This is unsustainable and costly to society, as it amounts to resource misallocation and sows the seeds of the next banking crisis.

Figure 9: Broad money (M4) and nominal GDP indexed from 1970

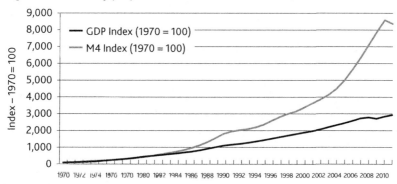

Source: Bank of England[110]

Credit that finances trading in existing assets, real or financial, does not contribute to GDP, but instead it can contribute to unsustainable asset inflation. Since the 1970s there has not been any direct oversight of whether credit contributes to GDP or not. Neither has there been any monitoring of whether credit creation funds investment in productive capacity or consumption transactions (the latter creating more direct inflationary pressure).[111]

The globalisation of capital flows and banking services saw a shift towards an international regime of banking regulation with policy being developed by the Basel Committee on Banking Supervision, whose secretariat is located at the Bank of International Settlements (BIS) based in Basel, Switzerland. Many observers consider the Basel Committee as being strongly influenced by the goals of the largest banks in the industrialised countries. Rather than focusing on liquidity, the Basel agreements (I, II, and more recently III) place emphasis on 'capital adequacy ratios' (see Chapter 5).

3.6.4.
The emergence of digital money

Just as important to our understanding of the modern monetary and banking system, however, have been developments in information and communication technology. These have changed not just the medium of exchange: from cash to cheques to debit and credit cards to internet banking, but the relative power of different actors in relation to the issuance of new money. As cash became less and less important as a medium of payment in relation to demand deposits that could easily be moved around with the use of debit cards or electronic transfers, so the macro-economic importance of the banking system as the main creator of new money in the economy increased.[112] As the European Central Bank stated in 2000:

> At the beginning of the 20th century almost the totality of retail payments were made in central bank money. Over time, this monopoly came to be shared with commercial banks, when deposits and their transfer via checks and giros became widely accepted. Banknotes and commercial bank money became fully interchangeable payment media that customers could use according to their needs. While transaction costs in commercial bank money were shrinking, cashless payment instruments became increasingly used, at the expense of banknotes.[113]

Today virtually all (most estimates are between 97 to 98 per cent) money in circulation is commercial bank money.[114] As shown in Figure 7, its growth has been exponential. As recently as 1982, the ratio of coins and notes to bank deposits was 1:12 – by 2010 this ratio had risen to 1:37.*

---

* Bank of England statistics: M4 (LPQAUYN) and Notes and Coins (LPMB8H4). Ratio calculated by dividing M4 by Notes and Coins for March 1982 and December 2010.

These figures and Figure 7 may appear to run counter to our everyday lived experience of using money. Most people, for example, have probably not noticed a decline in their use of cash over this period – we all still feel more comfortable going out with a tenner in our wallets. But it is important to distinguish between the frequency of transactions and the value of transactions paid for with each type of money. Cash is still used for what numerically is the majority of transactions, but the majority of transactions are very small, for example, less than £10. Digital money – in the form of transferring demand deposits (commercial bank money) from one account to another – is used almost exclusively for larger transactions and hence accounts for the majority of transaction *volumes*. This is because of the convenience of credit and debit cards and, increasingly, online banking where the volumes are considerably larger. None of these media of exchange involve notes and coins (state-money).

We have discussed how all money is credit. Nowadays, we can also say that, with the exception of a tiny fraction of cash, money is basically information. Huge volumes of money are moved around our economies simply by people typing data into computers. The 1s and 0s, the binary language of the computer, are the closest representation we have to what money is today. Money has never been a commodity, as we have seen, but in our digital world it is now even less tangible than it has ever been. Those with the power to create new money have enormous power – they can create wealth simply by typing figures into a computer and they decide who can use it and for which purpose.

Let us now examine in detail how this happens in the UK today.

References

1   Simmel, G., (2004/1907). *The Philosophy of Money*, 3rd Edition. London: Routledge, p.148

2   Ferguson, N., (2008). *The Ascent of Money: A Financial History of the World*. London: Penguin, p. 31

3   Kaminsky, G. L., (2003). *Varieties of Currency Crises, National Bureau of Economic Research*, Working Paper 10193. Retrievable from http://www.nber.org/papers/w10193

4   Davies, G., (2002). *A History of Money*. Cardiff: University of Wales Press, p. 27

5   Jevons, W. S., (1896/1875). *Money and the Mechanism of Exchange*. New York: Appleton and Company

6   Goodhart, C.A.E. (1998). The two concepts of money: implications for the analysis of optimal currency areas. *European Journal of Political Economy* 14: 407–432

7   Smithin, J., (2000). Introduction in *What is Money?* London and New York, Routledge, pp.1–16

8   Ingham, G., (ed). (2005). Concepts of Money: Interdisciplinary Perspectives from Economics, Sociology and Political Science. London: Edward Elgar.

9   Mill, J. S., (1871). *Principles of Political Economy*, p.341

10   Menger, C., (1892). On the Origins of Money. *Economic Journal* 2: 239–255

11   Jevons (1896/1875). op. cit.

12   Radford, R. A., (1945). The Economic Organisation of a POW Camp. *Econometrica*, Volume 12

13   Schumpeter (1994/1954). *History of Economic Analysis*. London: Allen & Union. p. 277

14   Walras, L., (1954-74). *Elements of Pure Economics*. London: Allen & Unwin

15   Pigou, A. C., (1949). *The Veil of Money*. London: Macmillan

16   Marshall, A., (1996-1899). Evidence to the Indian Currency Committee in Marshall, A. (n.d.). *Correspondence of Alfred Marshall, Economist*, Volume II, 1891–1902 at the Summit. Cambridge: Cambridge University Press

17   Pigou (1949). *op. cit.*

18   Sidrauski, M., (1967). Rational choice and patterns of growth in a monetary economy. Retrievable from http://en.wikipedia.org/wiki/American_Economic_Review *American Economic Review* 57(2): 534–544

19   Fisher, I., (1911). *The Purchasing Power of Money*. New York: Macmillan.

20   Clower, R., (1967). *A reconsideration of the microfoundations of money. Western Economics Journal*. Retrievable from http://www.carlostrub.ch/sites/default/files/Clower1967.pdf, in Walker D. (ed.) *Money and Markets*, Cambridge: Cambridge University Press, pp. 81–99

21   Hahn, F., (1965). On some problems of proving the existence of an equilibrium in a monetary economy, in Hahn, F., Brechling, F.P.R. (eds), *Theory of Interest Rates*. London: Macmillan

22   Lapavitsas, C., (2005). The emergence of money in commodity exchange, or money as monopolist of the ability to buy. *Review of Political Economy* 17(4): 549–569.

23   Werner, R. A., (2005) *New Paradigm in Macroeconomics*. Basingstoke: Palgrave Macmillan., pp. 20–24

24   Mauss, M., (1966). *The Gift*, London: Cohen & West.

25   Humphrey, C., (1985). Barter and Economic Disintegration *Man*, 20 (March): 48-72, p. 56.

26   Marx, K., (1976-1867). *Capital, Volume 1*, Harmondsworth: Penguin

27   Minsky, H.P., (1986-2008). *Stabilizing an Unstable Economy*. Yale: McGrawhill, pp. 159-160

28   Dodd, N., (1994). *The Sociology of Money*, Cambridge: Polity Press, p. 12

29   Keynes, J. M., (2008/1936). *The General Theory of Employment, Interest and Money*. BN Publishing

30   Werner (2005). *op. cit.* pp. 17–18

31   Keynes, J. K., (1930). *A Treatise on Money: Volume 1 A Pure Theory of Money*, Chapter 1

THE NATURE AND HISTORY OF MONEY AND BANKING

32 Goodhart, C.A.E. (1998). The two concepts of money: implications for the analysis of optimal currency areas. *European Journal of Political Economy* 14

33 Smithin, J., (2000). Introduction in *What is money?* London: Routledge, pp. 1–16

34 Ingham, G., (2004). *The Nature of Money.* Cambridge: Polity Press

35 Leyshon, A., Thrift, N., (1997). *Money/Space: Geographies of Monetary Transformation,* Routledge: London

36 Mellor, M., (2010). *The Future of Money: From Financial Crisis to Public Resource,* Chapter 1. London: Pluto

37 Davies (2002). *A History of Money.* Cardiff: University of Wales Press. pp. 50–55

38 Ibid. pp. 50–1 quoting from Orsingher, R., (1964). *Banks of the World: A History and Analysis.* Paris: viii

39 Davies (2002). *op .cit.* p. 50

40 Innes, A.M., (1913). What is Money? *Banking Law and Journal* May: 377–408

41 Davies (2002). *op. cit.,* p. 663

42 Wray, L. R., (1998). *Understanding Modern Money: The Key to Full Employment and Price Stability,* Chapter 3. Cheltenham: Edward Elgar p. 43

43 Grierson, P., (1977). *The Origins of Money,* London: Athlone Press, pp. 19–21

44 Wikipedia (n.d.) Retrievable from http://en.wikipedia.org/wiki/Wergeld

45 Greirson (1977). *op. cit.* p. 43

46 Innes (1913). *op. cit.*

47 Wray (1998). *op. cit.* Chapter 3

48 Innes (1913). *op. cit.* p. 398

49 Mosler, W., (2010). *Seven Deadly Innocent Frauds of Economic Policy.* Valance Co. Inc., p. 18

50 Knapp, G. F., (1905). *The State Theory of Money.* London: Macmillan

51 Eladio, F. (2009). Three difficulties with neo-chartalism, *Journal of Post Keynesian Economics* 31 (3): 523–541. Retrievable from http://www.ucm.es/info/ec/ecocri/cas/Febrero.pdf

52 Innes (1913). *op. cit.*

53 Davies (2002). *op. cit.,* pp. 203–8 quoted in Ingham (2004) *op. cit.* p. 123

54 Wray (1998) *op. cit.* pp. 57–61

55 Tolstoy, L., (1904). *What Shall We Do Then? On the Moscow Census Collected Articles.* London: J.M. Dent & Co.

56 Zelizer, V, 1997 (1994). *The Social Meaning of Money: Pin Money, Paychecks, Poor Relief, and Other Currencies.* Princeton, New Jersey: Princeton University Press, p. 17

57 Ferguson (2008). *op. cit.,* p. 31

58 See Ingham (2004) *op. cit.* pp.107–33 for a guide to developments at a European level and Davies (2004) *op. cit.* pp. 238–83 for a British focus. See Werner, R.A., (2005). *op. cit.* Chapter 12, for an overview of the history of banking and its implications

59 Carruthers, B. G., (1996). *City of Capital.* Princeton: Princeton University Press, p. 62

60 Davies (2002). *op. cit.* p. 249

61 *Ibid.* p. 251

62 *Ibid.* p. 252

63 Percy, R., (1824). *Interesting Memorials of its Rise, Progress, & Present State, Volume 3* (Google eBook).

64 Ferguson (2008). *op. cit.* pp. 43–4

65 Werner (2005). *op. cit.* Chapter 12

66 Withers, H., (1909). *The Meaning of Money*. London, p. 20

67 Huerta de Soto, J. (2006-1998). *Money, Bank Credit, and Economic Cycles*, translated from the Spanish by Stroup, M.A., Alabama: Ludvig von Mises Institute., Chapter 2, pp 37–111

68 Grignon, P. (n. d.) Money as Debt. Retrievable from http://video.google.com/videoplay?doc id=-2550156453790090544

69 Rothbard, M., (1974). *The Case for a 100 Percent Gold Dollar*. Washington, DC: Libertarian Review Press; Huerta de Soto (2006-1998) *op. cit.*

70 Marx, K., (1894). *Capital*, Volume III, part V, Chapter 29. Retrievable from http://www.marxists. org/archive/marx/works/1894-c3/ch29.htm [accessed 10 April 2011]

71 Werner (2005). *op. cit.* p. 168

72 El Diwany, T., (2003). *The Problem with Interest*, 2nd Edition. London: Kerotac, pp. 8–10

73 Pettifor, A., (2006) *The Coming First World Debt Crisis*, Basingstoke: Palgrave Macmillan. Chapter 5, pp. 120–144

74 Davies (2002). *op. cit.* p. 252

75 Ferguson (2008). *op. cit.* pp. 165–18

76 Shaxson, N., (2010). *Treasure Islands: Tax Havens and the Men Who Stole the World*. London: Random House.

77 Ingham (2004). *op. cit.* p. 129

78 Carruthers, B. G., (1996). *City of Capital*. Princeton: Princeton University Press, pp. 71–83

79 Carruthers (1996) *op. cit.*, p. 130

80 *Ibid.*

81 Ferguson (2008). *op. cit.* Chapter 2

82 Pressnell, L.S., (1956). *Country Banking in the Industrial Revolution*. Oxford: University Press / Clarendon Press

83 Davies (2002). *op. cit.* pp. 286–92

84 *Ibid.* p. 311

85 Galbraith (1975) op. cit. pp. 48–9

86 *Ibid.*

87 Retrievable from http://en.wikipedia.org/wiki/Bank_Charter_Act_1844

88 Bagehot, W., (1876). *Lombard Street: A Description of the Money Market*, New York: Scribner, Armstrong and Co., p. 25

89 Werner (2005). *op. cit.* p. 179

90 Cobbett, W., (1828). *Paper Against Gold*, p. 5, quoted in El Diwany (2003) op. cit.

91 Davies (2002). *op. cit.* p. 321

92 Nichols (1992-61). *op. cit.* p. 3

93 Davies (2002). *op. cit.* p. 372

94 Remarks by Governor Ben S. Bernanke at the H. Parker Willis Lecture in Economic Policy, Washington and Lee University, Lexington, Virginia, 2 March 2004

95 Eichengreen, B.J., (2008). *Globalizing capital: a history of the international monetary system*. Princeton University Press; 2nd edition, p. 82

96 Eichengreen, B. J. and Sachs, J. (1985). Exchange Rates and Economic Recovery in the 1930s. *Journal of Economic History* 45: 925–946

97 Choudhri, E., Kochin, L.A., (1980). The Exchange Rate and the International Transmission of Business Cycle Disturbances: Some Evidence from the Great Depression. *Journal of Money, Credit, and Banking* 12: 565–574

98 Davies, R., Richardson, P., Katinatire, V., (2010). Evolution of the UK Banking System. *Bank of England Quarterly Bulletin* 4: 321–332

99 Croome, D. R. and Johnson, G. J., (eds) (1970). *Money in Britain 1959–69: The papers of the 'Radcliffe report – ten years after' conference at Hove, Sussex*, October 1969. London: Oxford University Press, p. 225

100 Bank of England interactive database, M4 (code LPQAUYN), Central Bank Reserves (code LPMBL22), notes and coin (code LPMAVAB). Retrievable from http://www.bankofengland. co.uk/boeapps/iadb/newintermed.asp

101 Davies (2002), *op. cit.* p. 408

102 Reid, M. (1978). The secondary banking crisis – five years on. *The Banker* 128(634): 21–30

103 Davies, R., Richardson, P., (2010). Evolution of the UK Banking System. *Bank of England Quarterly Bulletin* 4: 321–332. Retrievable from http://www.bankofengland.co.uk/publications/ quarterlybulletin/qb1004.pdf p. 328

104 Davies (2002). *op. cit.* p. 409

105 *Ibid.*

106 Monetary Policy Committee and Bank of England. (1999). The Transmission mechanism of monetary policy, *Bank of England*. Retrievable from http://www.bankofengland.co.uk/

107 *Ibid.*

108 Davies (2003). *op. cit.* p. 414

109 Pettifor (2006). *op. cit.* p. 62

110 GDP statistics from Bank of England, *The UK Recession in Context, 3 centuries of data*. M4 statistics from Bank of England interactive database, M4 (code LPQAUYN)

111 Werner (2005). *op. cit.*

112 Huber, J., Robertson, J., (2000). *Creating New Money: A Monetary reform for the information age*. London: nef

113 ECB. (2000). *Domestic payments in Euroland: commercial and central bank money*. Speech by Tomasso Padoa-Schioppa, Member of the Executive Board of the European central bank, at the European Commission Round-Table *Establishing a Single Payment Area: State of Play and Next Steps, Brussels*, 9 November 2000, quoted in Werner, R., (2009). *op.cit.*, p. 5

114 For example, the Bank of England estimated notes and coins to be 3 per cent of money in circulation in 2007 – see Berry, S., Harrison, R., Thomas, R., de Weymarn, I. (2007). Interpreting movements in Broad Money. *Bank of England Quarterly Bulletin* 2007 Q3, p. 377. Retrievable from http://www.bankofengland.co.uk/publications/quarterlybulletin/qb070302.pdf

MONEY AND BANKING TODAY

Few phrases have ever been endowed with such mystery as open-market operations, the Bank Rate, the rediscount rate. This is because economists and bankers have been proud of their access to knowledge that even the most percipient of other citizens believe beyond their intelligence.
J.K. Galbraith (1975)[1]

We have now critically examined the common public and textbook understanding of money and banking and showed how banking in the UK has developed over the past three centuries. We have seen that today the bulk of the UK's money supply is created not by the state, the Bank of England, the Treasury, or the Royal Mint, but by a small collection of private, profit-oriented companies that are commonly known as banks.

These are the fundamentals. However, it is important also to have a grasp of the workings of the present-day money and banking system in the UK. In particular, we need to understand that there are some constraints on the quantity of credit that banks can create even though they effectively have a licence to create new money.

The next two chapters provide a detailed overview of the way that commercial banking works today in the UK and how it interacts with the central bank, the payment system and the money markets. To start, we need to address the concept of liquidity.

4.1.
Liquidity, Goodhart's law, and the problem of defining money

In Section 3.1, we saw that acceptability as a means of exchange and of final settlement were key functions of money. History suggests that one useful way of judging acceptability of money is whether you can use it to pay taxes and, more generally across the economy, to buy goods and services. However, when defining money mainly as private sector assets, there is no sharp dividing line between money and non-money. There are some assets which can be much more easily converted into money than others; this quality is referred to as liquidity. More liquid assets are those that can be more certainly realisable at short notice without loss.

For example, my house is very illiquid because I am unlikely to be able to sell it quickly unless perhaps I offer it for sale at a huge discount. In contrast, if I can find a pawnbroker then I can quickly convert my watch into cash. If other people realise that my watch is quite a liquid asset, they might even accept it in exchange for selling me something, because they know they can easily convert it into cash. In this case, my watch has taken on some of the functions of money – we might call this 'near-money'. Because liquidity changes gradually across different assets (i.e. there is a spectrum of liquidity – see Figure 10); drawing a line at any particular point will always to a certain extent seem arbitrary.[2]

Figure 10: Liquidity scale

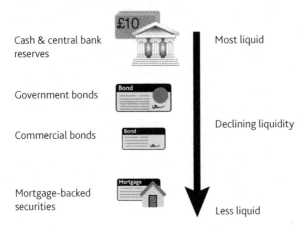

Banknotes are the most liquid asset, and can be used immediately to perform economic actions like buying, selling or paying debts, thus meeting immediate wants and needs. Central bank reserves, which function as electronic banknotes for commercial banks trading with one another, are equally liquid.

To this we can add commercial bank money, the electronic money in my bank account, because with electronic banking and debit cards my bank deposits are certainly widely accepted. Indeed bank deposits are sometimes more acceptable since it is actually easier and more convenient to use electronic payment for many routine obligations, including utility bills and taxes, than it is to use cash. As far as the deposit holder is concerned, electronic money appears to be just as liquid as cash, even if, technically, it isn't.

This seems straightforward for current accounts, or 'demand deposits', but what about savings accounts, or 'time deposits'? An instant-access savings account is really just as liquid as a current account. But what if I have to give seven days' notice? This particular bank deposit is less liquid, but once I have given the bank notice it will be transformed into a more liquid deposit in my current account. This helps explain why the Bank of England uses several different measures of money supply, which are set out below in a simplified form:

Central bank money (also known as M0, high-powered money, monetary base, or narrow money)
1. Notes and coins in circulation (sometimes referred to as cash).
2. Reserve balances at the Bank of England.

Broad money
M1 Notes and coins in circulation with the non-bank public plus sterling current accounts.

M2   M1 plus sterling time deposits with up to three months' notice, or up to two years' fixed maturity.

M3   M2 plus repurchase agreements, money market fund units, and debt securities up to two years – estimated by the European central bank (ECB) for the UK to be consistent with the M3 measure used by the ECB for the euro area.

M4   M3 plus other deposits at UK banks or building societies.

Further complications arise from the capacity of modern capitalism to continuously create new forms of credit/debt that are not perfectly liquid.[3,4] Economist Charles Goodhart argued that defining money was inherently problematic because whenever a particular instrument or asset was publicly defined as money by an authority in order to better control it, substitutes were produced for the purposes of evasion[5] (this is known as 'Goodhart's law').[6] We revisit the question of where to draw the line around 'money' later in Chapters 5 and 7.

The process of defining money becomes easier when we focus on the question of when and how new money is created. Then the definitional problems become irrelevant. When a bank makes a loan it invariably credits the borrower's current account and from there the money is spent. When a bank grants an overdraft facility, it promises that it will make payments on my behalf even though I have no deposits. In this case, new deposits are created for the person to whom I have made a payment. Thus new commercial bank money enters circulation when people spend the credit that has been granted to them by banks (Section 4.2).

Others also sometimes point out that commercial bank money is credit and then proceed to distinguish this from 'money' and measures of the money supply. Such an argument is mere smoke and mirrors. It is impossible for anyone else to distinguish between a balance on my current account that got there because I paid in £1,000 in cash over the counter, and the same balance that got there because the bank advanced me a £1,000 loan. Even the cash I pay in over the counter had to be withdrawn from another bank account, which may have been funded by a loan or an overdraft. In any event, as the opinion polls referred to in Chapter 2 demonstrate, if you stopped someone in the street and told them that the balance in their current account was not actually money at all, they might well think you had taken leave of your senses.

The Bank of International Settlements describes it as follows:

> *Contemporary monetary systems are based on the mutually reinforcing roles of central bank money and commercial bank monies. What makes a currency unique in character and distinct from other currencies is that its different forms (central bank money and commercial bank monies) are used interchangeably by the public in making payments, not least because they are convertible at par.*[7]

In the next sections, we go through the credit creation process by private banks and the relationship between private banks, the central bank and the payment system.

4.2.
Banks as the creators of credit money

A customer, whom we'll call Robert, walks into a branch of Barclays Bank and asks to borrow £10,000 for home improvements. Barclays makes a check of Robert's income and evaluates his credit rating, and decides that he can be relied upon to keep up repayments on the loan.

Robert signs a loan contract promising to repay the £10,000, plus the interest, over the next three years, according to an agreed monthly schedule. This loan contract legally binds Robert to make repayments to the bank. As such, it has a value of £10,000 (plus the interest) to the bank. Upon signing, Barclays records it as an asset on its balance sheet (T-chart 1):

T-chart 1: Loan by Barclays Bank

Barclays Bank Balance Sheet (Step 1)	
Assets	Liabilities
(What the borrowers owe to bank + bank's money)	(What the bank owes to the depositers + bank's net worth)
Loan to Robert £10,000	

Of course, double entry bookkeeping (Box 5) requires an equal and opposite accounting entry, and besides, Robert now wishes to get access to the money. So Barclays creates a new bank account for him, and gives it a balance of £10,000. This account is a liability of the bank to Robert, so it is recorded on the liabilities side of Barclays' balance sheet (T-chart 2):

T-chart 2: Bank simultaneously creates a loan (asset) and a deposit (liability)

Barclays Bank Balance Sheet (Step 2)	
Assets	Liabilities
(What the borrowers owe to bank + bank's money)	(What the bank owes to the depositers + bank's net worth)
Loan to Robert £10,000	Robert's new account £10,000

Note that the bank has expanded its balance sheet and all it has done is added some numbers to a record in a computer database, recording that it has a liability to Robert and also an asset in the form of Robert's agreement to repay his loan. This is the process of extending credit or, more accurately, of creating credit. This credit authorises Robert to make payments of up to £10,000 from this account, using his debit card, cheque book, or bank transfer. The numbers that the bank typed into Robert's account can be used to make payments, and therefore function as money. The process of creating commercial bank money – the money that the general public use – is as simple as a customer signing a loan contract, and the bank typing numbers into a new account set up for that customer.

Box 5: Double-entry bookkeeping and T-accounts

A double-entry bookkeeping system is a set of rules for recording financial information where every transaction changes at least two different ledger accounts.

The name derives from the fact that financial information used to be recorded in books – hence 'bookkeeping' (whereas now it is recorded mainly in computer systems). These books were called ledgers and each transaction was recorded twice as a 'debit' and a 'credit'.

The accounting equation serves as an error detection system: if at any point the sum of debits does not equal the corresponding sum of credits, an error has occurred. It follows that the sum of debits and credits must be equal. Double-entry bookkeeping is not a guarantee that no errors have been made, for example, the wrong nominal ledger account may have been debited or credited, or the entries completely reversed.

On the balance sheet of a bank, the debits and credits are termed assets and liabilities respectively. A bank's capital (or equity) is derived from the accounting equation: Equity = Assets – Liabilities. By convention, it is recorded on the liability side (see also figure 15 and the explanation of bank solvency in box 10).

In this guide, we use T-accounts to show what banks' balance sheets look like. T-accounts split the bank's assets (conventionally shown on the left) from liabilities (shown on the right). Assets can be thought of as legal contracts that entitle the bank to a stream of future income (interest received) in return for payment of an initial sum (principal) which will eventually be recovered by the bank. Liabilities can be considered as a promise to pay a certain sum in the future, which incurs a stream of expenses (interest paid) until that time.

Commercial banks and the Bank of England do not normally use T-accounts but instead list assets first and then liabilities underneath, but we shall use T-accounts as it is easier to compare multiple bank balance sheets (e.g. a commercial and the central bank) using T-accounts next to one another.

The process is similar if Robert has an overdraft facility, but in this case no new deposit is created in his account. Instead, a new deposit is created for someone else when he makes a payment to them. The overdraft operates as a variable loan of which the borrower can determine the timing and amount within the limit agreed.

When a bank buys securities ('tradable loans') such as a corporate or government bond, it adds the bond to its assets, and increases the company's bank deposits by the corresponding amount. Similarly, the bank creates new money when it buys assets, goods or services on its own account, or pays its staff salaries or bonuses.

These newly created demand deposits represent new spending power – or money – in the economy. It is not spending power that has been taken out of someone else's savings. As shown in T-chart 2, Robert is free to spend his 'deposit' however he wants. However, if Robert spends his credit with customers of other banks, then the other banks will come to Barclays asking it to settle with them. This process of settlement is described next. In Chapter 5, we analyse the extent to which the need for central bank reserves and interbank settlement will limit the willingness of banks to create credit or money in the manner just described.

4.3.
Payment: using central bank reserves for interbank payment

If you and I both have an account at the same bank, it is a very simple process for me to transfer £500 to you. I simply instruct my bank to do so and it makes an accounting entry on its computer that shows £500 leaving my account and £500 entering your account. There is no need for any cash to be handed over, or any reason to involve the Bank of England. This clearing or payment function within the same bank has, as we saw in Chapter 3, been going on since Babylonian times. All that is required is for some numbers to be typed into a computer (or written on a clay tablet, in former times) and removed from another account.

But what if we bank with different banks as in the example in Figure 11? Given that a demand deposit, as we have seen, is no more than a contract with a promise to pay, how does it get transferred, as a means of final payment, from one bank to another? One option is for me to withdraw £500 in the form of cash and give it to you to pay into your own account. Most of us would find this highly inconvenient.

Principally, there are two ways for banks to get around this problem. The first is for banks to use their accounts with other banks to settle transfers directly, having netted out transactions in opposite directions. This is called 'bilateral settlement'.

An alternative method is for banks to use their accounts with the central bank. The Bank of England has its own clearing system with its own equivalent of demand deposits that have the status of final means of payment, just as cash or legal tender. Just to recap on Section 2.3, we call this type of money **central bank reserves**. Together with currency in the form of notes and coins which is circulating outside the banking sector, this makes up **high-powered money**, also known as **base money**, **monetary base**, or **central bank money**.

In the same way that you have a bank account with a particular bank, the banks themselves have bank account(s) with the Bank of England called reserve accounts (Figure 12). Just as you must maintain enough balance in your account to ensure all your payments go through, so private banks must maintain reserve balances in their Bank of England account in order to enable payments to other private banks requested by customers. It should be noted that commercial banks have been using central bank reserves as means of settlement with other banks since the 1770s, as discussed in Sections 3.4 and 3.5.

In Figure 11, Richard makes a payment of £500 to his landlord Stuart. The result, as shown in the simplified graphic, is simply a transfer between their respective banks' reserves accounts (HSBC and Barclays).

Figure 11: Commercial banks and central bank reserve account with an example payment

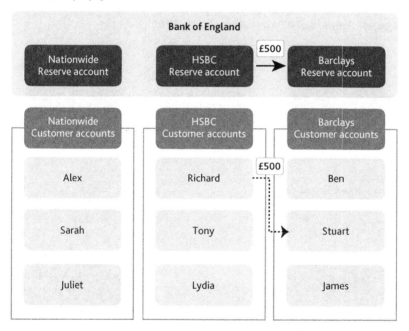

The quantity of central bank reserves is determined by the central bank. It adjusts its reserves to try to always ensure that there are enough in the system for commercial banks to access to make the necessary payments to each other. It ensures there is enough 'liquidity' in the clearing system. Commercial banks cannot 'own' central bank reserves in just the same way as you and I cannot 'own' demand deposits. Instead commercial banks borrow central bank reserves from the central bank to finance their reserves balances. So commercial banks have a liability to the central bank in the form of these loans and the central bank has an asset as it is owed money by the commercial bank (T-chart 3). Alternatively, they can sell securities to the central bank and receive reserves as payment.

T-chart 3: Balance sheet of private banks and central bank showing reserves

Private banks		Central bank	
Assets	Liabilities	Assets	Liabilities
(What borrowers owe to the bank)	(What the bank owes to customers)		
Loan to customers	Deposits of customers	Loans to private banks	Reserve deposits of private banks
Central bank reserves	Loans from central bank		

Now, let us work through our example of Richard paying his landlord Stuart in more detail. Follow the steps in Figure 12 to understand how this payment is made.

Figure 12: Payment of £500 from Richard to Landlord

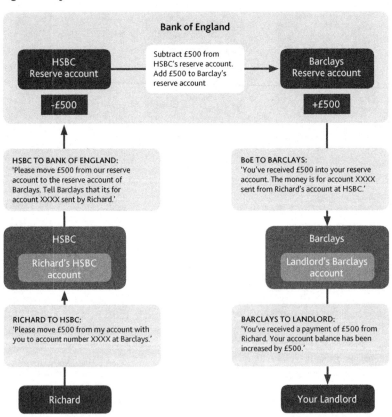

After the transaction, HSBC's and Barclays Bank's balance sheets will have changed in the following way:

T-chart 4: Private banks balance sheet

HSBC		Barclays	
Assets	**Liabilities**	**Assets**	**Liabilities**
-£500 central bank reserves to Barclays	-£500 (from Richard to Stuart)	+£500 central bank reserves (from HSBC/Richard)	+£500 (owed to Richard's Landlord)

Central bank reserves, like bank deposits, are not tangible. They are simply numbers stored by a computer (Box 6). We can see from T-chart 4 that the total amount of reserves in the central bank reserve accounts has not changed by Richard paying his landlord £500; £500 has been taken out of HSBC's reserve account and £500 has been added to Barclays' account. Barclays receives an increase in its reserves of £500 and also adds £500 to the Landlord, Stuart's, demand deposits. Again, the accounts are separate but mirror each other.

So there is no need for any additional money anywhere in the system.

Box 6: Money as information – electronic money in the Bank of England

A reserve account at the Bank of England is not a physical vault where coins and paper money can be kept. It is just an accounting record in a computer database – in technical terms it is no more complex than a number in an Excel spreadsheet. Central bank reserves refer to the numbers stored in this computer record. Central bank reserves are not tangible, and cannot be stolen in the way that physical cash can. Central bank reserves cost nothing to produce, as one billion can be created in the same length of time that it takes to type out the following numbers: 1,000,000,000.

It is important to appreciate the fact that all money, bar a small amount of paper notes and coins, is no more than a digital record in a computer database. In fact, if you were able to access the database that holds the central bank reserve accounts, it may look like this:

Account Name	Balance
Barclays Plc	£125,352,003,023.54
Lloyds Banking Group	£250,015,135,010.24

The central bank reserves are no more tangible than the £375 billion typed out above. The entire record of balances of the central bank reserve schemes will take up less space on the Bank of England's computer hard drive than the average song on an MP3 player.*

---

* The full record of the billions of transactions from and to each account will of course take up many thousands of times more space than the simple record of the total balance.

4.3.1.
Interbank clearing: reducing the need for central bank reserves

The fact that HSBC's reserves balance has fallen by £500 and Barclays' has risen by £500 could be taken to imply that HSBC needs to replenish its balance, to have sufficient funds for other payments, and Barclays could reduce its balance.

In practice however, there are millions of people across the country all transferring money to each other across only a few major banks (Figure 13). These banks can keep a tally on their computer systems, and usually many of the movements cancel each other out at the end of each day – this is called **intra-day clearing**. Hence the actual amount of central bank reserves that needs to be transferred between banks at the end of the day or overnight (shown in Figure 13 as movements of liquid between the central bank reserve 'buckets') is a small proportion of the total value of the transactions that have taken place between their customers. The larger any individual bank is as a proportion of the total value of customer payments, the fewer reserves it is likely to need because so many transactions take place between its own customers and not between it and the other banks.

Figure 13: Simplified diagram of intra-day clearing and overnight trading of central bank reserves between six commercial banks.

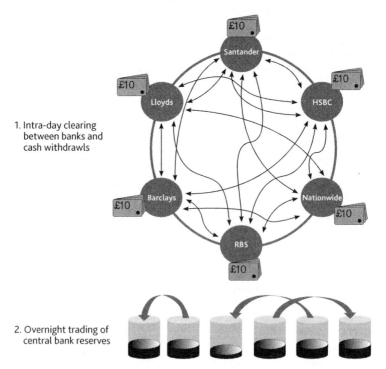

1. Intra-day clearing between banks and cash withdrawls

2. Overnight trading of central bank reserves

For example, just before the financial crisis in 2007, Lloyds Bank (now merged with HBOS) had 19 per cent of the personal current account market.[8] That means that 1 in 5 people in the UK banked with Lloyds and so it could clear a significant number of transactions between its own customers with no need for any central bank reserves or without any need to use its balances with other banks. Furthermore, whilst tens of millions of pounds were leaving its accounts every day to go to different banks, so tens of millions would be coming back to it from the same banks. The difference between these inflows and outflows is obviously much smaller than the total gross value of the flows. Hence Lloyds only needed to keep a small proportion of central bank money as a proportion of total payments, conferring a commercial advantage to scale. Other things being equal, the smaller the bank, the relatively larger the amount of central bank reserves it requires to settle its customers' transactions, and so the lower the amount of more profitable assets it will be able to hold.

At the end of each day, commercial banks will either be 'short' of central bank reserves and need to borrow more or they will be 'long' on central bank reserves and have 'excess' liquidity. As in Figure 13, we can imagine banks' reserves with the central bank as buckets with different volumes of liquid. Some banks will have too much and others too little, so they will trade with each other to balance this out in preparation for the following day's trading. To adjust its reserves, a bank can either borrow funds directly from the central bank or, more usually, it will engage in overnight trading with other banks on the interbank money market. Banks that have excess reserves will typically lend them to banks in need of reserves in return for highly liquid interest-bearing assets, usually gilts (government securities) (see Chapter 3, Box 3 on bond issuance). The rates of interest on loans between banks will typically be better than banks could attain when borrowing directly from the central bank.

If central bank reserves are withdrawn from one account, they must go up in some other account. What this means is that the 46 banks within the clearing system know that there should always be enough money in aggregate to meet all the necessary payments. There may not be enough reserves to meet liquidity requirements, if the central bank imposes such a rule (we examine liquidity regulation in Section 5.2). This means that if a bank finds itself with too few reserves to make a payment, it can borrow central bank reserves from another bank within the loop, which, by definition, will have excess reserves. And the opposite also applies – if a bank has excess reserves, it can lend these to a bank in need of more reserves. The one vital caveat, as we discuss later, is that banks have enough confidence in one another to be happy to lend to each other. These transfers are made on the interbank money market (Box 4) at the interbank market rate of interest, known as LIBOR (Box 7). We explore how the Bank of England attempts to influence this rate in Chapter 5.

Box 7: What is LIBOR and how does it relate to the Bank of England policy rate?

The London Inter-Bank Offered Rate, or LIBOR for short, is an average of the interest rates that leading banks say they would be charged if they were to borrow from other banks. LIBOR is not a single interest rate; it is calculated and published each day for ten currencies and fifteen different maturities of between 1 day and 1 year.

To calculate LIBOR, a panel of between 8 and 16 banks, depending on the currency, submit answers to the following question: "At what rate could you borrow funds, were you to do so by asking for and then accepting interbank offers in a reasonable market size just prior to 11 am?"

These submissions are annualised (e.g. a quote for a 1 day maturity would be multiplied by 365 to give the yearly maturity). The top and bottom 25% of quotes are then discarded, and the average is calculated out of the remaining 50%. The results are then reported at around 11.30am. The process and the calculations are carried out daily by Thomson Reuters on behalf of the British Bankers Association, the trade group representing British banks.

LIBOR is important, because a substantial volume of financial contracts are priced in relation to it (amounting to many trillions of pounds) and banks – often those participating in determining it – are counterparties in these contracts and their derivatives or proprietary trading desks also bet on the movement of LIBOR.

In theory, if the Bank of England is operating a corridor system (see Appendix 1) then the LIBOR rate should not exceed the boundaries set out by the corridor. We would expect that no bank would deal in the market on worse terms than it could receive from the Bank of England. However, in practice this need not be the case – during 2007-08 LIBOR moved significantly above the Bank of England base rate, despite the fact banks could borrow reserves for lower rates from the Bank of England. Why did they elect to borrow from the markets at higher rates? In short, they were worried that turning to the Bank would make them appear as though they were in trouble, which could spark a run on their deposits or make other banks less willing to lend to them. Essentially, the Bank of England lending facilities had a stigma attached to their use.

Many of the banks participating in the setting of LIBOR have been sued by investors for market abuse.* US and subsequently UK and European regulators have investigated various reporting banks and in the summer of 2012 more than a dozen major banks on three continents were found guilty of manipulating the LIBOR rate, including Barclays which was fined $290m.

The problem has been that LIBOR is not based on actual transactions and the banks are conflicted in their interests; they are counterparties in large transactions and at →

---

* See, for instance, the anti-trust litigation filed in April 2012 by the Mayor and City of Baltimore and others in the District Court of New York.[9]

the same time price-setters who are able to influence future LIBOR, which will determine the profit on those transactions. Basing LIBOR on actual transactions may not be enough, however, if the reported rates are not weighted by transaction size. It could be possible for banks to influence the average weight by undertaking and reporting small transactions at preferred rates.

The UK government set up an independent review and on September 27th 2012 the Director of the Financial Services Authority, Martin Wheatley, reported the findings. He recommended that sponsorship of LIBOR should move from the British Bankers Association, a trade body for UK based banks, to a fully independent and regulated administrator. In addition, he called for five currencies and 130 of the 1,540 daily fixings to be dropped and for the rate-setting process itself to be regulated by the Financial Services Authority.[10]

4.3.2.
Effects on the money supply

Commercial banks can increase or decrease their reserves with the central bank in a number of ways. They can borrow additional reserves from other banks or borrow reserves from the central bank, usually by posting gilts as collateral. The central bank effectively creates such reserves when it lends them to the commercial banks. The banks can also sell securities to the central bank or other banks in exchange for additional reserves.

Commercial bank money does not have to be obtained from the central bank, however, and can be created at will by banks themselves. As Keynes argued, if all the banks 'move in step' and all create new loans, which is quite typical during times of economic confidence, the aggregate amount of money will increase in the economy and the central bank may be forced to increase the aggregate amount of reserves in the system to ensure the payment system does not collapse.[11] This dynamic is commonly described in academic terminology as an 'endogenous reserve (or money) supply' and will be explored further in Chapter 5.

Just as banks create new money when they make loans, this money is extinguished when customers repay their loans as the process is reversed. Consequently, banks must continually create new credit in the economy to counteract the repayment of existing credit. However, when banks are burdened by bad debts and are more risk averse, more people will repay their loans than banks are willing to create new ones and the money supply will contract, creating a downturn.

4.4.
Cash and seigniorage

The Bank of England clearing payment system is a closed loop (Figure 13). As a customer, I cannot withdraw my bank deposits in the form of central bank reserves. I can, however, withdraw from the banking system in the form of cash. One of the commercial banks' key functions is to provide cash on demand to customers who have positive balances in their accounts, subject to certain limits such as the limit of withdrawals from cash-machines to £250 a day in the UK.

Where does this cash come from? Just like central bank reserves, it comes from the central bank. To meet customer requests for cash the commercial bank turns some of its central bank reserves into cash. Hence, when a customer withdraws cash the bank's liability falls by the same amount as the fall in its cash holdings (see T-chart 5). A commercial bank's balance sheet will record cash 'holdings' as assets held with the central bank, along with reserves.

T-chart 5: Private and central bank balance sheet

Private banks		Central bank	
Assets	Liabilities	Assets	Liabilities
Loans to customers (owed to the bank)	Deposits of customers		
Central bank reserves and cash holdings	Loans from central bank	Loans to private banks	Reserve deposits of private banks and banknotes issued to banks

Every bank must hold enough cash on its premises to ensure its account holders can get access to it on demand. The need to hold cash on demand thus places a concrete liquidity constraint on banks, but it is a constraint that has become less and less significant as the proportion of cash used for payments in the economy has declined (see Section 3.6).

4.4.1.
Is cash a source of 'debt-free' money?

Given that bank notes are still created by the Bank of England, some monetary analysts have concluded that there are two 'money supplies'. Firstly a supply of cash, created by the Bank of England and injected into the economy by being lent to commercial banks, and secondly a much larger supply of bank-created money. This second type of money is created as banks make loans to, and buy assets from, businesses and members of the public. Indeed, as we discussed in Section 4.1, Bank of England statistics do distinguish between cash and the 'broad' money supply, which includes commercial bank money.

However, the reality now is slightly different. While it is true that cash has a different status from bank deposits – as the run on Northern Rock demonstrated, people have more confidence in banknotes – it is only possible for members of the public to get hold of cash via their bank deposits. In this sense one could describe cash as a physical representation of commercial bank money, over which the Bank of England retains the branding rights. The reason for this is as follows: when the Bank of England creates bank notes, it does not give them to the Government for spending directly into the economy. Instead it sells them to commercial banks in exchange for either gilts (government bonds) or central bank reserves. Bank notes therefore do not represent debt-free money for the Government, although the Bank of England does make a profit on the sale of banknotes, parts of which accrue, eventually, to the Treasury (see Box 8).

Commercial banks effectively 'sell' the cash to the public; when you take money out of a cash machine you are not literally withdrawing the cash from your account. Instead, you are swapping banknotes for banks deposits (the numbers in your account). From the bank's perspective, they initially had an asset (the £10 note) and a liability to you, recorded as your bank balance. When you withdraw cash from the ATM, the bank's assets and liabilities both fall by £10 as they hand the cash over to you and reduce the balance of your account by £10 (T-chart 6).

T-chart 6: Withdrawal of £10.00

Private bank A	
Assets	**Liabilities**
Cash holdings = £100	Alex's deposits = £100
Alex withdraws £10 cash from the machine	

Private bank A	
Assets	**Liabilities**
Cash holdings = £90	Alex's deposits = £90

The significance of this is that collectively members of the public can only access cash if they have commercial-bank money in their accounts, or if they sell assets (e.g. bonds) to the central bank. The only way in which the money supply can be increased by the Government or central bank is through the purchase of assets from the non-bank private sector, or, in the case of the Government, by borrowing from the commercial banks in the form of loan contracts.*

---

* As Werner has argued since 1994. See, for instance, Werner (2000)[12] or Werner (2005).[13]

Box 8: Seigniorage, cash and bank's 'special profits'

The Bank of England sells bank notes to commercial banks. They sell these notes at face value (a £10 note sells for £10), yet the cost of printing a £10 note is just a few pennies. The difference between the face value and cost of production gives the Bank of England a substantial profit. This profit from the creation of money is known as 'seigniorage', and is paid over to the Treasury, where it can be used to fund government spending or to reduce taxation. Between 2000 and 2009 this seigniorage amounted to nearly £18 billion.[14]

The growth of digital commercial bank money, vis-à-vis government issued cash, can be seen to have the effect of significantly reducing this seigniorage profit to the Government proportionate to the total money supply.[15] Commercial banks do not generate seigniorage themselves as they issue credit which will, at some point, be repaid in full. However, as we discussed in Section 3.4 on Fractional Reserve Banking, commercial banks can be seen to generate 'special profits' from their power to issue money in the form of credit through the interest charged upon loans and used overdraft facilities.

Huber and Robertson[16] suggest the interest charged on the issuance of money by banks can be viewed as a 'money tax', since the Government could issue non-interest bearing money directly in to the economy. They also argue that banks enjoy a form of additional 'special profit' because they don't have to first borrow this money like other organisations. This 'special profit' can be thought of as equivalent to the central bank's base rate over the course of the loan.

The total profits arising are then the rate of interest charged on the loan (e.g. 8 per cent), added to the base rate (e.g. 2 per cent) = 10 per cent, minus any interest paid by the bank to the customer on any portions of the loan that the customer has not yet spent. This is opposed to an interest rate 'spread' profit of 8 per cent - 2 per cent = 6 per cent. Using this methodology, Huber and Robertson calculated that in 2000 the 'special profits' generated through this were £21 billion.[17]

4.5.
How do banks decide how much central bank money they need?

How might banks decide then on how much central bank money (reserves and cash) to keep aside for payments? Let's run through an example:

Barclays issues Mrs Jones a loan of £10,000. This creates an interest-bearing asset of £10,000. Simultaneously, it creates an interest-bearing deposit for Mrs Jones of £10,000 which she can spend as money.

However, Barclays knows that Mrs Jones may want to convert some of this £10,000 into cash. And also that she may transfer some to other banks electronically which will mean that Barclays will need some additional central bank reserves.

So Barclays could sell some of its liquid assets (government securities) on the money markets, replenishing its stocks of central bank reserves when it receives payment, from other banks, for the assets it sold. By how much should it increase its cash and central bank reserves in order to remain sufficiently 'liquid' to service this new loan? Given that the ratio of physical cash to customer demand deposits in 2010 was 1:37[*], the bank decides it only needs an additional £270 (£10,000/37) in cash. In addition, since the ratio of central bank reserves to deposits in 2010 was 1:15, it decides to increase its reserve account by £667 (£10,000/15), which requires borrowing the additional reserves on the interbank market. So out of the total loan of £10,000, the bank accesses just £937 of additional central bank money, equivalent to less than 10 per cent of the total loan.[†]

On average, prior to the financial crisis of 2008 onwards, the banks had £1.25 in central bank money for every £100 of customers' money. In the more cautious, post-crisis environment, the banks still have on average only £7.14 for every £100 of customers' money.[‡]

4.6.
Is commercial bank money as good as central bank money?

Let us revisit briefly the popular conception of banking as a safe-deposit box that we set out in Chapter 1. If you had £500 in your bank account, it might be logical to assume that the bank must have £500 in central bank money, ring-fenced for you and ready to use. But this is not the case. As the customer of a bank, you do not have access to any central bank money, any more than there is a bundle of cash with your name on it lying in the vaults. For your £500, as we have seen, the bank will only hold a small proportion of central bank reserves. Like goldsmiths before them, banks know that at any one time not many customers are likely to demand all of their money in cash. The banks also know that within the closed loop of the Real Time Gross Settlement (RTGS), see Box 9, as well as payments and central bank reserves leaving them, a similar volume will be coming back to them.

---

[*] Authors' calculations from Bank of England statistics, ratio calculated by dividing M4 by Notes and Coins for December 2010.

[†] Authors' calculations from Bank of England statistics, M4 versus notes and coins 2006.

[‡] Authors' calculations from Bank of England statistics, M4 versus Reserve Balances, 2010.

Box 9: Real time gross settlement (RTGS)

Forty-six banks currently have reserve accounts with the Bank of England.[18] Around £780 billion of transfers are made on average each day between these reserve accounts[19]. With all 46 reserve accounts, there are a total of 2,070 different payment flows in both directions between the accounts (money can be transferred from each individual bank to every other bank).* Rather than each bank having to deal with 45 other banks in order to make payments between them, they can simply send payment instructions to the Bank of England's RTGS (real time gross settlement) processor.

Established in 1996, the RTGS is a computer system that stores the balance of each bank's reserve account and the transactions going to and from each reserve account. The RTGS processor handles transfers of money by reducing the balance of the paying bank's reserve account, and increasing the balance of the receiving bank's reserve account.

RTGS executes the full transfer of the total payment, made instantly between reserve accounts through the RTGS processor. This is in contrast to 'multilateral net settlement' systems, whereby transactions between banks are queued, cancelled out as much as possible, for example Bank A's payment to Bank B might cancel out another payment that Bank B needs to make to Bank A. The net difference is transferred at regular intervals such as every two hours for 'faster payments services', or daily for transfers such as BACS.

---

* Forty-six banks that can each send payments to 45 other banks, assuming one counts every direction of payment as one 'flow', rather than counting each bilateral relationship as one 'flow' (in which case it would be half as many: 1,035).

Your money is *not* central bank money, and nor is it backed pound for pound by central bank money. Your money is a 'promise to pay' by a commercial bank, but as we saw in Chapter 3 on the history and nature of money, even central bank money is only a promise to pay that is enforced by the Government. The difference between the credibility of central bank money (including cash) and commercial bank money is further blurred by the insurance of commercial bank money by the state.

4.6.1.
Deposit insurance
Commercial banks are in a rather privileged position compared with ordinary businesses. Not only are they allowed to create money and allocate purchasing power, but someone else guarantees to pay their liabilities for them if they are unable to. That someone else is you, the taxpayer, via the Government. As we described in Chapter 2, the Financial Services Compensation Scheme (FSCS) guarantees that the first £85,000 of any money deposited in UK licensed banks will be repaid in the event the banks are unable to make the payment. This £85,000 is risk-free. It has been transformed by the state from an IOU issued by a bank to an IOU issued by the Government. For any deposit above £85,000, if the bank went into liquidation you would join the queue of general, unsecured creditors (behind the secured and senior creditors) hoping to get some of their money back.

So, in summary, your account with a bank provides you with the right to request a transfer to another bank, guaranteed up to £85,000.

These institutional arrangements reinforce the notion that bank credit is money, and because banks can extend credit, they can create money as effectively as when the Bank of England rolls the printing presses to produce more banknotes.

4.7.
Managing money: repos, open market operations, and quantitative easing (QE)

Towards the end of Chapter 3, we discussed how, during the 1970s, a fundamental shift occurred in the way the Bank of England conducted monetary policy. As new kinds of financial institutions – secondary banks (see section 3.6.3) – began lending aggressively, the Bank decided that rather than try to regulate the quantity of credit provided by the banking system as a whole, it would attempt to influence the price of credit. The price or cost of credit is the interest rate charged on it when it is lent out. This makes sense in a world of perfect information, complete and competitive markets, flexible prices, zero transaction costs, and utility-maximising agents, which are the conditions required for markets to clear, or reach equilibrium. In such a world, higher interest rates should lead to a reduction in the demand for credit and vice versa, as the credit market, like all markets, would be in equilibrium.

Every commercial bank may need to borrow reserves and cash from the central bank, so by changing the rate of interest charged on central bank reserves, the Bank of England can, in theory, influence the demand for loans from banks, as banks will pass on this change in interest rate to customers.

Banks access reserves indirectly via the interbank or wholesale market (Box 4) by selling or lending government securities (gilts) (Box 3). Banks lend reserves to each other at the market rate of interest applicable to them – which will vary by bank and may diverge from LIBOR. The closer the market rate of interest is to the policy rate set by the Bank (Bank Rate) the more effectively changes in the Bank Rate will carry through and the more 'reliably monetary policy is implemented' (see also Section 5.2 and Appendix 1).[20]

The central bank cannot directly determine the market rate of interest in the interbank market, but it can affect the market rate of interest by lending and borrowing reserves itself on this market to try and keep this rate close to the policy rate. These loans are conducted via repurchasing agreements (repos) and other open-market operations or through providing 'standing facilities'.

Figure 14: Open market operations by the Bank of England

A. Withdrawing liquidity

1. Bank of England sells government bonds to the interbank money market.

2. It receives central bank reserves/cash in return, withdrawing reserves from commercial banks' accounts at the central bank reducing liquidity in the system.

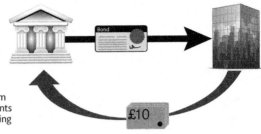

B. Increasing liquidity

1. Bank of England buys government bonds to the interbank money market.

2. It provides central bank reserves/cash in return, increasing reserves at the commercial banks' and increasing liquidity in the system.

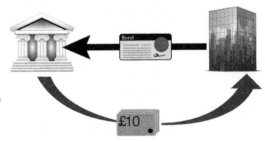

4.7.1.
Repos and open market operations

As shown in Figure 14, the central bank may have to make loans to commercial banks to fund their reserve account deposits. The primary objective of the Bank's Open Market Operations (OMOs) is therefore to supply a sufficient quantity of reserves. Nowadays it does this primarily via secured loans or repos, rather than buying or selling government bonds, or gilts, from the banks for cash. Repos are collateralised loans in which the commercial banks have to provide high-quality collateral, such as gilts, in exchange for receiving the loan.* With repos and reverse repos, central banks can add or subtract liquidity from the financial system very quickly and precisely. Nevertheless, they only constitute one example of central bank transactions. In practice, central banks are always engaged in purchase and sale operations, and their true quantitative monetary policy stance can be observed by netting out all their transactions.

In the UK, in normal times (i.e. prior to 2008), the banks decide the quantity of central bank reserves they wish to hold every month to accommodate their payments with other banks.[21] So the central bank knows exactly how much to lend, in aggregate, to the banking system. And these reserves are then distributed between banks via the money market (see Appendix 1 for developments since the financial crisis of 2007-8).

---

* Legally a repo involves the security being sold in exchange for cash with an agreement to resell the security in the other direction at a pre-specified later date, but this effectively implies a collateralised loan.

Since the rate charged on the loans is the Monetary Policy Committee's policy rate, and the demand for reserves is met by the supply from the central bank, traded rates in the money market tend to be close to the policy rate. However, in some instances market rates can deviate from the policy rate. This is usually due to some kind of market friction or loss of confidence, or could result from a bank being short of reserves and unable to meet its commitments in the interbank market.

If the central bank believes there is merit in supplying extra liquidity in the interbank market – normally indicated by the interbank rate (LIBOR or the actual rate paid by banks which may be known to the Bank of England) going significantly above the policy rate – it can make additional loans to the banks, collateralised by government securities, or it can engage in outright asset purchases.

Once it decides that the market no longer needs these extra reserves, it can wait for the loans to mature or it can absorb the excess reserves sooner by selling securities into the market.

The RTGS system (see Box 9) requires large stocks of reserve-like assets, i.e. government securities. Hence, its implementation in the late 1990s saw a massive uptake in repos and short-term (overnight) OMOs to ensure that liquidity was maintained. From the perspective of the central bank, when it grants the repo, it is a secured loan, as it is backed by a government security. The government securities given to the central bank as collateral will continue to appear as assets in the balance sheets of commercial banks. An asset of additional central bank reserves will appear with a matching liability to the central bank.

4.7.2.
Standing facilities

The Bank of England has a range of facilities designed to help deal with unusual market conditions. For example, it offers standing facilities in which a bank can always lend or borrow additional funds to or from the central bank at a penal rate relative to the policy rate. Typically, the borrowing and lending rates have been 1 per cent above and below the policy rate, respectively.

Lending facilities allow banks to borrow reserves directly from the central bank, again in return for government securities, and **deposit facilities** allow banks to deposit reserves directly with the central bank.[22]

If a commercial bank receives 'new' central bank money, then the aggregate amount of reserves in the system will have increased. With this in mind, the Bank of England will only exchange gilts for central bank reserves in one of two places:
1. The **Operational Lending Facility** exists primarily as a conduit for monetary policy in normal times. It allows commercial banks to exchange gilts for central bank reserves overnight, at a spread of 25 basis points above the Bank Rate. This short-term lending is primarily intended to facilitate borrowing if a

bank suffers temporary payment difficulties, or if the interbank overnight rate has become particularly volatile. However, the penal rate and the short-term nature of the lending are designed to ensure that the extra reserves are not used to enable more lending.

2. The **Asset Purchase Facility** (also referred to as **Quantitative Easing**, see Section 4.7.3) allows the central bank to purchase gilts and other types of assets outright, for which it issues newly created central bank reserves. This may help drive down interest rates in asset markets and increase liquidity, with the intention of incentivising banks to begin lending again. However, it may also result in more money circulating in the economy, thus stimulating economic activity, even if interest rates remain unchanged. It is important to note that, in order to comply with the Maastricht Treaty, Article 101 (see Section 6.1), the gilts purchased by the Bank of England in exchange for reserves are not bought directly from the Government.

As well as exchanging gilts for reserves, the Bank of England also exchanges other assets for gilts through its **Discount Window Facility** (See Section 4.7.4).

4.7.3.
Quantitative Easing

Central banks tell us that monetary policy is conducted mainly through interest rates. The official description is along the following lines: when the Bank of England believes that the economy is heating up it will raise interest rates to dampen economic activity. Conversely, if too little economic activity is taking place the Bank will lower the policy rate on the basis that, since interest rates are the driving force of economic activity, this will stimulate growth.

This official narrative has been criticised, as there is very little empirical evidence to support it; interest rates tend to follow economic growth and are positively correlated with it.[23,24] The problem with this official narrative become especially obvious when interest rates have been lowered so many times – and without the desired effect – that they approach zero. The same economic theory would then suggest that interest rates would need to fall below zero, becoming negative – in effect punishing banks for holding reserves with the central bank by requiring them to pay a fee. This is not difficult to implement in practice, as has been shown in Switzerland and Sweden, but Werner has argued that after banking crises one can reduce interest rates to zero or below and this will not produce an economic recovery, since interest rates are not the determining factor of bank credit creation. When the Bank of Japan faced this situation in the 1990s it re-iterated the official description of monetary policy, arguing that ever further interest rate reductions were both necessary and the only policy available. When it had reduced short-term interest rates from 7% at the beginning of the 1990s to 0.001% at the end of it, the results were not impressive: Japan remained mired in deflation. Thus in March 2001 the Bank of Japan adopted the monetarist policy of expanding bank reserves, a policy common among central banks in the early 1980s, but abandoned due to its ineffectiveness. This policy was also ineffective, but thanks to using a label originally defined as expanding credit creation – 'quantitative easing' – it caught the imagination of investors and commentators. Thus today often monetarist reserve or base money expansion is referred to as 'quantitative easing', or QE.*

Unlike the Bank of Japan, the Federal Reserve implemented a policy more directly aimed at expanding bank credit creation, as explained by Chairman Bernanke.† This paid off in 2012 as bank credit growth recovered.

In contrast, the Bank of England adopted the Bank of Japan's monetarist reserve expansion under the label 'quantitative easing', and did not target bank credit creation directly, although it has made substantial efforts to ensure that bond purchases take place (to a significant extent) from the non-bank sector. Between 2009 and September 2012, the Bank of England has created £375bn of central bank reserves through four successive rounds of QE; £200bn between March and November 2009; £75bn between October 2011 and January 2012; £50bn between February and May 2012 and £50bn announced in July 2012. QE was introduced following the same logic as in Japan: the Bank of England had already reduced interest rates to 0.5% - the lowest level in the Bank's history – and the economy is still contracting.

The Mechanics of bond purchase operations, including QE

The process is best understood through the use of accounting T-charts (see T-charts 7-10 below[31]).

T-chart 7: QE on central bank balance sheet

Assets	Liabilities
+ Loan to APF	+ Additional reserves

T-chart 8: QE on Asset Purchase Facility (APF) balance sheet

Assets	Liabilities
+ Gilts purchased	+ Loans from central bank

T-chart 9: QE on pension fund balance sheet

Assets	Liabilities
– Gilts sold + Deposits	[no change]

T-chart 10: QE on commercial bank balance sheet

Assets	Liabilities
+ Central bank reserves	+ Deposits (belonging to pension fund)

---

* The term QE had been proposed in 1994 and 1995 by Richard Werner to recommend a policy that would expand credit creation. The Bank of Japan is usually thought of as commencing QE on March 19th 2001, but it did not use the expression 'quantitative easing' in its official descriptions of its policy in March 2001, and its scheme differed in key respects to Werner's scheme of quantitative easing. In fact, Werner had predicted that mere reserve expansion would not work after banking crises – neither would interest rate reductions or fiscal policy that is not monetised.[26,27,28]

† Federal Reserve governor Ben Bernanke, who was an active participant of the debates around the Bank of Japan policy in the 1990s, chose to distance his own policies at the Federal Reserve in 2008 from others by calling them "credit easing", an expression much closer to Werner's original definition of QE[29]. Bernanke (2009)[30] seems to agree that a policy of "changing the quantity of bank reserves [uses] a channel which seems relatively weak, at least in the U.S. context".

Firstly it should be noted that the Bank of England created a new body to handle the purchases of gilts – the Asset Purchase Facility (APF).* The Bank makes a loan to the APF which uses this to purchase gilts (see T-charts 7 and 8 overleaf) from the non-bank investment sector, such as from a pension fund. The pension fund's holdings of gilts are reduced, with a corresponding increase in its holdings of commercial bank deposits. This is a change in the composition of the assets in the fund, with no change to liabilities – see T-chart 9. The pension fund's bank gains additional central bank reserves from the APF on the asset side of its balance sheet and a matching increase in deposits on the liability side as it credits the pension funds bank account (T-chart 10). So QE does create new purchasing power when the APF buys gilts from the non-bank sector, and the proceeds are not used as idle reserves or bank deposits, or to buy bonds from the banking sector.

How is QE supposed to affect the economy? QE may have an impact on the economy via multiple channels. First, as commercial banks hold significantly higher levels of central bank reserves , it is hoped the additional liquidity will enable them to increase their lending to the real economy, creating credit for new GDP transactions (the 'liquidity effect'). This is however the weakest part of the argument, as in the past, as evidenced by Japan's experience, this has not been possible due to banks' higher risk aversion, triggered by large amounts of non-performing assets.†

Secondly, due to central bank purchases of such large quantities of government bonds, their availability in the markets decreases. It is then hoped investors will turn to other forms of investment which would support businesses (the 'portfolio rebalancing' effect), however, only the purchase of newly issued corporate bonds and equity in the primary market will increase purchasing power of businesses and the primary market is only a fraction of the overall turnover of capital markets.

Thirdly, by purchasing gilts on such a large scale, the Bank of England hopes to push up their price and thereby push down the interest rate received by investors. Again, it is anticipated this will make other types of financial assets more attractive and stimulate growth: the 'wealth effect'.

All three channels are indirect, and all attempt to stimulate the real economy by acting through the financial sector. Thus bond purchase operations by central banks, including what is styled as QE, do not create new credit or deposits (purchasing power) directly in the hands of households, businesses or the Government. New credit may be created in the non-bank financial

---

* The creation of the Asset Purchase Facility enables the Bank to keep a clear distinction between QE and more standard Open Market Operations (see section 4.7), although essentially the same activity is taking place. Perhaps more importantly, it allows the central bank to avoid marking those investments to market on its balance sheet, while it can maintain that it is applying mark-to-market rules.

† Indeed, one recent empirical study found that the Bank of England's QE had no impact on the economy.[32]

(or investment) sector. The investment sector may choose to invest this new purchasing power in newly issued corporate bonds or equity that may allow companies to increase their spending. However, it may also choose to buy government or corporate bonds from outside the UK, or it may invest in existing financial assets such as previously issued bonds or equities, or derivatives based on commodities such as oil or food, which will have the effect of inflating the prices of these assets. Or it may simply sit on these deposits because of concerns about the future of the economy.

Meanwhile, companies that are able to raise additional funds through bond or equity issuance may choose to use the money to simply pay off existing bank debt rather than invest in productive activity. If so, this will have the paradoxical effect of reducing credit creation, and the money supply, by exactly the same amount as QE increased it.

The banking sector, flooded with new central bank reserves, also has multiple options. It can choose to expand its lending to the real economy. However, it can also simply sit on the reserves. Banks are paid 0.5% interest on reserves by the central bank and they are the most liquid form of asset they can hold (see section 4.1).* Furthermore, if banks do use this additional liquidity to create credit, it might be for transactions that are profitable but do not contribute to GDP, e.g. mortgage lending or foreign currency or commodity speculation.

So, bond purchase operations and QE do not involve creating (or 'printing') money if by 'money', we mean more money in the real economy that is being used in GDP-related transactions. Although it may well have pushed down medium to long term interest rates and made it easier for the Government to borrow by creating significant additional demand for gilts, since at least 2010 the main criticism of QE has been that it has failed to stimulate bank lending in the real economy. Bank credit creation shrank in 2011 and the UK economy moved into a double-dip recession in 2012.†

---

* As explained in Appendix 1, prior to the commencement of QE, a demand-based 'corridor' system of reserves management was in operation, whereby banks would borrow a pre-defined quantity of reserves via repos from the central bank at a rate equivalent to the bank rate. The net cost of holding reserves was thus zero. With QE, however, the banking system was flooded with reserves and banks no longer needed to borrow from the Bank via repos. This means they are being effectively paid by the central bank to hold reserves. This has prompted former Monetary Policy Committee member Charles Goodhart to call for the central bank to stop paying interest on reserves or even charge a tax on such reserves.[33] One reason the Bank may be reluctant to take up Goodhart's suggestion is that there would then be nothing to stop the overnight LIBOR rate falling below 0.5% which is effectively the 'floor' set by the Bank for LIBOR. Such a drop would call into question the Bank of England's control over market interest rates.

† For a detailed recent evaluation of QE on the UK economy by the Bank of England, see Bridge and Thomas (2012)[34]; for a critique of QE in term of its failure to stimulate GDP-related transactions (and hence growth), see Lyonnet and Werner (2012).[35]

4.7.4.
Discount Window Facility

The Discount Window Facility is a permanent facility to provide liquidity insurance to the banking sector. This allows banks to borrow gilts from the Bank of England in exchange for other less liquid collateral and then exchange these gilts for central bank reserves on the interbank market. However, they have to pay higher fees that reflect the type of collateral and the size of the drawing relative to the size of the borrowing bank. Gilts are supplied rather than lending additional reserves directly to avoid affecting the amount of central bank reserves available to the banking sector as a whole.

4.8.
Managing money: solvency and capital

We have so far explored how banks and the central bank try to ensure there is sufficient liquidity in the banking system, and how the central bank tries to manage the quantity of credit creation through influencing interest rates and, when these are close to zero, undertaking QE. We now take a closer look at the regulation of solvency and how this relates to liquidity.

Liquidity involves the ability to be able to meet demand for withdrawals when many people want to withdraw money at the same time. In contrast, solvency is the long-term stability of a bank's finances, and is related to its capital.

Capital can be in the form of equity, or 'own funds', which constitutes the initial investment by shareholders plus retained profits. It also includes additional equity issued to investors over time (Figure 15). Because it can use retained profits as capital, every time a bank makes a profit, it can set some aside to increase its capital. Capital also contains a substantial third component: provisions. These principally cover depreciation and amortisation, which are typically reported as negative entries on the asset side, and bad loans. Between 2004 and 2010 provisions constituted virtually the whole of UK banks' retained earnings: £159.6 billion out of £160 billion. Only the retained profits portion (earnings after provisions) is equity capital.

Figure 15: Balance sheet for commercial bank including capital

Balance sheet for commercial bank		
Assets £	**Liabilities £**	
Loans to customers	Customer deposits	
Reserves at the BoE		
Cash	Loans from other financial institutions	
Financial assets (e.g. government securities)	Capital	Equity capital:
Other assets (e.g. buildings, investments)		• share capital
		• retained profits
		Provisions
		Subordinated debt
		(liability to
		bondholders)
Total liabilities = Total assets		

The equity capital proportion of capital is a liability of the bank to itself or its shareholders. In contrast to deposits it cannot be drawn down by its owners. Instead, the own funds are reduced when a borrower defaults on a loan. In that case, an amount equal to the default would be reduced from loans on the asset-side and from the 'own capital' on the liability side (Figure 15). When bad loans become too large as a proportion of total assets, own capital – that is, the net worth of the bank – can become negative. In this case, the bank has become insolvent. This is quite feasible, since capital is commonly less than 10 per cent of bank assets. This means that a mere 10 per cent fall in values of assets held by banks will wipe out most banks.

Another way of putting this is that the own capital shows what would be left over for shareholders if the bank was wound up and all its assets used to pay off all its liabilities. This is relevant because if a bank becomes bankrupt, its creditors (those with claims to the bank's liabilities) take precedence over its equity holders, who are last in the queue.

Capital can also include liabilities that are, for regulatory purposes, allowed to be substituted for equity capital, such as subordinated (long-term) debt. Subordinated debt is the liability banks owe to the purchasers of their bonds, who have accepted the risk that if a bank falls into difficulty it may default on its bonds which may therefore become worthless.

The most recent international regulations (Basel III) incorporate subordinated debt as an allowable form of capital (Chapter 5). Note that capital does not represent a physical pool of cash, as the funds are in practice invested. It is an entirely different concept from liquidity.

- *Solvency* is determined by whether you have sufficient capital to cover losses on your assets.

- *Liquidity* is determined by whether you have sufficient liquid assets to meet your liabilities.

This said, a lack of liquidity can cause a bank to become technically insolvent. In an attempt to convert its assets into cash, the bank might have to sell them at such a discount that its losses exceed its capital (see box 10).

Box 10: If banks can create money, how do they go bust? Explaining insolvency and illiquidity

To stay in business, banks must ensure their assets (loans) are greater than or at least match their liabilities (deposits). If the value of assets falls below their liabilities, they will become insolvent. This means that even if the bank sold all its assets, it would still be unable to repay all its depositors and thus meet its liabilities. Once a bank is insolvent in a balance sheet sense, it is illegal for them to continue trading.

There are two main types of insolvency:

1. A solvency crisis
If customers' default on their loans to a large enough extent - as happened during the 2007-08 financial crisis with subprime mortgages - banks become insolvent because their assets are less than their liabilities. In the hope of preventing this kind of insolvency, banks hold a capital - or equity - 'buffer', and indeed are required to hold them by international and domestic regulators (see Section 5.1), which will absorb the initial losses on assets. For example, if it has equity of £10bn the bank can absorb up to £10bn of defaults on its loans before it becomes insolvent. However, this buffer will be exceeded if enough customers default.

In this situation, creating money in the form of deposits through making loans will not help the bank at all. This is because making loans increases the assets (the loan contract) and the liabilities (the newly-created deposits) by exactly equal amounts, but does not affect the net difference between assets and liabilities. To become solvent again, a bank must find a way of reducing its liabilities, or increasing its assets, or both.

2. A liquidity crisis
Banks can also become insolvent in an accounting sense if they are unable to meet the demand for their liabilities as they fall due, even if their total assets appear greater than their liabilities. This is known as a 'cash flow insolvency' or, in banking terminology, a 'liquidity crisis'. To use the technical term, there is a 'maturity mismatch' between the rate at which loans (assets) are repaid and the rate at which deposits (liabilities) are withdrawn. How might this happen?

Typically, a bank will have many long-term and thus illiquid assets (e.g. 25 year-mortgage loans) whilst at the same time having many short-term liquid liabilities (i.e. customer deposits) which can be drawn down on demand. If confidence in a bank falls, this mismatch can become a problem. Customers may decide to rapidly withdraw their →

---

deposits en masse (a 'bank run'), either by withdrawing cash, or by requesting electronic transfers across to accounts at other banks. In this situation, the bank can rapidly run out of both cash and central bank reserves.

The bank can try to quickly sell off its loans in order to bring in the central bank reserves it needs to pay other banks, but if investors have concerns about the quality of the loans they are likely to force down the price of the loans and pay below the 'book' value of those loans. The bank may then be forced in to a 'fire-sale' of all of its assets in order to meet depositors' demands for withdrawals. If the price of its assets keeps falling, this will eventually lead to the type 1 insolvency explained above, whereby the total value of a bank's assets is less than its liabilities.

In a liquidity crisis, the ability of banks to create money by making loans is of no help. In fact, it would make the situation worse, because every loan creates new liabilities (the new bank deposits), which the borrower could then pay away to customers of another bank. This would mean that the bank would need to find even more central bank reserves to settle the transaction with other banks.

4.8.1.
Bank profits, payments to staff and shareholders and the money supply

As discussed, bank profits, including interest payments, are added to the bank's equity capital. When this happens, the money supply is effectively reduced since equity capital does not circulate in the real economy. So if I repay a loan of £1,000 plus £100 interest, there will be a total reduction in the money supply of £1,000 for the principal repayment plus £100 for the interest repayment.

However, the bank adds this £100 to its equity capital. It may then choose to use a proportion of this to pay its staff or pay out dividends to shareholders, as well as maintaining the levels of buffer capital required by capital adequacy rules (section 5.1). So if a bank chooses to pay £80 of that £100 to its staff, £80 of new deposits will be effectively 're-created'.[36,37] The net effect on the total money supply of the repayment of the loan will thus only be a reduction of £1,020 (=£1,100-£80).

It should be clear, however, that this mechanism is not the same as a credit expansion as explained in section 4.2. Instead of creating a new asset and liability, the bank's equity on the liability side contracts as it charges expenditure against it and new deposits are created for the recipients of the expenditure. Conversely, when the bank receives income it reduces the deposits of its customers when they make payment.*

---

* This raises an interesting question of causality in terms of where the money to pay interest to banks comes from in the first place. It might appear that the more money the banks pay out to staff, the more can be repaid as interest and the more profits the banks can realise in the aggregate. This also has implications for the nature of growth and stability in capitalist economies where banks are constantly removing a proportion of the money supply from circulation in the form of equity. For an interesting discussion see Binswanger (2009).[38]

The ability of a bank to create money in this way is limited by regulatory requirements and the value of its shareholder capital. For example, if a bank has £100 of equity capital, but is required by Basel Capital Accords (section 5.1) to maintain £80 of that against its assets, then it can only pay out £20 in wages or dividends.

4.9.
Summary: liquidity and capital constraints on money creation

So in summary, there are two main liquidity constraints on the creation of new commercial bank money that may affect individual banks:

1. Having enough central bank reserves to ensure cheque, debit card or online payments can be made to other banks in the Bank of England closed-loop clearing system at any one time.
2. Keeping enough of their demand deposits in the form of cash so that solvent customers can get access to cash whenever they wish.

In practice these constraints are weak under the current monetary policy regime as we explain in Chapter 5. Individual banks have a number of ways of boosting the reserve balances, including borrowing from other banks on the interbank market.[39,40]

Every bank also has a capital constraint – it must ensure it has enough own funds so that if customers default on their loans, it can absorb these losses without threatening the bank's solvency. However, in aggregate, banks are not constrained by capital, as they create the money that circulates and this can be used to increase capital.

This chapter concludes our exploration of the mechanics of the modern banking system. The next chapter explores in more depth recent developments in commercial bank credit creation, including its relation to the financial crisis and how authorities have attempted to regulate the monetary system through the use of capital and liquidity rules.

References

1. Galbraith, J. K., (1975). *Money: Whence it came, where it went*. London: Penguin, p. 50

2. Dodd, N., (1994). *op. cit.* pp. 12

3. Harvey, D., (2006-1982). *The Limits of Capital*. London: Verso

4. Ingham, G., (2004). *The Nature of Money*. Cambridge: Polity Press

5. Dodd, N., (1994). *op. cit.* p. xx

6. Goodhart, C.A.E., (1989). *Money, Information and Uncertainty*. London: Macmillan, p. 100

7. BIS. (2003). *The role of central bank money in payments systems*, Basel: Bank for International Settlements. Retrievable from http://www.bis.org/publ/cpss55.pdf

8. Office of Fair Trading. (2008). *Personal Current Accounts* in the UK, p. 17. Retrievable from http://www.oft.gov.uk/shared_oft/reports/financial_products/OFT1005.pdf

9. United States District Court, S.D. New York. *Re Libor-based financial instruments anti-trust litigation*. 2012 WL 1522306 (S.D.N.Y.) (Trial Pleading) Retrievable from http://newsandinsight.thomsonreuters.com/uploadedFiles/Reuters_Content/2012/05_-_May/Libor_Consolidated_Amended_Complaint.pdf

10. Financial Times (2012). *Total overhaul for 'broken' Libor*, 28th September 2012

11. Keynes J. M., (1930). *A Treatise on Money*, op. cit., Volume 1, p. 26

12. Werner, R.A., (2000), Japan's plan to borrow from banks deserves praise, *Financial Times*, 9th February 2000

13. Werner, R.A., (2005). *New Paradigm in Macro-economics*, Basingstoke: Palgrave Macmillan

14. Bank of England Annual Reports, 2000-01 to 2008-09. In each annual report, the Issue Department accounts state the amount payable to HM Treasury

15. Robertson, J. and Huber, J., (2000). *Creating New Money*. London: **nef**. Retrievable from http://www.neweconomics.org/publications/creating-new-money

16. *Ibid.* p. 80

17. *Ibid.* p. 2; see also Appendix, table 4, footnote 3, p. 89

18. List of Reserve Scheme Participants. Retrievable from http://www.bankofengland.co.uk/markets/money/documentation

19. Bank of England, *Payment Systems Oversight Report*, Retrievable from http://www.bankofengland.co.uk/publications/psor/index.htm

20. Clews, R., Salmon, C., Weeken, O., (2010). The Bank's money market framework. *Bank of England Quarterly Bulletin* Q4: 292–301, p. 293

21. Clews et al. (2010). *op. cit.*

22. *Ibid.* p. 295

23. Werner, R.A., (2005). *op. cit.*

24. Werner, R.A., (2005). *op. cit.*

25. Werner, R.A., (1995), Keiki kaifuku, ryōteki kinyū kanwa kara, (How to Create a Recovery through 'Quantitative Monetary Easing'), *The Nihon Keizai Shinbun* (Nikkei), 'Keizai Kyōshitsu' ('Economics Classroom'), 2 September 1995 (morning edition), p. 26; English translation by T. John Cooke (November 2011), retrievable from http://eprints.soton.ac.uk/340476/

26. Werner, R.A., (1995). *op. cit.*

27. Voutsinas K. and Werner, R. A. (2010). The Effectiveness of 'Quantitative Easing' and the Accountability of the Central Bank in Japan. Paper presented at *The 8th Infiniti Conference on International Finance*, Trinity College, Dublin, 14-15 June 2010; *The 27th Symposium in Money Banking and Finance*, Université Montesquieu-Bordeaux IV, 17-18 June 2010; *The MMF 2010 Annual Conference* at the Cyprus University of Technology, Limassol, 1-2 Sept. 2010

28   Lyonnet, V. and Werner, R. A., (2012) Lessons from the Bank of England on 'quantitative easing' and other 'unconventional' monetary policies. *International Review of Financial Analysis,* Volume 25, December 2012, Pages 94 - 105

29   *Ibid.*

30   Ben Bernanke (2009). Speech given at the London School of Economics on 15 January 2009.

31   Adapted from Bridge, J., and Thomas, R. (2012) *The impact of QE on the UK economy – some supporting monetarist arithmetic.* Bank of England, Working paper No. 442, January 2012. London: Bank of England

32   Lyonnet, V. and Werner, R. A., (2012) *op. cit.* pp. 94 - 105

33   Financial Times, *Negative interest rates in the UK?,* May 15th 2012, Money Supply blog. Retrievable from http://blogs.ft.com/money-supply/2012/05/15/negative-interest-rates-in-the-uk/#axzz24wbFtZ4c [accessed 29 August 2012]

34   Bridge, J. and Thomas, R. (2012). T*he impact of QE on the UK economy – some supporting monetarist arithmetic,* Working Paper No. 442, January 2012. London: Bank of England. Retrievable from http://www.bankofengland.co.uk/publications/Documents/workingpapers/wp442.pdf [accessed 5 September 2012]

35   Lyonnet, V. and Werner, R. A., (2012). *op. cit.*

36   Binswanger, M., (2009) Is There a Growth Imperative in Capitalist Economies? a circular flow perspective, *Journal of Post-Keynesian Economics,* Volume 31, No. 4 707, p. 713

37   See also the explanation by campaigning group Positive Money. Retrievable from http://www.positivemoney.org.uk/how-banks-create-money/balance-sheets/#destroying

38   Binswanger, M., (2009) *op. cit.*

39   Goodhart, C.A.E., (1989). *op. cit.*

40   Werner, R.A., (2005). *op. cit.*

THIS PAGE IS INTENTIONALLY LEFT BLANK

5

REGULATING MONEY CREATION AND ALLOCATION

There can be no doubt that besides the regular types of the circulating medium, such as coin, notes and bank deposits, which are generally recognised to be money or currency, and the quantity of which is regulated by some central authority or can at least be imagined to be so regulated, there exist still other forms of media of exchange which occasionally or permanently do the service of money ... [I]t is clear that, other things equal, any increase or decrease of these money substitutes will have exactly the same effects as an increase or decrease of the quantity of money proper, and should therefore, for the purposes of theoretical analysis, be counted as money.

Friedrich Hayek, 1931[1]

In Chapters 3 and 4 we described the deregulation, digitisation, and emergence of the modern payment system. We also introduced the concepts of liquidity and solvency, and explained some theoretical misconceptions about the nature of credit markets. In this chapter we examine the external constraints on the creation of new commercial bank money. In particular, we examine regulations imposed on banks' liquidity and their provision against insolvency. We shall see that, for a number of reasons from deregulation to the emergence of the 'shadow banking' system, both liquidity and capital ratios fell relentlessly in the period from 1970 to the start of the financial crisis of 2007–08. Finally, we consider implications for the regulation of credit creation and allocation in theory and practice.

5.1.
Protecting against insolvency: capital adequacy rules

In Chapter 4, we discussed the theory that by making banks hold a certain amount of capital they should be able to survive a significant number of their assets becoming non-performing, for instance, due to default on loans. If most banks in an economy have this buffer, then it is hoped that banks will retain enough confidence in other banks to continue lending reserves on the interbank market and that individuals will not rush to withdraw their deposits. Solvent banks should therefore be less likely to suffer a liquidity crisis.

The Basel Committee on Banking Supervision (BCBS) has formulated recommendations concerning required bank capital. The Committee is a private body of central banks and regulators linked to the Bank for International Settlement (BIS).* Commonly referred to as the Basel Accord, the BCBS rules, while formally non-binding on any national regulator, are in practice adopted by national and European Union financial regulatory authorities and thus have become binding on banks.† First introduced in 1988, their goal is to assure the solvency of banks and limit credit creation indirectly. There is no intention to help authorities maintain consistency between the quantity of credit created and underlying economic activity, or to ensure a particular allocation of credit. The recent banking crisis, however, has shown that they do not fulfil even the limited goals of assuring bank solvency. It remains to be seen whether the latest round of revised Basel rules (known as Basel III) is an improvement.

According to the rules, banks must set aside a certain amount of capital every time they make a loan. Capital can be derived from retained profits or money raised from investors, including, as we discussed in Chapter 4, the owners of the bank: the shareholders. This is also called the **own capital** or **own funds** of the bank. Just like deposits or credits, own funds are an accounting entry, but in contrast to deposits they cannot be withdrawn – funds becoming corporate

---

* The BIS itself developed out of the Reparations Committee established under the leadership of JP Morgan after WWI.

† For a detailed history of the Basel Rules pre-Basel II, see Goodhart (2011)[2].

equity are handed over to the company in perpetuity, in exchange for ownership rights over the firm. Instead, equity capital is used when the bank suffers losses, such as when a borrower defaults on a loan. In that case, the same amount would be reduced from loans on the asset side and from the own capital on the liability side. Since capital usually is less than a tenth of assets, which include bank loans, sovereign debt, and derivatives such as Exchange Traded Funds* and Collateralised Debt Obligations† a 10 per cent default of loans would wipe out all capital and render the bank insolvent. A smaller loss would leave it in breach of capital adequacy rules, requiring it to shrink its lending or raise more capital. When the proportion of bad assets becomes too large, own capital – that is, the net worth of the bank – can become negative.

Being able to use retained earnings as capital means that every time a bank makes a profit, it can set some aside as capital, which enables further lending, which leads to further profits, which further increases capital. Therefore, under a stable capital ratio, a bank's balance sheet can expand at the same rate of increase as its retained profits.

In the current system of Basel regulation, loans are given a risk weighting depending on how risky the regulators perceive the loan to be. Under Basel II rules, large banks can further refine the regulators' risk weighting to suit their own particular risk profiles. The bank uses sophisticated risk management systems to self-assess its own risk and hence its capital requirements. This resulted in large banks choosing a lower level of capital before the crisis. As a result, the level of capital required is under review by domestic and international regulators and is set to go up. In the UK, following the Independent Commission on Banking's final report published in September 2011, it is expected to be raised to 10 per cent for the retail banking subsidiaries of large banking groups. The risk weighting applied to different categories of loan have a considerable impact on the amount of capital required to be set against them, and hence on their profitability. For example, business loans are given a 100 per cent risk weighting whereas mortgages are currently weighted at 35 per cent on the grounds that if the homeowner cannot pay, the bank can repossess the house and sell it to recover its loan. The impact on capital levels for an overall capital requirement of 8 per cent is shown below:

Loan type	Loan amount (£)	Risk weighting	Capital ratio	Capital amount (£)
Business	100,000	100%	8%	8,000
Business	35,000	100%	8%	2,800
Mortgage	100,000	35%	8%	2,800

As we can see, a £100,000 mortgage would only require £2,800 of capital; the same level of capital will support a business loan of only £35,000. From this

---

* Exchange Traded Funds allow investors to track the prices of a bundle of different assets.

† Collateralised Debt Obligations combine parts of a large member of loans into a new 'composite' asset.

it follows that unless a business loan makes three times as much profit as a mortgage, the bank will prefer to extend mortgages.

5.1.1.
Why capital adequacy requirements do not limit credit creation

Because retained profits can count as capital, the more profitable a bank is, and the more of those profits that are retained as capital, the more loans it can make and still meet the Basel capital requirement.

It should be clear by now that increasing capital adequacy ratios will not necessarily prevent an increase in bank credit creation when times are good. There are three main reasons for this:

1. An economic boom, and particularly rising asset/collateral values, will encourage each individual bank to lower its estimates of risk, and hence of the level of capital it requires.
2. A more favourable view of economic prospects will also encourage the bank to make more loans, generating additional profits which increase its capital and allow it to make more loans.
3. If regulators in the future impose higher capital adequacy requirements as a counter-cyclical 'macro-prudential' policy, banks will find it easier to raise more capital, as the money to purchase newly issued preferred shares, for instance, is ultimately created by the banking system, and an increasing amount is created during boom times (hence the boom in the first place).

Furthermore, different dynamics come into play when we distinguish between an individual bank and the banking system as a whole. As we argued in Section 4.3, if the banks expand their balance sheets in step, there is little to restrain them. If only one bank continues to lend, it will find that it bumps up against its capital adequacy and liquidity limits, but if all banks are lending and creating new deposits, provided they remain willing to lend to one another, the banking system in aggregate will generate enough additional capital and liquidity.

In other words, the Basel capital adequacy arrangements reinforce the pro-cyclicality of the banking system. At best, the delay before growth in earnings from new lending shows up as capital and will act as a 'drag' on balance sheet growth. The same applies the other way round: if banks become concerned about the economy and their balance sheets, they will be less keen to make loans that might default and reduce their capital adequacy.

So the trouble is that the design of capital adequacy rules usually neglects the crucial fact that banks are the creators of the money supply. Requiring banks to raise more capital in the boom times won't stop the boom. The boom is caused by increased bank credit, and some of the expansion in the money supply can be tapped by banks to fund higher capital ratios.[3,4]

5.1.2.
Leverage Ratios: a variant of capital adequacy rules

In 2009, the G-20 Committee of Finance Ministers and central bank governors and the Financial Stability Board, an international committee of central bank regulators and national finance ministries, proposed to introduce a 'leverage ratio' to supplement the risk-based regulatory capital adequacy ratio.

There are two common definitions of a leverage ratio. Firstly, the Canadian definition which is total assets to total capital including equity and subordinated debt. This is to say that the leverage ratio is simply the inverse of Basel capital adequacy requirements but without the risk-weighting procedures. The US and European definition has been even more similar to the Basel capital adequacy, as it defines the leverage ratio as equity capital as a proportion of adjusted assets.

The discussion of leverage ratios is thus similar to a discussion of capital adequacy rules. Stricter capital adequacy rules require banks to hold more capital, which is to say that the banks will have lower leverage. As such, this proposal is not a new suggestion, but is continuing the long Basel tradition of the 1980s which, critics argue, has failed to prevent banking crises in Japan, Asia, the USA and Europe.

Leverage ratios are therefore also an indirect and inadequate means of trying to control bank credit. Historically the only effective method of controlling bank credit has been via direct credit controls. These work as follows: the central bank tells commercial banks that they can extend credit for transactions that are not part of GDP, such as financial asset transactions including lending to hedge funds, only by a certain absolute amount, expressed as a fraction of GDP; say 5 per cent. At times they may even entirely forbid credit for such purposes. Banks then have to focus more on creating credit for transactions that are part of GDP. Under such a system there would be either no credit ceiling, or very high credit growth quotas, for investment in the production of goods and services and productivity enhancements, as these are non-inflationary and growth-enhancing. We review some historical example of credit controls in section 5.7.

Unlike direct control of credit, the leverage ratio or capital adequacy may not achieve the goal of avoiding asset bubbles or may not enable the authorities to achieve the desired amount of credit creation. Indeed, leverage can give a misleading picture of both the state of the banking system and that of the economy.

The leverage ratio has actually been imposed in the US for many years, but it failed to prevent the subprime crisis. The reason is that the leverage ratio can fall while bank credit creation in total (as well as credit creation for financial transactions not contributing to GDP) rises unabated. This is what happened in the US, according to a World Bank report on this topic.*

5.2.
Regulating liquidity

If capital adequacy rules only weakly constrain credit creation can liquidity rules do any better?

We saw in Chapter 4 that there is a relationship between a bank's reserves with the Bank of England and the amount banks can lend. However, this is not a relationship that is compatible with widespread public perception of 'banks as intermediaries' or the 'money multiplier' model in economics and finance textbooks. Banks do not intermediate the deposits they receive. Banks create brand new money at will by extending credit or buying assets. As discussed in Section 4.5, the size of their reserves is mainly determined in consultation with the Bank of England by banks' own estimates of what is needed to cover their every-day payment requirements.

Banks have not always made good decisions with regard to their liquidity and have regularly required the central bank to step in and provide injections of liquidity in order to prevent the collapse of the system. Figure 16 (overleaf) illustrates this, showing changes in the Bank of England's balance sheet as a percentage of GDP.

In the mid-nineteenth century, UK banks held on average 60 per cent of liquid assets as a proportion of total deposits, a ratio partly explained by the frequency of liquidity crises around that time.[7] Banks halved this ratio following the 1866 Overend and Gurney crisis when the Bank of England accepted a role as 'lender of last resort', committing to supply sufficient reserves to prevent future liquidity crises.

---

* During 2009 the World Bank wrote a proposal to introduce a leverage ratio: 'One argument against the leverage ratio has been that the United States, despite having a leverage ratio in place, was at the epicentre of the global financial crisis. Why did the U.S. leverage ratio fail to provide the right warning signs? To answer this question, a good starting point is to analyse the evolution of leverage in the years running up to the financial crisis. Over the past decades financial innovation has fundamentally changed the structure of the financial system... Banks funded a growing amount of long-term assets with short-term liabilities in wholesale markets through the use of off-balance-sheet vehicles, exposing themselves to credit and liquidity risk by providing facilities to these vehicles. Moreover, they also held structured credit instruments on their own balance sheet, exposing themselves to embedded leverage and increasing their asset-liability mismatch and their funding liquidity risk. For major European and U.S. investment banks, balance sheet leverage multiples (measured as total assets divided by equity) increased during the four years preceding the global financial crisis (Figure 2). For Japanese and U.S. commercial banks, by contrast, aggregate balance sheet leverage did not increase over this period, and in some instances it even fell.'[5]

Figure 16: Bank of England balance sheet as a % of GDP

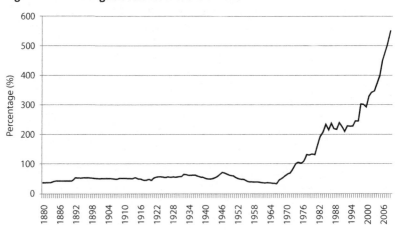

Note: The definition of UK banking sector assets used in the series is broader after 1966, but using a narrower definition throughout gives the same growth profile

Source: Sheppard, D. K (1971) and Bank of England

5.2.1.
Compulsory reserve ratios

The first agreement on liquidity between the Bank of England and commercial banks occurred in 1947, when the privately owned Bank of England was nationalised. It involved a requirement to hold a minimum ratio of highly liquid assets, such as central bank reserves, cash or Treasury bills, to deposits of 32 per cent. This was lowered to 27 per cent 16 years later. The regime prevailed until 1971, when the Competition and Credit Control policy regime (CCC) introduced a minimum reserve ratio of 12.5 per cent. As we saw in Chapter 4, CCC led to a massive decline in liquidity reserve ratios (Figure 8, Chapter 4).

After twice lowering the minimum requirement, the Bank of England finally abolished the compulsory reserve ratio regime with the cash ratio deposit regime in 1981, which did not directly require a minimum level of liquid assets.

5.2.2.
Sterling stock liquidity regime (SLR)

The SLR, introduced in 1996, focused on holding sufficient liquidity to meet a particularly severe liquidity stress. It was calibrated to ensure that a bank had enough highly liquid assets to meet its outflows for the first week of a liquidity crisis without recourse to the market for renewed wholesale funding, in order to allow the authorities time to explore options for an orderly resolution.

In the words of Nigel Jenkinson, responsible for financial stability at the Bank of England in 2008, the SLR was:

> ...designed as one component of a wider crisis management regime, and not as a means for a bank to manage its precautionary buffer for addressing liquidity strain on a going-concern basis.[8]

From 2006 up to 2009, the UK operated a 'corridor' system in which banks set their own reserve targets every month.[9]* Reserve balances, that on average over the month fell within a relatively narrow range around those targets, were remunerated at Bank Rate. Outside this range, surplus reserves, which had been moved to the deposit facility, were remunerated at the lower deposit rate. In contrast, banks with insufficient reserves had to borrow those reserves at the higher lending rate.

The system worked for a short period with the money market rates staying relatively close to the Bank of England's rate, but from the summer of 2007, the financial crisis began to unfold and interbank market interest rates moved significantly above the Bank of England's rate. The Bank responded by making extra loans available, since some banks were hoarding reserves and so the interbank market was not working efficiently. In addition, the Monetary Policy Commission (MPC) started rapidly cutting the Bank Rate, but whilst overnight interbank rates remained close to the policy rate, longer term interbank rates (for three-month loans, for instance) continued to be inflated.

The system of voluntary reserves was suspended in March 2009 following the decision of the Bank to embark on the purchase of financial assets funded through the creation of new central bank reserves, more popularly known as Quantitative Easing (explained in Section 4.7.3).[10,11] The corridor system has now been replaced by a 'floor' system with the level of reserves initially being increased in line with asset purchases and all reserves remunerated at Bank Rate.

In December 2009, the Financial Services Authority (FSA) announced a new liquidity regime. Under this, each bank would have to hold a buffer of central bank reserves or gilts. Banks would be required to hold an amount determined by various 'stress tests', including an inability to access wholesale funding or rollover loans over a two-week period and a 'sizeable retail outflow', in other words unusually large levels of withdrawals by bank customers.[12] At the time of the announcement, the FSA said it would wait until the recession was over and banks' balance sheets had improved before imposing the rules, and agreements have not yet been put in place for individual banks. Persistent funding gaps between banks' current holdings of highly liquid assets and the new requirements suggest it may be some time before the regulations come into full force.[13]

---

* For a full explanation of the changes in the Bank of England's interest rate regime, see Appendix 1

This is not the case in many other countries. In the United States, for example, there is still a requirement for larger banks to hold central bank reserves of 10 per cent against certain defined categories of liabilities.[14]

At the international level, there is a proposal to tighten liquidity regulations by insisting that all banks hold enough easy-to-sell assets to withstand a 30-day run on their funding (similar to the crisis that engulfed Lehman Brothers in 2008) and this is due to come in to force in 2014. At the time of writing, however, it appears likely that this 'liquidity coverage ratio' will be softened by the Basel Committee on Banking Supervision, as very few banks in Europe are near reaching these kind of liquidity levels given their exposure to the European sovereign debt crisis.[15]

5.3.
Securitisation, shadow banking, and the financial crisis

Prior to the financial crisis, banks discovered a means to circumvent the Basel regulations on capital adequacy. This new method allowed them to preserve their capital adequacy and maintain liquidity whilst continuing to expand credit creation and is known as 'securitisation'. Securitisation is the process of selling on a loan, or a package of loans, and passing the risk and reward onto someone else in exchange for cash. By taking loans off the bank's balance sheet, it can create capacity for new lending while staying within the required capital ratios.

Depending on the quality, quantities, and streams of interest accruing to them, the bank can make a judgment as to whether it will be profitable to hold a loan or set of loans or to sell them. Because banks 'originate' the loans in the first place – and larger investment banks in particular have huge teams of analysts spread across the world looking at the latest developments in financial markets – they are quite often in a better position to judge the quality of a loan or set of loans than the buyer of the securitised loans. This is referred to as an 'asymmetry of information'; the seller has better information than the buyer. Banks which merely originate loans which they intend to sell on to others have less of an incentive to be careful in their analysis of credit risk and the sustainability of these loans. As a result, the banks can play the market to ensure capital adequacy levels are kept up whilst they continue to expand lending, increasing systemic risk in the economy as a whole. This is another example of the problem that arises when banks are given the privilege of creating new money without any guidance as to how this should be done in the public interest in order to contribute to general prosperity and stability. Each individual bank might pursue an 'optimal' strategy, but the collective result for the economy as a whole is far from optimal.

The financial crisis has been widely attributed to the 'originate and distribute' model of banking that investment banks began engaging in on a large scale from the early 2000s. In particular, there was rapid growth in the market for residential mortgage-backed securities (RMBSs). This involved the creation of packages of different mortgage loans of different levels of riskiness which were securitised and sold on to investors – often long-term investors such as insurance companies and pension funds and even local and regional authorities. However, many of these securities were backed by American 'subprime' mortgages, that is, loans to high-risk borrowers. These began to default when house prices in the USA collapsed in 2006.

Because no one knew where exactly in these complex securities particular subprime mortgages were held or how widely they had been spread, banks suddenly became very risk-averse about the true value not only of other banks' balance sheets but also of their own. They became reluctant to lend to each other in the interbank market, which created severe balance sheet problems for all banks.

Box 11: The 'shadow banking' system

The 'shadow banking system' is a loose term used to cover the proliferation of financial activities undertaken by banks off their balance sheets, largely beyond the reach of regulation. No solid definition yet exists, but it conventionally includes non-depository money market funds and the use of securitisation and credit derivatives by many institutions as well as private repo transactions.[16]

What all these have in common, aside from their extraordinary expansion over the last decade, is the creation of forms of credit that have no relationship to traditional banking. As discussed previously, it is quite possible for banks to create money and credit out of nothing. In a myriad of ways, the shadow banking system hugely extends that principle. For example, securitised collateral, typically in the form of loans repackaged to receive AAA grade ratings, could be used in a repo transaction. The asset would be sold to another institution, with an agreement to buy back at a later date, at a higher price. The seller would, in effect, be 'borrowing' the money, with the difference in price being equivalent to the interest rate. Repo transactions have therefore been called another type of privately created money[17] and form a crucial part of the shadow banking system.

By virtue of its nature, estimating the size of the shadow system can be difficult,[18] although it is now likely to be somewhat larger than conventional banking. As of early 2007, Timothy Geithner, then President of the Federal Reserve Bank of New York* suggested the US shadow banking system had assets under management to the value of $10.5 trillion - about $500 billion larger than the US deposit banking system at the time.[19]

This was close to the peak of the market; the crash of 2007-08 has been described as a 'run' on the shadow banking system: and confidence in the complex structures of unregulated credit creation evaporated, leaving the US banking system 'effectively insolvent for the first time since the Great Depression' as the crisis spread into ➔

---

* The Federal Reserve Bank of New York is one of 12 regional central banks that are privately owned by the member banks and together comprise the Federal Reserve System in the USA. The New York bank is the key institution in the system because it is the main locus of open market operations.

conventional banking.[20] Colossal injections of government funds in those countries worst affected by the crash have stabilised and restored confidence to the system, promoting a further boom in its activities. Meanwhile, banking bailouts have increased government borrowing and national debt, whereas bailouts funded by the central bank would not have created any liabilities for taxpayers. Despite, or perhaps because of the success of internationally co-ordinated government action to avoid widespread banking collapses, the underlying weaknesses of an unregulated, off-balance-sheet credit system have not been addressed. Since the crash, Basel III and other efforts at regulatory reform have instead focused very heavily on the capital and liquidity provisions of commercial banks.

5.4.
The financial crisis as a solvency and liquidity crisis

The financial crisis revealed both the fragility of depending too much on the interbank lending market for liquidity and, hence, the weakness of the Bank's dependence on attempting to influence commercial bank money creation indirectly through changes to Bank of England rate and open market operations (OMOs), as described in Chapter 4.

The credit creation process requires banks to utilise the interbank market to shift excess central bank money and/or bank money to those banks in need of it. This only works if banks can assume their solvency is largely unquestioned. However, question marks over bank solvency began to appear in 2007. Problems in the US housing market and in particular doubts about the quality of subprime loans led to concerns spreading throughout the global banking system wherever these assets had been repackaged, securitised and sold on. Rumours spread and banks that were more dependent on such wholesale funding became the target of short sellers, while depositors increasingly shifted their funds away from them. By trading with a bank suspected of being insolvent, other banks were endangering their own solvency.

Very rapidly, banks lost confidence in each other's solvency. Banks also showed a reluctance to borrow reserves directly from the Bank of England using standing facilities, which prompted the creation of the Discount Window Facility (Section 4.7.4). The explanation for this also lies with confidence: it appears banks feared the reputational damage caused by borrowing from the standing facility was too great.

As a consequence the interbank market virtually froze; the interbank interest rate in London shot far above the Bank Rate and the central bank was no longer able to control the interbank rate. During investigations into the LIBOR scandal, evidence given by Barclays created the impression that the Bank of England may have encouraged banks such as Barclays to under-report LIBOR, so as to downplay the worries about the fragility of the banking system – a claim strongly denied by the Bank's Deputy Governor, Paul Tucker.[21]

As we have seen, banks cover most of their borrowing needs in the interbank market. So this sudden rise in the market rate of interest and credit rationing between banks caused a liquidity crisis that threatened the payment system and the stability of the banking system in general.

When queues formed outside Northern Rock, the Bank of England was forced to step in, lending billions to Northern Rock directly and buying increasing amounts of assets from the banks in exchange for Bank of England reserves and cash that would enable them to make payments and rebuild their capital. Only by flooding banks and the interbank market with central bank reserves on a massive scale was the Bank able to avert financial collapse.

5.5.
Endogenous versus exogenous money

We have seen then that the central bank cannot control bank money creation through adjusting the amount of central bank reserves which banks must hold (as is implied in the multiplier model discussed in Chapter 2). Such control might be possible if people used cash for all their transactions, since banks are not permitted to create new banknotes. But as we have seen, people use their demand deposits for the greater majority of payments and banks are permitted to create demand deposits. Provided the interbank markets are functioning smoothly, enabling banks to manage their liabilities, they can always obtain the necessary funds to settle their customers' payments.

In reality, the tail wags the dog: rather than the Bank of England determining how much credit banks can issue, one could argue that it is the banks that determine how much central bank reserves and cash the Bank of England must lend to them (Section 4.3). This follows on from the Bank's acceptance of its position as lender of last resort, even though it has not fully played this role in the recent bank rescues, such as Northern Rock and RBS, since it passed on the cost of initial central bank money injections to the Government and hence to tax-payers. When a commercial bank requests additional central bank reserves or cash, the Bank of England is not in position to refuse. If it did, the payment system described above would rapidly collapse.[22]

In academic terminology, this process is often described as **endogenous money creation**. The term 'endogenous', loosely used in this context, means that the process is intrinsic to the workings of the economy.[23] Because cash and central bank reserves must be created on demand by the central bank whenever commercial banks request it, there is no obvious limit to the amount of this 'high-powered' money that the central bank must create. In this way, the narrow money supply could be viewed as demand driven. This contrasts with the notion of exogenous money, whereby the money supply can be determined externally to the workings of the economy – for example, by the central bank adjusting its reserve ratio or interest rate. This latter approach, widely associated with monetarism and Milton Friedman,[24] was popular as a policy framework in the 1980s but has fallen out of favour. But while reserve money may be endogenous, the broad money supply can be exogenously influenced by central banks through a regime of credit guidance.

Thus, there are inconsistencies when attempting to describe the money creation process as purely endogenous. Whether the central bank is able to influence money creation depends very much on how it chooses to intervene. While the central bank is likely to be forced to inject whatever reserves are needed to prevent banking activity from triggering monthly liquidity crises and interest rate volatility, this does not mean that the central bank is never in control of the money supply. The Bank of Japan, for instance, has been a strong supporter of the endogenous money approach. It has argued for much of the past 20 years that it cannot stimulate the economy because money creation is demand-driven. Allegedly, there simply has been very little demand for money in Japan, yet record amounts of money were demanded by the Japanese government to fund fiscal expenditure whilst SMEs in Japan were demanding credit and receiving none.[25]

The Bank of Japan could have injected more money into the economy than required by the reserve needs of banks. There is nothing to prevent it simply purchasing assets from the non-bank sector and thus bringing new money into circulation. For instance, it was proposed as early as 1995 that the Bank of Japan should simultaneously boost the economy, rescue the property market (where values had fallen by about 80 per cent) and strengthen the banking sector, while increasing the quality of life in the large cities. Tokyo, for instance, is a major city with one of the lowest ratios of park acreage per capita. It could do this by purchasing, at attractive prices, unused or empty real estate and creating new public parks.[26,27] This would inject new purchasing power, support the property market and thus, by boosting collateral values, also help the banking system. In fact, the Japanese central bank has purchased properties in the past, albeit exclusively for the use of its own staff, such as beach resorts, golf courses, restaurants and clubs in central Tokyo. The central bank has drawn on the endogenous money argument to maintain its policy stance even as Japan's recession has entered its third decade.

The second pillar of the endogenous money argument is that banks' credit creation always responds to the demand for bank loans. Anyone whose loan application has been turned down knows for sure that this is evidently not the case – banks ration credit, as will be discussed in Section 5.6. Consequently, credit creation is not purely endogenous to the economy, but it can be said that the central bank and the commercial banking sector together can determine credit creation and hence shape economic activity.

5.6.
Credit rationing, allocation and the Quantity Theory of Credit

The concept of credit rationing provides another explanation of why adjustments to the interest rate are likely to be a weak tool in controlling credit creation. We discussed in Chapter 2 why the idea of markets automatically clearing makes little sense as a description of reality. Without perfect information, there is nothing to ensure that demand will equal supply and that transaction prices are equilibrium prices. In a world such as ours, with imperfect information, markets do not automatically clear – so we are in a state of disequilibrium.* This means that markets are rationed and outcomes are determined by quantities, not prices.[28,29,30,31]

The outcome of these markets follows the short-side principle: whichever of demand or supply is smaller, that quantity will be transacted.[33] If I am a supplier of apples but only have ten apples, then I can only trade a maximum ten apples with you, even if you want one hundred – and I may choose to sell you fewer. On the other hand, if you want just one apple I cannot sell you more than just one apple. Whoever is on the 'short side' has a major advantage, namely market power. This is perhaps most obviously felt when you are applying for a job. Could the job market for television news readers, for instance, ever be thought of as being in equilibrium? Since many people can read, the pay and perks are attractive and the positions limited in number, there are likely to be more applicants than jobs available.

The ubiquity of rationing also becomes obvious when we are trying to obtain tickets for the theatre, or, indeed, the Olympic Games. If, in aggregate, the amount supplied in a market is smaller than the amount demanded, the supply side is the short side and has market power. It could push up the price of the apples or gain other advantages and benefits and the buyers would have to put up with it. Market power is again often felt in the labour market, or in the allocation of orders to contractors, where the decision-makers often demand – and obtain – what could be described as 'non-market' benefits or 'rents'. For example it is becoming increasingly necessary to be willing to work for no salary for an extended period in order to gain entry into some professions.[34]

Is the credit market also rationed? This does not appear to fit with the idea of endogenous money we discussed earlier, which implies that, at the right level of interest, whatever money is demanded will be automatically supplied by the banks. In turn the Bank of England will supply sufficient reserves and cash and the credit market will 'clear'.

Common sense, however, tells us money and credit are different from apples and, indeed, every other kind of commodity (in fact, as we have seen, money is not a

---

* See Goodhart (1989) for a good summary of theoretical and empirical debates on credit rationing.[32]

commodity at all). Suppose you would like to have more pairs of shoes; eventually you will simply run out of space for shoes. Even if you are a princess living in a castle you will want things other than shoes to be taking up your castle space. Economists call this declining marginal utility; each additional pair of shoes adds less utility than the last. However, having more money does not affect what other things you can or cannot have. It just means you can have more of anything. The demand for credit, and hence money, appears far less subject to diminishing marginal utility.[35]

Under the endogenous money theory, it is assumed that banks make loans, and credit 'clears' at a given interest rate. A riskier loan will incur a higher rate of interest but if the demand for credit is always very high (or even infinite), the theoretical market-clearing interest rate would be so high as to leave banks with only risky projects, while sensible projects could not generate sufficient returns to service the loans.[36] It is therefore more important for a bank to avoid defaults on its loans than it is to earn a higher rate of interest. Higher rates may bring an extra few percentage points' profit, but a default could lead to a 100 per cent loss. As a result, and as US economists Jaffee and Russel showed in 1976 and as Stiglitz and Weiss showed in 1981, banks prefer to ration and allocate credit – even in the best of times.[37] Paul Tucker, Deputy Governor of the Bank of England, appears to agree:

> ... [households and companies] ... are rationed in their access to credit, given that borrowers know a great deal more about their conditions and prospects than do risk-averse lenders, and that lenders face obstacles in ensuring that borrowers honour their contracts.[38]

An interesting example of how credit rationing affects the macro-economy arises when comparing banks' incentives for mortgage lending vis à vis lending to small business. The owners of a small business may have limited liability; this means that if they take out a loan but the business fails, they will not be held personally liable in excess of their stake in the company. There are 'asymmetric' incentives between the business owner and the bank. The risk to the business owner of taking the loan is much smaller than for the bank.[39] In practice, banks often attempt to circumvent limited liability by seeking collateral from the directors or shareholders of the business, usually by taking a charge on their house. Thus, business loans may not even be granted to applicants who cannot provide such personal guarantees. Figure 17 suggests that banks in the UK have been moving increasingly in this direction in their lending activity – as can be seen in the huge growth in secured loans to individuals compared with lending to the productive sector.

Figure 17: Net Bank Lending by Sector, 1997-2011, Sterling Billions

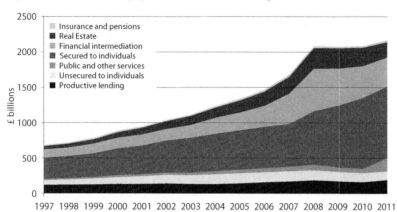

Source: Bank of England[40]

In contrast, if a bank issues a mortgage, it knows that if the borrower defaults, it will be able to repossess their house. The bank has access to the collateral. In the real world of imperfect information and hence lack of market clearing and credit rationing, a large bank that is focused on reliable and high profits will usually prefer to loan against collateral than against future cash flows. This discriminates against business investment because even in cases where the bank obtains collateral from the businesses owners or managers, the loan repayments will be made from the future cash flows that arise from the investment being funded by the loan. This requires careful scrutiny of the business case, and, crucially, good judgement from an experienced professional. The existence of market failure in the form of imperfect information suggests that some form of market intervention will be required to change these incentives.

As economists Blanchard and Fischer point out, if credit rationing exists…

> …it is possible that the interest rate is not a reliable indicator of the impact of financial variables on aggregate demand. It is quite likely in this case that variables measuring quantities, such as the amount of credit, have to be looked at in appraising monetary and financial policy.[41]

Empirical work on the Japanese economy, where interest rates were kept at very low levels throughout the 1990s in an effort to encourage lending and growth, but banks continued to heavily ration credit, supports this thesis [42,43] – as indeed, does the current situation in the UK, where the Bank Rate has been kept at a record low level of 0.5 per cent since early 2009. Yet net bank lending to small businesses in particular has continued to decline, becoming negative in September 2009 (Figure 18, overleaf).[44] This is the case in spite of the interbank rate also eventually returning to a level close to the Bank Rate.

Figure 18: Change in Lending to Small and Medium-sized Enterprises, 2004-12

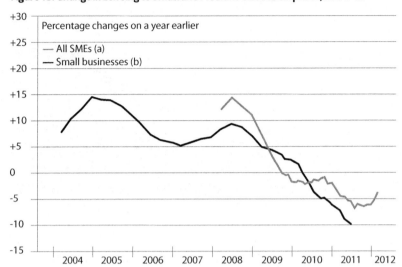

(a) Source: monthly BIS survey and Bank calculations. Lending by four UK lenders to enterprises with annual bank account debit turnover less than £25 million. Data cover lending in both sterling and foreign currency, expressed in sterling terms.

(b) Source: BBA. Lending by seven UK lenders to commercial businesses with an annual bank account debit turnover of up to £1 million. Sterling only. This survey terminated at June 2011.
Retrievable from www.bba.org.uk/statistics/small-business.

Sources: Bank of England, BBA, BIS and Bank calculations.

Reproduced from Bank of England, 'Trends in Lending', July 2012 [45]

Credit rationing by the banking system in aggregate will also lead to rationing in other markets.[46] If the credit being lent to small businesses is reduced, this will lead the businesses themselves to reduce their investment, their pay or the numbers they employ. These actions will have knock-on effects. As Werner has argued:

> ...the quantity of credit becomes the most important macro-economic variable, delivering 'exogenous' (external) budget constraints to any particular market.[47]

With a rationed and supply-determined credit market, it follows that adjusting interest rates is a policy that has a limited impact on credit-creation and hence the economy. With a limited role for reserve requirements and the abolition of bank credit guidance through the central bank, there are minimal external liquidity constraints on commercial banks. And finally, we have argued that capital adequacy rules are only a weak constraint on the creation of new commercial bank money, particularly with the advent of securitisation and other methods that allow banks to manipulate their balance sheets.

So, we can perhaps conclude the endogenous versus exogenous money debate as follows: in modern economies, where new money is created by the banking system, the supply of money is driven by credit creation, but credit creation is not driven by the demand for credit. Instead, the credit market is determined by the supply of credit and credit is rationed. It is the quantity of credit supplied, rather than the price of credit, which will determine macro-economic outcomes and without even perhaps being aware of it, banks are thus in a very powerful position. The total increase, or decrease, in the nation's money supply is the collective result of their individual lending and asset purchase decisions. In other words, because commercial banks ration and allocate credit, and they create new money in the process, they have a decisive influence over the allocation of new money in our economy. Macro-economic policy and analysis should be guided by an understanding and monitoring of these processes, as argued by Richard Werner in his 'Quantity Theory of Credit' (box 12).

Box 12: The Quantity Theory of Credit

The link between money and the economy is a central pillar of economic theories and models. The 'equation of exchange' offers such a fundamental link, as it says that *The amount of money changing hands to pay for transactions is equal to the value of these transactions.*

The most common application in most major economic theories is as follows:
$MV = PY$
which says that money (M) times the speed of its circulation (velocity - V) is equal to prices (P) times nominal GDP (Y)*

When combined with further assumptions, this equation has become known as the 'Quantity Theory of Money'.[48] An important assumption is that velocity is constant or at least stable. However, empirically velocity has been unstable and since the 1980s has frequently and significantly declined in many economies. The net result is a lack of reliable or predictable links between measures of money and nominal GDP. Consequently, economic theories that do not include money or banks increased in popularity and came to dominate mainstream economics (as explored further in section 2.2.2). However, such theories and models have been much criticised since the financial crisis of 2008.[49,50]

Co-author, Richard Werner, suggests a solution to the empirical problems faced by the above quantity equation. He points out that the original formulation, as cited in italics above, considers all transactions, but financial and asset transactions (e.g. mortgage finance) can be substantial and are not part of nominal GDP. Hence when money is increasingly used to pay for such non-GDP transactions, the traditionally defined velocity appears to decline. However, traditional monetary measures, such as M1 or M2 cannot be divided up and Werner argues that they are not the correct way to measure money in any case, since they measure stocks of money rather than money in circulation and used ➡

---

* 'nominal' means not adjusted for inflation; in contrast 'real' GDP would be GDP adjusted for inflation.

for transactions. Noting that money is created by the banking system as credit, he proposed his 'Quantity Theory of Credit', which disaggregates monetary flows into two streams: credit creation (C) used for (1) GDP transactions and (2) financial transactions – noted with subscripts R and F for real and financial circulation, respectively: In the equations below, 'Q' (rather than Y) is used to represent the quantity of transactions in either the real (Q_R) or the financial sector (Q_F).

$$CV=PQ$$
$$C=C_R+C_F$$
$$C_RV_R=P_RQ_R=P_RY \text{ (i.e. nominal GDP)}$$
$$C_FV_F=P_FQ_F$$

Based on empirical observation and institutional analysis Werner argues that banks ration credit and hence the credit supply is the driving variable. This has been theoretically as well as empirically supported in a variety of studies and cases. In this framework, "the standard `quantity theory' monetary model is a special case of a more general `quantity theory of disaggregated credit'."[51] In fact the old 'quantity theory of money' "would really have to be re-labelled the quantity theory of credit"[52, 53].

Werner has argued that the theory has important implications for development, growth and unemployment.[54-59] Developing economies should not be dependent on external borrowing, he suggests, since they can achieve non-inflationary growth by creating credit in their own banking system and guiding it towards productive use. The high growth witnessed by many East Asian economies in the post-war era (Japan, Taiwan, Korea, China after 1982) was achieved by the implementation of such a credit guidance regime. Indeed, Werner argues that if properly implemented unemployment could be eradicated using this approach.

5.7.
Regulating bank credit directly: international examples

The analysis set out in the previous sections, and international examples described here, suggest that the appropriate regulation of the total quantity of credit creation and the quality of its use (i.e. the allocation of credit for different types of use) are key variables that economic policymakers should monitor and, indeed, seek to control. The quantity and allocation of credit across different uses will shape the economic landscape.

Indeed, during their history, almost all central banks have employed forms of direct credit regulation variously called: credit controls, the direction of credit, the guidance of credit, the framing of credit, window guidance or moral suasion.

5. REGULATING MONEY CREATION AND ALLOCATION

We discussed the example of the UK in Section 3.6.2 and it is also useful to have a brief discussion of other international examples in the twentieth century, in particular Asia.

First implemented by the German Reichsbank in 1912, credit controls were copied by the Federal Reserve in the 1920s (and had the greatest impact in economic history when adopted by the Japanese, Korean and Taiwanese central banks in the early 1940s during WWII) and then continued for many decades in the post-war era.[60] Called 'window guidance' in these countries, the central bank determined desired nominal GDP growth, then calculated the necessary amount of credit creation to achieve this and then allocated this credit creation both across the various types of banks and across industrial sectors.[61]

Unproductive credit creation was suppressed because financial credit creation, such as today's large-scale bank lending to hedge funds, simply produces asset inflation and subsequent banking crises. Thus it was difficult or impossible to obtain bank credit for large-scale, purely speculative transactions. Likewise, it was difficult to obtain consumer loans on a significant scale as these would increase the demand for consumer goods but not necessarily result in a direct increase in goods and services available, hence triggering consumer price inflation instead. Most bank credit was allocated to productive use, which meant either investment in plant and equipment to produce more goods, or investment to offer more services or other forms of investment that enhanced productivity (such as the implementation of new technologies, processes, and know-how) – and often a combination of these. Such productive credit creation turned out to be the least inflationary, since not only was more money created, but also more goods and services with more value added.

The banks were quite willing to participate in such a system of credit guidance, as by way of return they also achieved unrivalled stability and a much greater degree of certainty concerning their market shares or even profits. Banks were recognised to be public utilities, and thus bonuses were also far more modest than, for instance, in the UK at the same time.*

In a 1993 study The World Bank recognised that this mechanism of intervention in credit allocation was at the core of the East Asian Economic Miracle.[63] Deng Xiao Ping had recognised this earlier and made Japanese-style window guidance the core of the Chinese economic reforms that led to decades of extremely high economic growth in China. Western central banks have meanwhile downplayed the importance and efficiency of such intervention in the credit market by the central bank (perhaps because it is out of kilter with the 'efficient market hypothesis' otherwise favoured by these countries' central banks and finance ministries). The Chinese central bank officially states that window guidance is

---

* For more on the institutional and political economy details of the East Asian credit guidance regime, see Werner (2003).[62]

one of its key monetary policy tools and empirical research has revealed this to be the case.[64] Window guidance could also be cited as a key reason why the Chinese economy has not fallen victim to the Asian economic crisis or to the international banking crisis of 2008.[†]

Detailed research on the efficacy of window guidance by the Bank of Japan has shown that this monetary policy tool has always worked extremely effectively, even when the goals set by the central bank were the wrong ones, such as the expansion of financial and speculative credit in the 1980s. In other words, credit guidance is an effective tool, although this is no guarantee that the policy goals selected will be the right ones. Economic history thus provides evidence that a simple regime of credit guidance, combined with adequate incentives (both carrots and sticks) for the banking system is an attractive avenue for delivering stable and high economic growth that is sustainable and, crucially, without recurring banking crises. Equally, this suggests that by severely limiting or entirely banning bank credit for transactions that do not contribute to GDP, asset bubbles and banking crises could be avoided in future. To be sure, such a measure would not stop speculation; instead, it would not allow speculators to use the public privilege of money creation for their speculative transactions, which may be sufficient to avoid banking crises.

---

† However, it seems China allowed credit to expand too far in the aftermath of the Lehman collapse in 2008, boosting financial credit as well as productive credit. This seems to have created asset price inflation, including in property, which is likely to cause problems in the future if no corrective policy action is taken.

References

1 Hayek, F., (2008-1931). *Prices and Production*. Auburn, Alabama: Ludwig von Mises Institute, p. 289. Retrievable from http://mises.org/books/hayekcollection.pdf

2 Goodhart, C., (2011). *The Basel Committee on Banking Supervision: A History of the Early Years, 1974-97* [Hardcover]. Cambridge University Press: Cambridge

3 Werner, R.A., (2010a). *Comment: Strengthening the Resilience of the Banking Sector*, submission to the Basel Committee on Bank Supervision, April 2010. Retrievable from http://www.bis.org/publ/bcbs165/universityofsou.pdf

4 Werner, R.A., (2010b). A simple rule is needed to prevent future banking crises, Letter to the Editor, *Financial Times*, 17 November 2010

5 D'Hulster, K., (2009). *The Leverage Ratio: New Binding Limit on Banks*. Crisis Response, Note 11. Washington World Bank. Retrievable from http://rru.worldbank.org/documents/CrisisResponse/Note11.pdf

6 Alessandri, P. and Haldane, A. G., (2009). *Banking on the State*, presentation delivered to the Federal Reserve Bank of Chicago twelfth annual International Banking Conference, p. 26

7 Jenkinson, N., (2008). *Strengthening Regimes for Controlling Liquidity Risk: Some Lessons from the Recent Turmoil*. Speech given at the Euromoney Conference on Liquidity and Funding Risk Management, Hyatt Regency, London, 24 April 2008

8 *Ibid.* p. 7

9 Clews, R., Salmon, C., Weeken, O., (2010). The Bank's money market framework. *Bank of England Quarterly Bulletin* Q4: 292–301, p. 293

10 Voutsinas, K., Werner, R.A., (2011a). *New Evidence on the Effectiveness of Quantitative Easing in Japan*. Centre for Banking, Finance and Sustainable Development Discussion Paper. Southampton: University of Southampton, School of Management

11 Lyonnet, V. Werner, R. A., (2012). Lessons from the Bank of England on 'quantitative easing' and other 'unconventional' monetary policies. *International Review of Financial Analysis*, Volume 25, December 2012, pp. 94-105

12 Financial Services Authority, (2009, October.) PS09/16: *Strengthening liquidity standards including feedback on CP08/22, CP09/13, CP09/14*, (para 6.27). Retrievable from http://www.fsa.gov.uk/pages/Library/Policy/Policy/2009/09_16.shtml

13 Financial Times, (15 February 2011). *Liquidity gap yawns at new reserves clause*. Retrievable from http://www.ft.com/cms/s/0/a75dbab2-385a-11e0-959c-00144feabdc0.html - axzz1MM2xlhBr

14 Board of Governors of the Federal Reserve System. Retrievable from http://www.federalreserve.gov/monetarypolicy/reservereq.htm - text2 [accessed 9 August 2011]

15 Financial Times, (2011). *Regulators poised to soften new bank rules*, p. 17, September 6th 2011

16 See, for example, the list provided by Turner, A.,(2011) *Reforming finance: are we being radical enough?*, 2011 Clare Distinguished Lecture in Economics and Public Policy, Clare College, Cambridge, 18 February 2011

17 Gorton, G. Metrick, A., (2010). *Regulating the shadow banking system*. London: Social Science Research Network

18 Singh, M. Aitken, J., (2010). *The (sizable) role of rehypothecation in the shadow banking system*. IMF working paper WP/10/172

19 Geithner, T. F., (June 2008). *Reducing systemic risk in a dynamic financial system*. Remarks at the Economic Club of New York, New York

20 Gorton, G. and Metrick, A., (2009). *Regulating the shadow banking system* NBER working paper 15223

21 BBC, (2012). Libor scandal: *Paul Tucker denies 'leaning on' Barclays*. Retrievable from http://www.bbc.co.uk/news/business-18773498

22 Goodhart, C.A.E., (1989). *Has Moore become too horizontal?* Journal of Post-Keynesian Economics 14: 134–136

23 For an account of endogenous money: Parguez, A., Seccareccia, M., (2000). *The credit theory of*

money: the monetary circuit approach. pp. 101–24, in Smithin (2000) *op. cit.*

24 Friedman, M., (1963). *Inflation: Causes and Consequences*. New York: Asia Publishing House

25 Werner, R.A., (2003). *Princes of the Yen, Japan's Central Bankers and the Transformation of the Economy*, Armonk, New York: M. E. Sharpe

26 Werner, R.A., (1995). *Liquidity Watch Report*, Tokyo: Jardine Fleming Securities

27 Werner, R.A., (2003). *op. cit.*

28 Werner, R.A., (2005). *New Paradigm in Macroeconomics*, London: Palgrave MacMillan.

29 Barro, R. Grossman, H., (1976). *Money, Employment and Inflation*. Cambridge: Cambridge University Press

30 Mullbauer, J., Portes, R., (1978). Macro-economic models with quantity rationing. *Economic Journal*, 88: 788–821

31 Malinvaud, E., (1977). *The Theory of Unemployment Reconsidered*, Oxford: Basil Blackwell

32 Goodhart, C., (1989). *Money, Information and Uncertainty*, Chapter VII: Credit Rationing

33 Werner, R.A., (2005). *op. cit.* p. 193

34 Milburn, A., (2009). *Unleashing Aspiration: Summary and recommendations of the full report*. The Panel on Fair Access to the Professions. London: Cabinet Office

35 Werner, R.A., (2005). *op. cit.* p. 193

36 Stiglitz, J. and Weiss, A., (1981). Credit rationing in markets with imperfect information. *American Economic Review*, 71: 393–410.

37 Stigler, G., (1967). *Imperfections in the Capital Market*. Journal of Political Economy, June 1967, 85, 287-92

38 Tucker, P., (2008). Money and Credit: Banking and the macroeconomy, speech given at the monetary policy and markets conference, 13 December 2007, *Bank of England Quarterly Bulletin 2008*, Q1, pp. 96-106. Retrievable from http://www.bankofengland.co.uk/publications/speeches/2007/speech331.pdf

39 Stiglitz, J. and Weiss, A., (1981). *op. cit.*

40 Bank of England Interactive Database – "Annual amounts outstanding of UK residential monetary financial institutions lending" to respective sectors: codes RPQTBVD, RPQTBVE, RPQTBVF, RPAB6PT, RPAB8F, RPATBVI and RPATBUA. Adjustments were made to figures on secured lending (code RPATBVX) to reflect changes in the Bank of England's reporting of covered bonds and securitised loans. Retrievable from http://www.bankofengland.co.uk/mfsd/iadb/notesiadb/Industrial.htm

41 Blanchard, O. and Fischer, I., (1989). *Lectures on Macro-economics*, Cambridge, MA: MIT Press, p. 479, quoted in Werner, R.A., (2005) op. cit. p. 193

42 Werner, R.A., (1997). Towards a new monetary paradigm: A quantity theorem of disaggregated credit, with evidence from Japan. *Kredit und Kapital* Volume 276–239. Retrievable from http://eprints.soton.ac.uk/36569/

43 Werner, R.A., (2005). *op. cit.*

44 Bank of England, (2011). *Trends in Lending*. Retrievable from http://www.bankofengland.co.uk/publications/other/monetary/trendsinlending2011.htm [accessed 27 September 2012]

45 Bank of England, (2012). *Trends in Lending*, July 2012. Retrievable from http://www.bankofengland.co.uk/publications/Pages/other/monetary/trendsinlending.aspx [accessed 27 September 2012]

46 Mullbauer, J. and Portes, R., (1978). Macro-economic models with quantity rationing. *Economic Journal*, 88: 788-821

47 Werner, R.A., (2005). *op. cit.* p. 198

48 Fisher, I. S, (1911). *The purchasing power of money: Its determination and relation to credit interest and crises.* New York, Macmillan

49 Kohn, D., (2009). *Monetary Policy Research and the Financial Crisis: Strengths and Shortcomings*, Speech by Vice Chairman Donald L. Kohn at the Federal Reserve Conference on Key

Developments in Monetary Policy on 9 October 2009. Washington: Federal Reserve Board. Retrievable from http://www.federalreserve.gov/newsevents/speech/kohn20091009a.htm

50 Buiter, W., (2009). The Unfortunate Uselessness of Most `State of the Art' Academic Monetary Economics, *Financial Times*, 3 March

51 Werner, R.A., (1998). Bank of Japan window guidance and the creation of the bubble, in Rodao, F. and Lopez Santos, A. (eds.). *El Japon Contemporaneo*. Salamanca: University of Salamanca Press

52 Werner, R.A., (2003). *Princes of the Yen, Japan's Central Bankers and the Transformation of the Economy*, Armonk, New York. M. E. Sharpe, p. 288, footnote 21

53 Werner, R.A., (2005). *op cit.*

54 Werner, R.A., (1992). *A Quantity Theory of Credit*, University of Oxford, Institute of Economics and Statistics, mimeo

55 Werner, R.A., (1993). *Japanese Capital Flows: Did the World Suffer from Yen Illusion? Towards a Quantity Theory of Disaggregated Credit*

56 Werner, R.A., (1997). *op cit.* pp. 276-309

57 Werner, R.A., (2005). *op cit.*

58 Werner, R.A., (2011). Economics as if Banks Mattered – A Contribution Based on the Inductive Methodology, *Manchester School*. Volume 79, September, pp. 25–35. doi: 10.1111/j.1467-9957.2011.02265_5.x

59 Werner, R.A., (2012). Towards a New Research Programme on 'Banking and the Economy' – Implications of the Quantity Theory of Credit for the Prevention and Resolution of Banking and Debt Crises. *International Review of Financial Analysis*, Vol 25, Dec 2012, pp. 1-17

60 Werner, R.A., (2005). *op. cit.*

61 Werner, R.A., (2002). Monetary Policy Implementation in Japan: What They Say vs. What they Do, *Asian Economic Journal*, Volume 16 no.2. Oxford: Blackwell, pp. 111-51

62 Werner, R.A., (2003). *Princes of the Yen, Japan's Central Bankers and the Transformation of the Economy*. Armonk, New York: M. E. Sharpe

63 World Bank, (1993). The East Asian Miracle, Economic Growth and Public Policy. Oxford: Oxford University Press

64 Chen, Y. and Werner, R.A., (2010). *The Monetary Transmission Mechanism in China*. Centre for Banking, Finance and Sustainable Development Discussion Paper. Southampton: School of Management, University of Southampton

6

GOVERNMENT FINANCE AND FOREIGN EXCHANGE

We have now completed our examination of the role of commercial banks in money creation and allocation and how national and international monetary authorities attempt to regulate this process. This chapter fills in some important gaps in the story, examining the role of governments and foreign exchange. We also show how fiscal and monetary policy cannot easily be separated in practice, particularly where choice of foreign exchange rate system has constrained monetary sovereignty. Further constraints on monetary and fiscal policy arise for nations, such those in the Eurozone, that have given up their own currencies and central banks.

We saw in Chapter 3 the vital role of the state in determining the unit of account and creating demand for a currency through taxation. We also reviewed how states have increasingly borrowed from investors via the issuance of tradable debt securities, namely government bonds. This chapter lays out how these activities and government spending – often collectively described as 'fiscal policy' – are conducted today and how the Government's accounts actually work.

We examine the effect of fiscal policy and the role of foreign exchange on the money supply, including debates on 'crowding out' and the dynamics of different exchange rate regimes. More technical detail on government accounts and foreign exchange is provided in Appendices 2 and 3. We begin, however, with an analysis of the legal limits placed upon the Government in terms of its money creation by the UK's membership of the European Union.

6.1.
The European Union and restrictions on government money creation

As we have seen in the UK, it is commercial banks, not the Government, that create the bulk of new money. As explained in Section 4.4, under normal conditions even cash, which is physically 'created' by the Bank of England, cannot enter circulation without customers first exchanging it for commercial bank money that they already hold.

We saw in chapter 3 how this situation arose due to legal and institutional developments over the course of three centuries. However, up until very recently it has still been legally possible for central banks to create money on behalf of governments (or 'monetise government debt') by lending to them. Indeed, up until 1997 it was standard practise in the UK for the central bank to provide the Treasury with an overnight 'overdraft' – known as 'Ways and Means' Advances - to provide flexibility with its cash flow. The sums involved were not insignificant, with the balance standing at £14.3 billion at the end of March 1997. When the UK joined the European Union, however, it gave up this right.*

---

* A consultation document published by HM Treasury states (paragraph 29) "...In line with the move to manage the Exchequer's cashflow separately from the Bank's operations, the Bank and the Treasury will freeze the size of the Ways and Means advance at the time of transition in cash management arrangements. Methods will then be explored to repay the balance. This is in accord with the Maastricht Treaty (Article 104) and will constitute a preparation for Stage 3 EMU entry by the Government."[1] n.b. Article 104 was amalgamated into Article 101/125 at a later stage.

The Treaty of Maastricht, approved by governments in December 1991, signed on 7 February 1992 and effective from November 1993, created the European Union and led to the creation of the European Central Bank (ECB), and the introduction of a single currency, the euro, from 2002. The Treaty, along with its subsequent revisions, specifies a set of economic and monetary rules which all members are obliged to adhere to, including the UK, even though it is not in the euro zone. This includes the statutory independence of the ECB from any government or democratically elected parliament, which is enshrined in the Treaty.

> *When exercising the powers and carrying out the tasks and duties*
> *conferred upon them by the Treaties and the Statute of the ECB, neither*
> *the European Central Bank, nor a national central bank, nor any member*
> *of their decision-making bodies shall seek or take instructions from Union*
> *institutions, bodies, offices or agencies, from any government of a Member*
> *State or from any other body.*
> **European Union (2008)**[2]

One of the most important rules of the Treaty in relation to money creation is Article 101 EC, now known as Article 123* of the Treaty on the Functioning of the European Union (TFEU)[3]. This prohibits the direct financing of government spending by the nation's central bank. This includes any overdraft or credit facility and the direct purchase of any debt instrument (i.e. gilts, treasury bonds) by the central bank. Article 101 EC does however allow the central bank to purchase debt instruments indirectly on the secondary market[†], after they have previously been issued to private investors and started to be traded in the money markets (see Chapter 2, Box 4). It is for the independent central bank, not the Government, to decide whether and when to do this.

Purchasing bonds on the secondary market is exactly what the Bank of England has been doing since it commenced 'quantitative easing' in 2009. It has purchased £375bn worth of existing government bonds mostly from institutional investors such as pension funds. New deposits have been created not in the Government's bank accounts, but in the accounts of these investors (section 4.7.3). Even when the central bank purchases bonds from banks, rather than institutional investors, this does not increase the money circulating in the economy. The Bank of England did not, and under Article 101 EC is not permitted to, purchase newly issued gilts *directly* from the UK government. Such an action would, of course, provide the Government with newly created money which could be spent directly in to the economy via government departments or used to reduce the national debt.

---

* Following the Lisbon Treaty of 2009, Article 101 EC was revised and is now known as Article 123 of the Treaty on the Functioning of the European Union, abbreviation TFEU or TEU. There were no substantive changes to policy however. Tables of equivalence retrievable from the EUR-lex website http://eur-lex. europa.eu/en/treaties/index.htm

† The initial sale of financial securities, such as the initial public offering (IPO) of a company's shares on the stock market, is referred to as 'primary markets'. Once securities have been issued for the first time all subsequent trading is known as the 'secondary market'.

These EU rules, in theory at least, ensure that when government spending exceeds taxes, governments are forced to borrow funds from the market and run up a deficit, rather than finance the deficit or increase public spending through new central bank money creation. This is why the interest rates on government debt of different European countries, particularly since the financial crisis, are the focus of so much media attention. If the interest rates on government debt reach a certain level, the markets may lose confidence in the Government's capacity to service its existing loans by keeping up interest payments, or roll over its debt, pushing interest rates even higher until eventually the country faces the prospect of default. Political economist Geoffrey Ingham argues that the Maastricht Treaty effectively removed the power of money creation from individual states and subjected them to 'market discipline'

> *The latter constraint [article 101] is aimed at preventing individual states from monetising their debt, in the time-honoured fashion, which would compromise the ECB's [European central bank's] absolute control of the production of money. Now that individual member central banks cannot monetise their states' debts, budget deficits must be financed directly in the money market – like those of any private corporation.[4]*

However, these restrictions on credit creation do not apply to 'publicly owned credit institutions' which have full credit creation powers and are treated in exactly the same way as private banks by the central bank. Also, as will be discussed below, the Maastricht rules do not prevent governments borrowing directly from commercial banks in the form of loan contracts, which also creates new money, to fund public sector borrowing, and hence remains a viable avenue to monetise government expenditure. Thus there are ways for governments to continue to exercise their powers of money creation, even under the restrictive Maastricht rules.[*]

Box 13: Could the Government directly create money itself?

There are many historical examples of governments funding fiscal shortfalls through the issuance of government money. This was done in the UK during WWI, and prior to this via the elaborate system of tally sticks deployed between the eleventh and nineteenth centuries[7] (see Section 2.3). Similarly, the Governments of Germany, Japan, and the USA issued at times significant amounts of government money, mainly during the nineteenth century. United States Notes were also issued in significant proportions by the US government during the twentieth century.[8]

While the issuance of government money to fund fiscal expenditure is often thought to be inflationary, this need not be the case, especially if limited by the amount of money-supply expansion needed to reach the growth potential of the economy. ➜

---

[*] As proposed by Werner since 1994 (see Sections 5.5 and 5.6 above). For sources on this proposal, see Werner (2012a)[5] and Werner (2012b)[6].

As has been argued by Huber and Robertson[9] and others, government-created money may represent an efficient use of the monetary system to minimise the tax burden and maximise value for tax-payers. No servicing costs in the form of interest, and interest on interest (compound interest), are incurred. This could be of substantial benefit at a time when many a government spends as much or even more on compounded interest on their debts than on their core government expenditure programmes (see also Box 8 on 'seigniorage'). Exploring alternative methods of creating new money is beyond the scope of this book, but these historical examples are important to illustrate that alternative systems are not just possible, but have been tested and found effective. We give a brief overview of this and other alternatives to the current money and banking system in Section 7.6.

6.1.1.
The Eurozone crisis and the politics of monetary policy

The European sovereign debt crisis, which commenced shortly after the North Atlantic financial crisis of 2008-09, has tested the rules governing monetary policy in the European Union to the extreme. The ECB has interpreted some of the rules 'flexibly', so that its credibility and enforceability in case of non-compliance by a member government are now somewhat more doubtful. The crisis has also revealed the enormous advantage of having a sovereign currency and central bank in times of crisis.

The UK, through its £375bn quantitative easing (QE) programme (section 4.7.3), can be seen to have, at least temporarily, monetised the Government debt 'by the backdoor'. The Bank of England maintains in official communications that the reserves will eventually be sold back into the market, but with such a vast figure it is not easy to see this happening in the near future. The reality is that the UK can only default on its debt if the central bank decides to stop buying government bonds and since there is no actual limit to the amount of reserves the Bank can create to buy bonds, there would appear little reason for this to happen. The fact that there are no restrictions on the Bank of England's ability to buy up government debt is one of the reasons that interest rates on UK government bonds have remained low.

In contrast, the Eurozone economies, locked in to a fixed exchange rate regime with 17 other countries, must depend on the European Central Bank (ECB) to prevent sovereign defaults. The ECB fears 'moral hazard' – that states will take ECB interventions for granted if interest rates on their borrowing become too high and lose 'fiscal discipline', i.e. continue to run up budget deficits safe in the knowledge the ECB will bail them out. There is also a free rider problem – in contrast to the UK where monetisation of debt will only affect the UK, in Europe the monetisation of debt will affect (and be paid for by) all countries. Therefore there is an incentive for any individual nation to go back on any agreement to reduce government spending.

Having said this, the ECB has bought billions of Euros worth of Greek, Irish, Portuguese, Spanish and Italian bonds from the secondary market in an attempt to prevent a loss of confidence in the European sovereign debt markets. It has also extended billions of euros at very low rates of interest to European banks via its Long Term Refinancing Operations (LTROs), announced on 8 December 2011. As in the UK, however, a large part of the funds provided to the banking system have become idle bank reserves with the central bank that do not stimulate the economy. Most recently, the ECB has announced that it is prepared to buy up the Government debt of struggling Eurozone members to an unlimited degree – via 'Outright Monetary Transactions' (OMTs). However, to access the funds, states will have to meet conditions set by the EU, the ECB and the IMF (the so-called Troika). All of these interventions can be seen to create an identical effect to QE.[10,11] The ECB's balance sheet has more than doubled in size since 2008 to €2.75 trillion via these interventions, although it has maintained the position that it has acted within its remit throughout and has not engaged in the monetisation of debt.[*]

6.2.
Government taxes, borrowing and spending (fiscal policy)

If the Government cannot borrow from the central bank or create its own money, how then does it 'spend'? Governments must, like me and you, obtain money from somewhere before they can spend.[†] Generally this spending is either funded from revenue, proceeds from profitable government-operated enterprises or services, national insurance contributions and taxes, or through borrowing.[‡]

6.2.1.
Taxation

How does taxation work? In principle the process is simple. When an individual is taxed, the value of their bank account is reduced (in the example below they bank with Nationwide), and central bank reserves are transferred from their bank's reserve account at the Bank of England to the Government's bank account at the Bank of England (known as the Consolidated Fund). When the Government spends, these reserves flow from the Consolidated Fund to the receiving person or organisation bank's reserve account (in this case Barclays). The person or organisation with whom the Government is spending sees the value of their bank account increase as a result.

---

[*] Most recently, for example, when announcing the unlimited government bond purchase intervention, the ECB President Mario Draghi stated: "Let me repeat what I said last month... we act strictly within our mandate to maintain price stability over the medium term; we act independently in determining monetary policy; and the euro is irreversible."

[†] Modern Money Theory (MMT) is an approach in macro-economics which argues against this[12]. MMT says that in nation states with fiat money, sovereign currencies and central banks; taxation is the means by which governments remove money from circulation (e.g. to prevent inflation or to create particular incentives within the private sector). There is no restriction on governments' ability to spend by creating new money.

[‡] The Government may raise funds through other means, for example by selling off national industries and assets, but these are one-off payments that cannot fund a permanent government deficit. There are also various other ways that governments can and have funded expenditure in the past, which we discuss further in Section 7.6.

Figure 19: Government Taxation and Spending

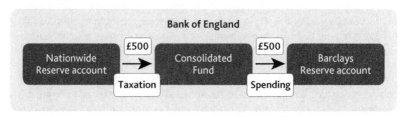

6.2.2.
Borrowing

If the Government is running a deficit, then spending outflows exceed tax inflows. To make the account balance, the difference can be made up by the issuance of government money – a practice not adopted since before 1945 (see section 7.6.3) – or else must be made up through government borrowing. The government borrows primarily by issuing government bonds, or 'gilts' (see section 3.4.3, box 3). Because the Government is perceived to be the safest borrower available as it need never default on debt denominated in its own currency (for reasons explained above), government bonds are usually sold with ease to investors. Indeed, investors find these assets a useful and desirable part of their investment portfolio, helping pension funds, for example, to match long-term assets against long-term liabilities.

What is the actual process through which the Government borrows? The process is summarised below and examined in detail in Appendix 2. The Government, through the Debt Management Office (DMO) sells gilts directly to a small group of banks known as Gilt Edged Market Makers, or GEMMs.* The GEMMs then sell these gilts on to clients on whose behalf they have bid in the gilt auction process, or to the wider investment community through the secondary market. The GEMM now has to pay the DMO for the new gilts by making a transfer from its own reserve account at the Bank of England, to the DMO's reserve account at the Bank of England. These reserves are then transferred to the Consolidated Fund at the Bank of England and from there they are spent into the economy, as shown in figure 20.

We can also trace customer deposits through this process. Members of the public, or the companies that employ them, make contributions to a pension fund. This results in deposits being transferred through the banking system from those individuals and companies to the bank account of the pension fund. When the pension fund purchases a newly-issued gilt from a GEMM, it sees a reduction in its own bank account. For a short while, it appears that the deposits have 'disappeared' and the money supply appears to have decreased. However,

---

* These include major investment banks such as Barclays Capital, Goldman Sachs and J.P. Morgan.[13]

Figure 20: Government Borrowing and Spending (no net impact on the money supply)

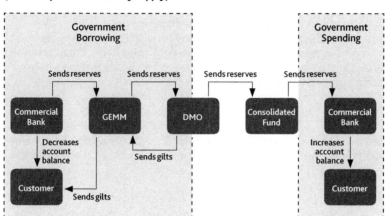

at the other end of the chain, the Government spends the proceeds of the recently-sold gilts, and the recipient will find their bank balance has increased. The deposits that 'disappeared' when the pension fund bought the gilt have now 'reappeared', and as a result there is no net change in deposits or reserves when the Government borrows.

Under current arrangements the only circumstance in which government borrowing leads to an expansion in the money supply is if a commercial bank directly purchases a government bond on its own account. In this case, unlike the scenario shown in figure 20, the bank will not reduce any of its customers' deposits as they are not involved in the transaction. However, the recipients of Government spending will have more bank deposits (assuming they are non-banks, such as households via public sector wages or companies via procurement of public services) and hence the overall supply of money has increased. In the UK, commercial banks hold a relatively small proportion of the stock of government bonds, ranging between zero and 16% over the past 25 years according to DMO figures, and so the current method of financing government spending through a combination of taxation and bond issuance results in a relatively small monetary expansion. However, there are two alternative methods of financing government spending that would ensure much greater expansion in the money supply, and these are discussed further in section 6.3.1.

6.2.3.
Government spending and idle balances

As shown in section 4.3, banks use central bank reserves in order to settle payments between themselves. When the Government borrows or taxes, reserves are withdrawn from the reserve accounts belonging to banks and moved to the Government's account at the Bank of England. When the Government spends, these reserves are transferred back to the banks. If the Government does not spend reserves as soon as it receives them, the banking sector as a whole may find that there is a shortage of reserves circulating in the system with which they can make payments. This could lead to an increase in the interest rate the banks charge each other for reserves on the interbank market (see section 4.3.1), making it difficult for the Bank of England to keep interest rates close to the target rate set by the Monetary Policy Committee (MPC).

Rather than allowing reserves that are not being used to sit idly in its bank accounts, the Government could lend them back into the market, and in so doing receive a rate of interest. Similarly, individual government departments bank with commercial banks and any idle deposits (and the reserve associated with them), which are not being used could be lent back into the markets. To mitigate these problems, any excess reserves held in any government accounts, including government department accounts held at commercial banks, are "swept up" at the end of the day into the Debt Management Office's (DMO) account at the central bank. Once there, the DMO lends these reserves back onto the money markets until they are needed. As a result, when the Government taxes or borrows and does not immediately spend, reserves are not drained from the banking system, as would initially seem to happen. Instead, the actions of the DMO ensure that the reserves are recycled back into the system.

6.3.
The effect of government borrowing on the money supply: 'crowding out'

Many economists argue that government borrowing affects the price and quantity of money available to the private sector – a process known as 'crowding-out'. The textbook crowding-out argument states that when a government borrows from the market, it has to persuade the private investment sector to give up resources so that it can use them. By borrowing money through issuing new government bonds, the Government effectively borrows a finite amount of money that otherwise could have been borrowed by the private sector. This has the effect of reducing the amount of investment available to businesses and the private sector and therefore drives up interest rates. This dampens the demand for loans for investment, thus reducing growth. [14]

However, empirically, this crowding-out effect via higher interest rates has been

---

* This is the quantity-crowding-out argument posed by Richard Werner - see Werner (1995)[17] and Werner (2003).[18]

difficult to prove.[15] This has been particularly obvious in the case of Japan, where during the 1990s fiscal expansion of record proportion was adopted. While this did not have the expected expansionary effect on the economy, interest rates did not rise as crowding-out theory would suggest.[16] As Werner has been arguing, when investors purchase newly issued government bonds with existing purchasing power, these funds are no longer available to be invested in the private sector. Instead they are given to the Government, who then spends them. The total stock of money in the economy has not changed. Hence, assuming government and the financial sector invest money in an equally productive manner, which we define here as resulting in GDP-related transactions, pure fiscal policy that is not connected to changes in monetary factors will be growth-neutral.*

So the crowding out does not take place via interest rates, as most economics textbooks suggest, but can even happen during periods of falling interest rates – via the rationing of available purchasing power.

However, the assumption that government and private sector investment are equally productive is unlikely to hold true in the real world. Government borrowing can be expansionary if the Government uses the money more productively than the original private investment holders would have done. The question then becomes how the composition of investment varies between public and private investment sectors. Will the Government actually use its borrowing to invest in the productive capacity of the economy, or is it simply borrowing to fund the ongoing expenses of running the public sector? Without the option of lending to government, would the financial sector (such as pension funds and insurance companies) have instead invested the funds in businesses and boosting productive capacity? Or would they have simply used the funds to bid up the price of existing financial assets? While a discussion of the Government's ability to spend money in a more economically productive manner than the private sector is beyond the scope of this book (and will probably remain a contested topic), a few points are worth considering.

Firstly, there are a number of reasons private investors might allocate money in less productive ways than the Government. Private investors, particularly institutional investors, will normally put their money where they receive the highest returns, including investing money in projects outside the UK. While this may result in a higher private return than if they had invested locally, the entire social benefit of the investment will fall abroad. In addition, the private investment sector can and does borrow money for non-productivity-enhancing purposes, such as commodity speculation and commercial property finance. This does not increase GDP transactions and will instead inflate asset prices (see discussion in section 5.6). A further example is when private investors fund private equity vehicles that take over productive manufacturers, fire local staff and outsource production to foreign low-wage countries. This reduces the number of low-skilled jobs available in the UK and contributes to unemployment. Finally, when private sector economic confidence is low, as during recessions, investors will tend to be risk averse and seek existing financial assets, including property, in which to store wealth in preference to providing funding for new commercial ventures. Trading existing assets does not stimulate GDP in the way that investment in new productive capacity and infrastructure does.

In contrast, government investment is bound to contribute to GDP transactions – there is little reason for the Government to invest in existing financial assets. Particular types of investment, such as in transport infrastructure, housing construction or low-carbon conversion and energy efficiency-enhancing investments, appear to have a positive long term growth impact but are often under-funded by the private sector because the initial costs of investment are high and the returns on investment are low or take many years to arrive. In addition, spending by the Government tends to also be redistributive; channelling funds towards lower income groups (e.g. via benefits) who may spend a larger proportion of any additional income than higher income socio-economic groups.[19]

Both the above features of government spending affect the flow of money in the economy in a way that could stimulate more GDP transactions later, even if the stock of money remains the same and initially there is no direct impact on nominal GDP. The 'velocity' of money, or the amount of times it changes hands in a given period, increases in this case. In terms of its effect on demand this is the equivalent of an increase in the quantity of money. In summary, it is possible that the Government could invest in a socially more beneficial way than the private sector, and that the nature of its spending would lead to money circulating faster and boosting economic activity. There is, however, no guarantee that governments will have the right information to invest productively, or even try to do so.

6.3.1.
Linking fiscal policy to increased credit creation

It is possible, however, to increase the impact of fiscal policy by linking it to credit creation. This can be done in a number of ways. The easiest would be for the central bank to purchase, indirectly, through the secondary market, the Government bonds newly issued to fund fiscal expansion, while not counteracting these purchases through any of its other transactions. In other words, when the Bank of England purchases £1 billion of existing gilts in the secondary market, the Government could take the opportunity to raise the same amount of funds by selling new gilts. Government spending would increase or taxation would fall, but the total stock of gilts owned by the private sector would remain unchanged.

When it cannot be sure of the long-term co-operation of the central bank, the

---

* This was first proposed by Richard Werner in 1994 – see Werner (1994,[24] 1998[25] and 2000[26])

Government can easily implement an alternative by ceasing the issuance of government bonds and borrowing instead directly from commercial banks in the form of long-term loan contracts.* This has the advantage of increasing bank credit creation, as well as strengthening the banking system by improving the quality of its loan book. Such a policy is a potential solution to many of the problems faced by countries such as Spain and Ireland presently: the prime rate, i.e. the interest rate banks charge borrowers with the best credit risk, is often far lower in Spain, Ireland, Portugal and Greece, than the sovereign bond yield of similar maturity. The reason is that bank credit is not tradable and hence not susceptible to speculative attacks, or downgrades by rating agencies – while being eligible as collateral with the ECB, not required to be marked to market and not requiring new capital from banks, according to the Basel rules.[20,21] As we saw in Section 3.6.2, a similar mechanism of the Government borrowing directly from banks was last adopted in the UK during World War II, when the Treasury forced banks to buy Treasury Deposit Receipts (TDRs) at 1.125% interest to help fund the war.[22] TDRs were valid for six months and therefore less liquid than Treasury bills but paid 0.125% higher interest than the Treasury Bills at the time.[23]

In response to the UK banking crisis, the Government chose to do the opposite: it borrowed money from the markets to finance a bailout of the banking system.* This has now been partially counteracted, however, by the central bank buying back government bonds through the programme of QE.

6.4.
Foreign exchange, international capital flows and the effects on money

A key feature of late twentieth Century globalisation has been the deregulation and liberalisation of international flows of money across national monetary regimes, which has had important consequences for government and central banks' ability to influence monetary policy. This section explains foreign exchange and what happens in relation to commercial bank money and central bank reserves, then goes on to look at exchange rate regimes and how states can intervene, or not, to achieve particular monetary policy goals. Again we shall see how international historical and institutional developments have left national bodies constrained in terms of monetary policy. More technical detail on how the foreign exchange payment system works is provided in Appendix 3.

6.4.1.
Foreign exchange payments

A foreign exchange market is simply a market place (physical or virtual) for buyers and sellers of different currencies and is essential to the modern globalised economy. Foreign exchange arises out of the need for people who are trading

---

* For further detail on the cost to the UK taxpayer of supporting the banking sector see Prieg, Greenham and Ryan-Collins (2011).[27]

across borders to get hold of the local currency in order to pay local sellers.

While the goods produced in a country are priced in terms of that country's currency (one loaf of bread = £1), the currency of a country is priced in terms of other currencies (£1 = $1.63 = €1.13). The price of currencies is known as the *exchange rate* and is quoted in pairs of currencies. For most individuals, the only time they will personally handle foreign exchange is when they are going on holiday. However, these transactions make up only a tiny proportion of all foreign exchange trades. The major private sector players in the foreign exchange markets are businesses, for import and export, and speculators.

Box 14: The Foreign Exchange Market

By 2010 the foreign exchange market had grown to be the largest and most liquid market in the world, with an average of more than $4 trillion of currency being exchanged (settled*) every day. 28 Banks located in the UK dominate the foreign exchange market, accounting for 37 per cent of all foreign exchange market turnover, with banks based in the United States accounting for 18 per cent, Japan 6 per cent, Singapore 5 per cent, Switzerland 5 per cent, Hong Kong SAR 5 per cent and Australia 4 per cent.

Of the currencies that are traded, the US dollar is the most prominent, accounting for 85 per cent of all transactions. The other key currencies are the euro, accounting for 37 per cent of all transactions, the Japanese yen accounting for 17 per cent and the pound sterling at 15 per cent†. 29

---

* In the forex markets the term 'settlement' refers to the completion of the transaction and fulfilment of the contract – i.e. for a spot transaction settlement would occur when both currencies have been delivered (electronically) to the buyer and the seller's bank accounts, normally two days after the deal was done (spot rates).

† Because two currencies are involved in each transaction, the sum of the percentage shares of individual currencies totals two hundred per cent instead of one hundred per cent.

Any large commercial bank that deals in foreign currencies, including nearly all major high street banks, will have reserve accounts not only in their home country's central bank but also at the central banks responsible for those foreign currencies. Let's look at what happens when one currency is exchanged for another in terms of commercial bank money and central bank reserves.

Let's say that Jim, an American, has just got a job in London and wants to buy a house that costs £1m. Jim banks with Citibank and has both a dollar account in the US and a sterling account in the UK (figure 21). Let's assume the exchange rate is US$1.50 = £1.00. He instructs Citibank to transfer $1.5m to his UK Citibank account. Jim will see his US dollar bank balance fall by $1.5m and his UK bank balance increase by £1m (after any fees from the bank)

Behind the scenes, his US Citibank will do a 'spot trade' (see Appendix 3.2.1), seeking out a UK bank, say Barclays, which wishes to buy dollars in exchange for sterling. The US Citibank will send dollar reserves from its account at the Federal Reserve (the US central bank) to Barclay's reserve account at the Federal Reserve. Both exchanges take place within the US monetary system.

In the UK, Barclays' will send sterling reserves from its account at the BoE to UK Citibank's account at the BoE (all in the UK system). In terms of reserves, Barclays in the US has received dollar reserves and in return, Barclays in the UK has sent pound reserves to Citibank in the UK. Thus in both countries the total level of reserves are the same.

Figure 21: A Foreign Exchange Transfer of $1.5m (£1m)

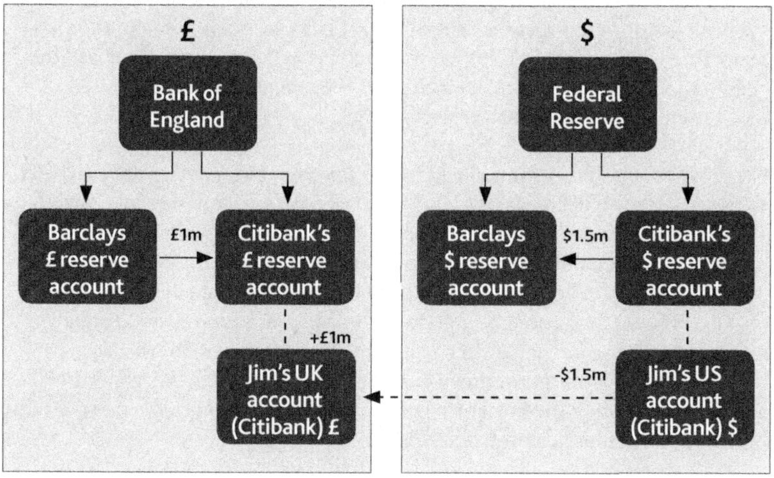

Jim's Citibank account in the UK now has £1m more and in exchange his Citibank account in America has 1.5m fewer dollars.

In reality, if both commercial banks have reserve accounts at both central banks it is likely that, bar a huge sum of money being exchanged, neither bank would need to adjust its reserves and, as with the UK interbank market, they would simply net out the change. The key point to note is foreign exchange transactions do not affect the level of reserves in aggregate in the banking system; they merely transfer reserves between banks.

6.4.2.
Different exchange rate regimes

As discussed in Section 3.6, the UK has moved from having a gold-backed currency to a pegged exchange rate and finally to a free-floating exchange rate. In this section we briefly review these different models and their relation to monetary policy.

When countries adhered to the gold standard, their exchange rate was determined by an agreement to exchange notes for a fixed quantity of gold. However, it is also possible to have a fixed exchange rate regime with a fiat currency, as was the case before in Europe just before the introduction of the euro.

When exchange rates are not freely set by markets, the most common arrangement is that of a pegged regime. Here the central bank sets the price of the domestic currency in terms of a foreign currency. To maintain this peg, sufficient foreign exchange reserves are required, and sufficient access to the securities in which the foreign exchange reserves are held. So for instance, in 1991 Argentina fixed its exchange rate against the dollar, so that one peso could be converted to one dollar on demand at the central bank. Likewise, many Asian economies maintained dollar pegs until 1997, however as central banks failed to adjust the pegs or their monetary policy appropriately, they ran out of sufficient foreign reserves and had to abandon the pegs.

Other types of pegged regimes include *crawling pegs* and *currency bands*. Under a *crawling peg*, the exchange rate is allowed to appreciate or depreciate slowly to allow for differing rates of inflation between the two countries. This stops goods in one country becoming relatively more expensive than in the other country, preserving the so-called real exchange rate (the exchange rate in terms of goods or 'purchasing-power-parity' to use the technical term). Conversely, *currency bands* allow the exchange rate to float freely, although only within a narrow range. Perhaps the most prominent currency band in recent history was the European Monetary System, which between 1978 and 1998 determined the value of exchange rates in the European Union.

These types of fixed exchange rate regimes often require central bank intervention to maintain currency stability. In contrast to fixed exchange rate regimes, *floating currency regimes* can in theory do away with central bank involvement in the foreign exchange market, with market forces determining the exchange rate. Currently most of the world's major currencies operate on a floating exchange regime, although the degree of intervention by central banks is not clear. In practice, central banks may intervene in order to stabilise exchange rates. For instance, following the earthquake that hit Japan on the 11 March, on 18 March 2011, the UK government and the other G7 countries intervened in order to prevent any further appreciation of the yen. These floating rate regimes are therefore sometimes known as 'managed' or 'dirty' floats. Under a floating regime, if Britons wish to invest in Europe they have to sell their pounds and buy euro. Unless there is a balancing flow of investment into pounds, the price of the pound against the euro will need to fall sufficiently to tempt new buyers of pounds into the market. This is known as an appreciation of the euro or, equivalently, as a depreciation of the pound.

6.4.3.

Government intervention to manage exchange rates and the 'Impossible Trinity'

So why is the choice of exchange rate regime important? Obviously it will directly affect those who wish to buy or sell foreign currency. However, the choice of exchange regime will also affect the ability of the central bank to pursue autonomous monetary policy. If a country chooses to have a fixed exchange rate and free capital flows, then monetary policy must be used to maintain the value of the currency. The central bank must stand ready to intervene in foreign exchange markets by buying and selling its own currency. For example, imagine you are the central bank of Argentina in 1991 and the exchange rate is fixed at one peso to one dollar. Due to a fantastic new investment opportunity in America, Argentineans start selling pesos and buying dollars, leading to downward pressure on the price of pesos in terms of dollars. Argentina's central bank steps in, selling dollars and buying pesos, and in doing so maintains the one-to-one exchange rate. For this to work, however, the central bank requires a sufficient stock of dollar reserves.*

It is widely acknowledged that it is not possible to simultaneously maintain free capital flows, a fixed exchange rate and a sovereign monetary policy, i.e. to use monetary policy as a policy tool to fulfil particular national requirements. This is known as the **Impossible Trinity** (Figure 22).

Figure 22: The Impossible Trinity

FREE CAPITAL FLOWS

The Impossible Trinity (a country can only choose two of these three)

FIXED EXCHANGE RATE

SOVEREIGN MONETARY POLICY

To see why this is so, consider a country with a fixed exchange rate regime. If the central bank of this country tried to lower its interest rate in order to stimulate the domestic economy, then residents of the country may look to transfer their savings into foreign assets, to take advantage of the relatively higher interest rate abroad. In order to do so, they would sell the domestic currency, likely leading to the price falling due to the sudden extra supply. However, the central bank is committed to maintaining the exchange rate. In order to stop the currency

---

* The process is actually far more complex than described here. Of particular importance is the fact that central bank reserves (in pesos) are transferred to the central bank, removing them from the system. Without any offsetting by the central bank the reduction in reserves can lead to an increase in the interbank rate.

depreciating, it has to sell its foreign exchange for domestic currency. However, people may continue to shift into foreign assets for as long as there is a difference between the interest rates. So unless the central bank increases the interest rate, the selling of the domestic currency may continue until the Bank's foreign exchange reserves are exhausted. At this point the central bank will no longer be able to support the currency – leading to its devaluation. Of course, this will break the central bank's commitment to the fixed exchange rate.

An example of this was the UK's response to 'Black Wednesday' - on 16 September 1992 - when the UK government was forced to withdraw the pound from the European Exchange Rate Mechanism (ERM) due to pressure from currency speculators. The Bank of England significantly raised interest rates twice in the same day in an attempt to stem capital outflows and maintain the exchange rate. This unprecedented action was ultimately unsuccessful as investors did not believe that the interest rate increases were sustainable.

Members of a currency union such as the eurozone are effectively operating a fixed exchange rate regime – so fixed that the currencies have been merged into a single currency. In a world of free capital flows this is why countries such as Greece, Spain, Portugal and Ireland are unable to pursue a sovereign monetary policy tailored to their individual economic circumstances (apart from the fact that they also do not have their own autonomous central banks any more). Without their own sovereign currency and central bank, they cannot adjust their interest rates to stimulate demand, nor create additional central bank reserves as the UK has been able to do via QE thereby helping to bring down interest rates.

Could a country restrict capital flows? Yes, it can if it has an independent currency and central bank. This strategy was successfully implemented by the Malaysia government after the outbreak of the Asian crisis and although this policy was initially opposed by the IMF, it has since reversed its opposition to capital controls[30]. China, India and Brazil have also all made routine use of such policies. However, the implementation of capital controls faces challenges, such as large firms attempting to disguise capital flows as current account transactions.

6.5.
Summary

This chapter has described the role of governments and foreign exchange in the money creation process, and in particular to what extent they can directly or indirectly influence the money supply through fiscal and monetary policies. EU legislation prevents member governments from expanding credit creation directly by borrowing from the central bank, or 'monetising government debt'. QE is sometimes seen as a means by which central banks get round these strictures, since the effect of buying up large quantities of government bonds with the creation of new reserves can be viewed as the monetisation of debt 'via the backdoor'. However, the effectiveness of QE has been widely contested, including by the authors[30,31,32,33,34] and in particular regarding its effectiveness in stimulating credit creation and GDP (see section 4.7.3). Furthermore, with independent central banks governments have no direct control over such policies.

The eurozone takes the Impossible Trinity to its logical conclusion, as the euro system is essentially a system of permanently fixed exchange rates. When a country adopts a fixed exchange rate regime with free capital flows, it must use monetary policy to manage the exchange rate rather than domestic credit creation. In the case of Eurozone members, they cannot use monetary policy for anything at all as they no longer have their own currency or central bank. Fiscal policy remains with national governments within the Eurozone (for now), who can raise funds through the issuance of bonds. The effect in terms of the money supply is neutral – funds are simply moved from one part of the economy to another. It may be possible to stimulate growth if the Government invests in a way that is significantly more productive than the private sector, but this is certainly not a given. This method of funding government deficits makes them dependent on the appetites of investors for purchasing government bonds; a deliberate feature of the system intended to subject governments to the fiscal discipline of international financial markets.

However, there could be other options for governments even under existing rules. An overview of alternative monetary systems is given in section 6.7, but it is worth highlighting two methods of direct government intervention in the credit creation process. Governments can expand the effective money supply by borrowing from commercial banks via loan contracts, as happened in the UK during World War II. It is also possible to issue government money directly as happened in the UK from 1914 to 1927 and in England from 1000 to 1826.[35]

These methods both align fiscal and monetary policy more closely, as the act of government spending directly expands the money supply, and would therefore be considered unconventional in terms of the current orthodoxy. However, the distinction and separation has come under intense strain since the financial crisis of 2008 and subsequent EU sovereign debt crisis. It would appear that previously unconventional policies, such as QE, can become conventional if the economic need appears sufficiently pressing.

Governments have intervened on a massive scale to bail-out the banking system, causing a strain on their fiscal position. Central banks have in turn used monetary policy to intervene on a significant scale in bond markets to support governments. This has contributed to lower interest rates and boosted demand for sovereign debt, thereby easing the strain on fiscal policy. The ECB's policies of 2012, in particular the OMT mechanism (see section 6.1) which places conditions on a government's fiscal policy before the ECB will embark on purchasing its bonds, challenge the idea that central banks can be truly 'apolitical'. Fiscal policy, monetary policy and the banking system, as the engine of credit creation, are inextricably intertwined.

References

1 HM Treasury, (1997). *The Future of the UK Government Debt and Cash Management: a response to consultation by HM Treasury*, 22nd December 1997. Retrievable from http://www.dmo.gov.uk/docs/publications/giltsmarket/consultationpapers/cons221297.pdf [accessed 30th August 2012]

2 Official Journal of the European Union, (2008). *Consolidated Version of the Treaty on the Functioning of the European Union*. Article 130 (ex article 108 TEC). Retrievable from http://eur-lex.europa.eu/LexUriServ/LexUriServ.do?uri=OJ:C:2008:115:0047:0199:EN:PDF [accessed 14 June 2011].

3 *Ibid.*

4 Ingham, G., (2004). *The Nature of Money*. Cambridge: Polity Press

5 Werner, R.A., (2012a). Towards a new research programme on 'banking and the economy' – Implications of the Quantity Theory of Credit for the prevention and resolution of banking and debt crises, *International Review of Financial Analysis*, forthcoming

6 Werner, R.A., (2012b). *How to end the European crisis – at no further cost and without the need for political changes*. Southampton, University of Southampton (Centre for Banking, Finance and Sustainable Development Policy Discussion Paper, 2-12). Retrievable from http://eprints.soton.ac.uk/341650/

7 Davies, G., (2002). *A History of Money*. Cardif: University of Wales Press, p. 663

8 Werner, R.A., (2005). *op. cit.* pp. 258–59

9 Huber, J. and Robertson, J., (2000). *Creating New Money*. London: nef. Retrievable from http://www.neweconomics.org/publications/creating-new-money

10 Financial Times (5 August 2011) *Market Unimpressed by ECB action*. Retrievable from http://www.ft.com/cms/s/0/fc04a956-bf71-11e0-898c-00144feabdc0.html - ixzz1ULKrwIT9 [accessed 6 August 2011]

11 European Central Bank, (7 August 2011). Press release. para 6

12 Wray, Randall, L., (2012). *Modern Money Theory, A Primer on Macro-economics for Sovereign Monetary Systems*. Palgrave Macmillan: London

13 UK Debt Management Office (n. d.) *Gilt Market: Market Participants*. Retrievable from http://www.dmo.gov.uk/index.aspx?page=Gilts/Gemms_idb

14 Spencer, R.W., and Yohe, W.P., (1970). *The 'Crowding Out' of Private Expenditures by Fiscal Policy Actions*, *Federal Reserve Bank of St. Louis Review*, October, pp. 12-24

15 Werner, R.A., (2005). *op. cit.*

16 *Ibid.*

17 Werner, R.A., (1995). Keiki kaifuku, ryōteki kinyū kanwa kara, (How to Create a Recovery through 'Quantitative Monetary Easing'), *The Nihon Keizai Shinbun (Nikkei)*, 'Keizai Kyōshitsu' ('Economics Classroom'), 2 September 1995 (morning edition), p. 26; English translation by T. John Cooke (November 2011). Retrievable from http://eprints.soton.ac.uk/340476/

18 Werner, R.A., (2003). *Princes of the Yen*. Armonk, New York: Sharpe, M.E.

19 Kuznets, S., (1953). *Shares of Upper Income Groups in Income and Savings*. National Bureau of Economic Research, New York, NY; Brown, C., (2004). Does Income Distribution Matter for Effective Demand? Evidence from the United States, *Review of Political Economy*, Volume 16, Number 3, 291–307

20 Werner, R., A., (2012c). *The Euro-crisis: a to-do-list for the ECB*. Southampton, University of Southampton (Centre for Banking, Finance and Sustainable Development Policy Discussion Paper 1-12). Retrievable from http://eprints.soton.ac.uk/341648/

21 Werner, (2012b). *op.cit.*

22 Howson, S. K., (1988). Cheap Money and debt-management in Britain 1932-51, in Cottrell, P. L. and Moggridge, D. E. (Eds), *Money and Power: Essays in Honor of L. S. Pressnell*. London: Macmillan, p. 252-3.

23 Tiley, G., (2007). *Keynes Betrayed*. Palgrave Macmillan: London, p. 205

24 Werner, R.A. (1994). *Liquidity Watch*, Jardine Fleming Securities (Asia) Ltd., May

25 Werner, R.A., (1998). *Minkanginkoukarano kariire de keikitaisaku wo okonaeba issekinichou* (Effective stimulation policy via government borrowing from commercial banks), The Economist, 14 July 1998

26 Werner, R.A., (2000). Japan's plan to borrow from banks deserves praise. *Financial Times*, 9 February 2000

27 Prieg, L., Greenham, T. and Ryan-Collins, J., (2011). *Quid Pro Quo: Redressing the Privileges of the Banking Industry*. London: **nef**

28 Bank for International Settlements, (2010). *Triennial central bank Survey of Foreign Exchange and Over-The-Counter Interest Rate Derivatives Market Activity in April 2010. Report on global foreign exchange market activity in 2010*. BIS - Monetary and Economic Department, p. 6

29 Bank for International Settlements (2010). *op. cit.* p. 12

30 Ostry D. et al., (2010). *Capital Inflows: The Role of Controls*. IMF Staff Position Note, 19 February 2010, SPN/10/04

31 Lyonnet, V. Werner, R. A., (2012). Lessons from the Bank of England on 'quantitative easing' and other 'unconventional' monetary policies. *International Review of Financial Analysis*, Volume 25, December 2012, pp. 94-105

32 Voutsinas, K. and Werner, R.A., (2010). *New Evidence on the Effectiveness of 'Quantitative Easing' and the Accountability of the Central Bank in Japan*, Centre for Banking, Finance and Sustainable Development, Discussion Paper, School of Management. University of Southampton, Southampton

33 Ryan-Collins, J., (2010). Quantitative easing is stimulating commodity trading, not the real economy. London: **nef**

34 Greenham, T., (2012). Quantitative easing: a wasted opportunity. London: **nef**

35 Davies, G., (2002). *op. cit.*, p. 27, p. 663

7

CONCLUSIONS

7. CONCLUSIONS

Banks create new deposits when extending credit, buying existing assets or by providing overdraft facilities which customers themselves turn in to deposits when they draw on them. These deposits are accepted by everyone, including the state, in payment for taxes. This is the process of credit creation, which enables banks to create money.

It is the ability of banks to create new money, independently of the state, which gave rise to modern capitalism and makes it distinctive. As political economist Geoffrey Ingham describes it, following Joseph Schumpeter:

> *The financing of production with money-capital in the form of newly created bank money uniquely specifies capitalism as a form of economic system. Enterprises, wage labour and market exchange existed to some small degree, at least, in many previous economic systems, but ... their expansion into the dominant mode of production was made possible by the entirely novel institution of a money-producing banking system.[1]*

7.1.
The history of money: credit or commodity?

The historical overview of the origins of modern banking laid out in Chapter 3 illustrates that money as credit pre-dates the period when commodities were used as money. The system has developed in such a way that today, with the increasing use of electronic payments instead of banknotes, it is commercial bank money that dominates the money supply.

The promissory notes and bills of exchange issued by the goldsmiths and merchants of seventeenth-century London were backed by nothing other than a claim on future income: they were promises to pay. But these bills would always be limited in their scale whilst they remained essentially personalised contracts. When the British state, desperate for funds to meet the cost for foreign wars and unable to mint silver fast enough to do so, also began to borrow from goldsmiths (instead of issuing government money, as had been done during the tally sticks era), the opportunity arose for modern money to emerge. These creditors, determined that the sovereign not renege on his debts, helped to establish a bank with monopoly powers to accept their promissory notes at a discounted rate. As Ingham argues:

> *... the privately owned Bank of England transformed the sovereign's personal debt into a public debt and then, eventually, in to a public currency ... The private money of the bill of exchange was lifted out from the private mercantile network and given a wider and more abstract monetary space based on impersonal trust and legitimacy.[2]*

Thus modern capitalism gave birth to a hierarchical form of regulatory control, with the central bank at the apex of the hierarchy, ensuring the continued link between the nominal value of commercial bank money and the real value of central bank money (Bank of England notes and coins). The hope was that the central bank could control the quantity of commercial bank money through its power of discounting and, as lender of last resort, rescue any bank which faced a run when depositors lost confidence, by emergency issuance of central bank money ('printing money'). For short periods of time, the system appeared to be stable, most obviously during the 1950s and 1960s, with a fixed exchange rate and strict national and international credit controls in place.

However, deregulation and developments in technology have brought us to a situation where commercial banks now completely dominate the creation of credit and, hence, the money supply. This is the case even though the acceptability of money is guaranteed by the state and the security of bank deposits backed ultimately by the tax-payer. In fact one could argue that demand deposits are even more liquid than pure cash, since today it is much easier and often cheaper to pay taxes (and virtually every other regular debt, for example household utility bills) by transferring demand deposits. Indeed if you do not have a bank account today, your life is considerably more complicated and expensive. Research has shown that lacking access to a bank account can lead to cumulative additional financial charges, excess interest and higher costs for energy and other utilities of up to £1,000 a year.[3]

7.2.
What counts as money: drawing the line

As we discovered in Chapter 4, identifying what counts as money is not easy. Financial innovation means that when an instrument is defined and controlled as 'money', Goodhart's Law suggests that substitutes will be found to enable evasion of tax and regulation.[4] Such instruments include derivatives based on loans that are secured on highly illiquid assets such as houses. Although never really considered as money, such instruments have been increasingly traded in a money-like fashion: moved around the world at great speed and frequency by investment banks, hedge funds and other global financial actors, but as the financial crisis has revealed, their acceptability among financial institutions ultimately depends upon the strength of the credit-debtor relationship. When it became clear during the financial crisis of 2007-8 that many of the mortgage-backed securities in the US were based on subprime loans whose borrowers were likely to default, the result was a fast and systemic collapse of confidence between banks as these debts had been spread over such a wide range of banks' assets. These mortgage-backed securities turned from being highly liquid and money-like; easily bought and sold, to being highly illiquid in a matter of days.

So expectations are central to liquidity and 'money-ness'. When expectations concerning future system-wide developments are stable and widely shared, then a wide spectrum of private liabilities will be regarded as liquid and will find a place in the portfolios of those financial institutions whose current operations generate a surplus of revenues over expenditures.[5] Thus liquidity itself becomes highly subjective and the potential for the type of systemic collapse in liquidity we have already seen significantly increases.

A further difficulty in defining money arises from the tension between its role as a means of exchange – where the more liquid the better – and its role as a store of value, where generally assets which are less liquid, such as homes, tend to hold their value more effectively against inflation.[6] It may be that different conceptions of money are partly driven by the relative importance that people place on the different functions of money at different times – whether they consider its usefulness as a store of value to be the most important aspect, or its usefulness and availability as a means of exchange. This tension merits further research, because it points to the possibility that no single form of money will perform all the functions of money equally well.

7.3.
Money is a social relationship backed by the state

The implications of the credit model of money are profound. Rather than being neutral or a veil over the 'real' activities of the economy (trade, exchange, the use of land and labour), it becomes clear that money – as an abstract, impersonal claim on future resources – is a social and political construct. As such, its impact is determined by whoever decides what it is (the unit of account), who issues it, how much of it is issued to whom and for what purpose.

The unit of account function continues to be determined primarily by the state, as it has been for at least four thousand years.[7] The state is able to do this simply because we live in societies where, even accepting the presence of vast efforts devoted to off-shoring and tax-haven activities, with the associated vast stores of wealth that simply never come within the oversight of the state in any real sense, most of us have to make regular payments to the state in the form of taxation. If people and firms know they must make regular payments denominated in a certain way, it makes perfect sense to use such a denomination equally for their own transactions. The medium of exchange may change – credit cards, cheques, online or mobile phone payments – but the unit of account remains the same, otherwise money loses its power of acceptability.

While money is really nothing more than a promise to pay, what distinguishes money from, say, an IOU note, is its general acceptability. Promises to pay that are accepted as tax will tend to be the most widely accepted for private debts and exchanges as almost everyone needs to make regular tax payments. The nature of the credit-debt relationship is abstract rather than specific.[8] As American economist Hyman Minsky has pointed out, "anyone can create money, the problem is getting it accepted"[9]. Since banks are the accountants of the economy, through whose computers the vast majority of all transactions are booked, they are uniquely placed to get their money – created though granting credit –

accepted. Part of the widespread acceptance of bank deposits as payment may be due to the fact that the general public is simply not aware that banks do indeed create the money supply.

People accept and hold money not because of its intrinsic value as a commodity but because of guarantees regarding its future re-exchangeability; the "satisfaction... of the holder does not depend on possession per se, but on possession with a view to future use for payment"[10].

Future exchangeability of money is guaranteed by the Government in three key respects:
1. Through its acceptability to pay taxes
2. By tax-payer-backed insurance of bank deposits*
3. By implicit tax-payer-funded guarantees that banks themselves will be bailed out if they get into trouble

We can therefore say that all money is credit but not all credit is money. Schumpeter recognised that what is required is a credit theory of money rather than a monetary theory of credit[11]. And, whilst no definition is perfect, Geoffrey Ingham's conception of money, which follows Simmel, Keynes and Schumpeter, seems appropriate: money is "a social relation of abstract value defined by a sovereign unit of account"[12]. Rather than 'appearing' or being 'called forth' by the natural operations of the market, money is in fact issued into circulation as a social relation of credit and debt between the state, its citizens and its banks[13]. As such, it can be fairly accurately accounted for when measuring credit creation in the banking system and credit creation by the central bank[14].

7.4.
Implications for banking regulation and reforming the current system

The power of commercial banks to create new money has many important implications for economic prosperity and financial stability and we highlight four that are relevant to understanding the banking system and any proposals for reform:
1. Although useful in other ways, capital adequacy requirements do not constrain money creation and therefore do not constrain the expansion of banks' balance sheets in aggregate. In other words, they are ineffective in preventing credit booms and their associated asset price bubbles.
2. In a world of imperfect information and disequilibrium, credit is rationed by banks and the primary determinant of how much they lend is not interest rates, but confidence that the loan will be repaid and confidence in the liquidity and solvency of other banks and the system as a whole.

---

* Although deposit insurance, as part of the Financial Services Compensation Scheme, is nominally funded by a levy on financial service firms, any significant banking failures or systemic crisis would quickly overwhelm its resources as it did in 2007-8.

3. Banks in effect decide where to allocate new credit in the economy. The incentives that they currently face lead them to favour credit creation for the purchase of existing assets or other financial speculation, rather than lending for investment in the creation of new assets. New money is more likely to be channelled into property and financial speculation than to small businesses and manufacturing, with profound economic consequences.

4. As the Quantity Theory of Credit shows, fiscal policy does not in itself result in an expansion of the money supply. Indeed the Government has in practice no direct involvement in the money creation and allocation process. This is little known but has an important impact on the effectiveness of fiscal policy and the role of the government in the economy.

7.5.
Towards effective reform: Questions to consider

We have seen that the roots of an unstable money and banking system may lie in a mistaken understanding of money's nature by successive sovereigns and governments. In Chapter 3, we showed how the Government's need for funds, combined with its belief that only gold and silver could be used as the basis for money, gave rise to the particular institutional arrangements we have today. The misunderstanding of money as a commodity rather than a creditor/debtor relationship has so dominated the imagination of our leaders and economists that they have allowed the development of a monetary policy regime that, despite repeated crises, remains steadfast.

Where Does Money Come From? reveals that a system where money creation is almost entirely dominated by commercial banks is not inevitable. This being so, any serious analysis of current monetary and banking arrangements gives rise to a plethora of unanswered questions, including:

- If the state's role is so crucial in determining what money is, why does it seem to have such trouble controlling the money supply, as the difficulties of monetarist policies in the 1980s demonstrated?

- Why has the state been unable to prevent the financial and banking crises we have seen over the past eight centuries?[15]

- Should the state have more power to determine how much money is issued in to the economy and for what purpose?

- As the money creation process has been privatised and banks hold the public privilege of money creation, should it not be incumbent upon them to ensure that this enormous power is used for activities that contribute to the common good? Should we continue to allow this public privilege to be used for the pursuit of banks' own short-term interests, when apparently banks cannot always successfully look after their own medium – to long-term interests?

7. CONCLUSIONS

- Does it make sense for shareholder-owned and profit-driven banks to have such powers of credit creation whilst financial institutions, such as credit unions, for example, which are owned co-operatively and primarily have a social purpose, are restricted in their credit-creating powers?[16]

- Does it make sense to regularly lay the costs of bankers' mistakes at the door of tax-payers without apparent punishment or serious deterrent for bankers? Should the Government and the central bank consider less costly alternatives of dealing with banking crises that do not burden the taxpayer with huge debts? For example, could the central bank, in its capacity as lender of last resort, be the one to purchase non-performing assets from banks at face value and keep them on its balance sheet?

- Have central banks been given the right monetary policy targets, the right mandates, and the right powers to carry out these tasks? Banking crises are caused by credit-driven asset bubbles and it is the role of monetary policy to prevent banking crises. Should the consumer inflation target be replaced or augmented with targets for asset price inflation, achieved via a regime of credit guidance?

- Should credit guidance, including the suppression of credit creation for speculative purposes, be reintroduced into the UK monetary policy toolset? Could this be one of the powers of the new Financial Policy Committee? And should such measures be combined with further policies to encourage productive credit creation (such as giving banks incentives to lend to small and medium-sized enterprises, for instance through rules about bank bonuses),[17] and policies that reshape the banking sector, such as encouraging more small, local or regional banks that are incentivised to develop long-term local relationships with customers?

- What part could complementary currencies play in improving the stability of the monetary system by providing alternative means of exchange during periods of credit contraction?

- Should the UK Government set up national banks able to create credit at zero or very low rates of interest for specific infrastructure projects?* Should the restrictions imposed upon direct government credit creation by the Maastricht Treaty be reviewed?

It is disappointing that so few of these questions have been addressed by national and international initiatives examining reform of the financial system so far. Indeed, in the UK the Independent Commission on Banking's reports included scant and inaccurate discussion of the key role played by banks in creating new money.

---

* See for example proposals for a British Investment Bank[18]

7.6.
Are there alternatives to the current system?

Whilst the primary purpose of this book has been to lay out how the existing money and banking system works rather than review and evaluate alternatives, the existence of such alternatives raises important questions for further research and, perhaps, policy innovation. Some of these have already been discussed in earlier chapters, and four key alternatives are summarised below:

7.6.1.
Government borrowing directly from commercial banks

Rather than funding borrowing through bond issuance (see chapter 3, box 3) governments or ministries of finance could borrow directly from commercial banks, for example through long term loan contracts at low rates of interest. A similar policy was last adopted in the UK during World War II, upon the advice of John Maynard Keynes. The Treasury borrowed from banks by issuing 'Treasury Deposit Receipts' (TDRs) at 1.125% interest (see section 6.3.1). Such an approach involves the creation of brand new purchasing power for the Government rather than a redistribution of purchasing power from the private sector as with bond issuance (section 6.3). The policy should also be popular with banks since governments are the safest possible borrower. Loans to governments would be classified as the highest class of risk-weighted asset under Basel III, so helping banks meet higher capital adequacy ratios.

Meanwhile governments borrowing in this way would not be subject to the whims of the bond markets and the rating agencies, the damaging effects of which have been made clear by the European Sovereign Debt Crisis. Indeed, as discussed in section 6.3.1, such a policy could be employed by southern European eurozone members to ease the current crisis.

7.6.2.
Central bank credit creation for public spending

Central banks, as we have seen, have the power to create money in the same way as commercial banks, via the expansion of their balance sheets. The QE policies of the Bank of England, the Federal Reserve, the ECB and the Bank of Japan show that, in times of crisis, there is nothing to stop central banks creating vast quantities of credit to support the existing financial system. However, the type of QE policies adopted do not appear to have been effective in boosting GDP growth and employment, as the additional purchasing power remains within the financial sector when bank and investor confidence is low (see section 4.7.3 on QE).

Historically, however, there are a number of examples of central banks creating new credit to be spent directly by the Government of the time in to the national economy. These include Australia from 1914-24 and New Zealand in the 1930s when central bank credit creation funded housing construction and the maintenance of food prices as well as the costs of war.[19,20,21] In Canada, the central bank played a key role in infrastructure investment, particularly via the Canadian Industrial Development Bank, from the 1940s through to the 1970s.[22,23]

As discussed in section 6.1, EU rules prevent central banks buying bonds directly from governments. However, these rules do not apply to buying bonds from 'publicly owned credit institutions', for example, in the UK the Green Investment Bank (GIB), the recently announced Business Investment Bank[24] or another nationalised bank could issue large quantities of bonds which could be purchased by the Bank of England in the same way it purchases Government bonds. Again this would create new purchasing power which could be directed into productive sectors.[25] If the central bank resisted taking these kinds of assets onto its balance sheet, they could be underwritten by the Treasury, as with the Government's 'credit easing' policy and the existing Asset Purchase Facility.[26]

7.6.3.
Money-financed fiscal expenditure

The core challenge common to both of the above options, when specifically focussing on the need to reduce fiscal deficits, is that the solutions must involve the creation of interest-bearing debt, although of course if the central bank is publicly owned, the interest will flow back to the Government itself. Most industrialised countries have substantial compound interest liabilities already, hence states might wish to consider alternatives to interest-bearing debt funding for fiscal expansion.

Historically, there are many examples of states directly creating money and putting it in to circulation free of interest.[*] Indeed, prior to the invention of modern banking at the end of the seventeenth century, most states used simple accounting techniques such as tally sticks in the UK (see section 3.3.1), minted coins or printed paper money to fund their activities and ensured their widespread adoption through taxation.[27,28,29] There are also numerous historical examples of governments funding fiscal shortfalls through the issuance of government money. These include the issuance of 'Greenbacks' by the US government during and after the Civil War and in the UK during World War I (the 'Bradbury Bills' – see Section 3.6.2).[30,31] Similarly, the Governments of Germany, Japan and the USA at times issued significant amounts of government money, mainly during the nineteenth century.[32]

---

[*] One could argue that state money is still 'debt' in the sense that its citizens must access it in order to pay taxes (their debt to the state) but it is the lack of interest and compounding interest which distinguishes this form of fiscal funding

A range of leading economists, including Irving Fisher[33], Milton Friedman[34], Henry Simons[35], James Tobin[36] and Herman Daly[37] have argued that a banking system where only the Government is permitted to expand the money supply would be more stable and could be implemented by instituting a 100% reserve requirement on bank accounts, with banks then playing a true intermediary role of matching savers and borrowers in the way that peer-to-peer lenders now do. This proposal has recently been endorsed by two research economists at the IMF who examined the 100% reserves proposal using state-of-the-art macro-economic modelling to show it would be effective in reducing existing debt and stabilising the economy.[38] While the issuance of government money to fund fiscal expenditure is often thought to be inflationary, this need not be the case, especially if limited by the amount of money-supply expansion needed to reach the growth potential of the economy.[39,40] This type of money issuance could be limited to specific sectors and for specific amounts of time and the Government could then tax it back out of circulation.

7.6.4.
Regional or local money systems

Finally, there are a range of historical and existing non-state based 'local' or 'community' currencies. These are exchange and payment systems whereby money is issued by non-state and non-bank actors. Such currencies have been described as 'common tender'[41] to distinguish them from fiat currencies or legal tenders and are also known generically as 'complementary currencies' to denote that they work in tandem with national fiat currencies rather than aiming to entirely replace them. They often specifically focus on fulfilling the `medium of exchange' function of money and have provisions to prevent people hoarding the currency as a store of value.

The best known examples are from the Great Depression era where in both the United States and Europe, 'stamp scrip' currencies were issued to support businesses and local production as national currencies became scarce because of deflation.[42] One of the survivors of this period is the Swiss WIR credit-clearing circle created in 1934. This is a mutual credit scheme, with the WIR co-operative bank creating credit lines, denominated in, but not exchangeable into, Swiss Francs. Loans are extended to members, currently numbering over 60,000 mainly small and medium size enterprises, and can be spent only within the network of these businesses. In 2008, the volume of WIR-denominated trade was 1.5 billion Swiss francs.[43] Evaluation of the system suggests it has a stabilising, counter-cyclical effect on the Swiss economy, as businesses use it more during recessions.[44] In such 'mutual credit' systems, credit is linked directly to the productive or spare capacity of the individuals or businesses involved as credits within the system are backed by delivery of goods and services by members.

Developments in technology have significantly reduced the transaction costs involved in such complementary currencies. Some thinkers have suggested encouraging their development could increase the resilience of a financial system that has become overly dependent on the type of state-monopoly, debt-based money that has been described and analysed consistently throughout *Where Does Money Come From?*[45]

7.7.
Understanding money and banking

The reforms and alternatives proposed herein are a useful starting point for further research and evaluation – the topic is, we hope, for development in further publications by enlightened students and researchers in academia, public policy and, perhaps, even in banks themselves. The main purpose of *Where Does Money Come From?* is to illustrate how the current system works so that such explorations can begin from a widely accepted set of assumptions.

The authors reveal a paradox at the heart of our monetary system: it is the state that essentially determines what money is and underwrites its value and yet it is predominately commercial banks that create it. In deciding who receives credit, commercial banks determine broadly how it is spent within the economy; whether on consumption, buying existing assets or productive investment, their decisions play a vital macro-economic role.

Many naturally resist the notion that private banks can really create money by simply making an entry in a ledger. Economist J. K. Galbraith suggested why this might be

> *The process by which banks create money is so simple that the mind is repelled. When something so important is involved, a deeper mystery seems only decent.*[46]

Where Does Money Come From? categorically establishes that there is no deeper mystery. We therefore must not permit our minds to be repelled, because it is only through the application of proper analysis and further public and policy debate, that we can collectively address the much more significant and pressing question of whether our current monetary and banking system best serves the public interest and, if not, how it should be reformed.

7. CONCLUSIONS

References

1   Ingham, G., (2008). *Capitalism.* Cambridge: Polity Press, p. 53

2   Ingham, G., (2004). *The Nature of Money.* Cambridge: Polity Press, p. 128

3   Thiel, V., (2009). *Doorstep Robbery.* London: **nef**

4   Goodhart, C.A.E., (1975). *Monetary Relationships: A View from Threadneedle Street.* Papers in Monetary Economics, Reserve Bank of Australia

5   Leyshon and Thrift (1997). *Money/Space: Geographies of Monetary Transformation*, p. 294

6   Dodd, N., (1994). *The Sociology of Money.* Cambridge: Polity Press, p. xix

7   Keynes, J.M, (1930). *A Treatise on Money: Vol 1, A Pure Theory of Money.* London: Macmillan, p. 3

8   Carruthers, B. G., (2005). *The Sociology of Money and Credit.* In Smelser, N. J., Swedberg, R. (eds). *The Handbook of Economic Sociology*, 2nd Edition. Princeton: Russell Sage Foundation.

9   Minsky, H. P., (2008-1986). *Stabilizing an Unstable Economy.* New York: McGraw Hill.

10   Knapp (1905). *The State Theory of Money*, London: MacMillan, p. 45

11   Ingham, G., (2004). *op. cit.*

12   Keynes, J.M, (1930). *A Treatise on Money, vol 1: A pure theory of money*, p. 3

13   Mellor, M., (2010). *The Future of Money*, London: Pluto Press

14   For more detailed formulae, see: Werner, R.A., (2005). *op. cit.*

15   Reinhart, C. M., Rogoff, K, S., (2009). *This Time is Different: Eight Centuries of Financial Folly.* Princeton: Woodstock

16   Werner, R.A., (2009). *Can credit unions create credit? An analytical evaluation of a potential obstacle to the growth of credit unions.* Discussion Paper Series, No. 2/09. Southampton: Centre for Banking, Finance and Sustainable Development, University of Southampton

17   Werner, R.A., (2010). *Comment: Range of Methodologies for Risk and Performance Alignment of Remuneration.* Submission to the Basel Committee on Banking Supervision, 31 December 2010. Retrievable from http://www.bis.org/publ/bcbs178/richardwerner.pdf

18   Skidelsky, R., Martin, F., and Wigstrom, C., W., (2011) *Blueprint for a British Investment Bank.* London: The Centre for Global Studies. Retrievable from www.skidelskyr.com/site/article/blueprint-for-a-british-investment-bank/ [accesssed 4th March 2013]; Dolphin, T., and Nash, D., (2012) *Investing for the future: Why we need a British Investment Bank.* London: Institute for Public Policy Research (IPPR). Retrievable from www.ippr.org/publication/55/9635/investing-for-the-future-why-we-neeed-a-british-investment-bank [accessed 4th March 2013]

19   Jauncey, L.C, (1933). *Australia's Government Bank.* Cranby and Day: London, p. 275

20   Greasley, D. and Oxley, L., (2002). Regime shift and fast recovery on the periphery: New Zealand in the 1930s. *The Economic History Review* 55(4): 697-720

21   Hawke, G. R., (1973). *Between governments and banks; a history of the Reserve Bank of New Zealand.* Wellington, Shearer, A. R., Govt. printer., p. 85

22   Ferguson, D. A., (1948). The Industrial Development Bank of Canada, *The Journal of Business of the University of Chicago*, Volume 21, No. 4 (October 1948), pp. 214-29;

23   Clark, R.E., (1985). T*he IDB: A history of Canada's Industrial Development Bank*, Published for the Federal Business Development Bank by University of Toronto Press.

24   The Guardian, (2012). Vince Cable reveals £1bn backing for business bank to help small firms, 24th September 2012, retrievable from http://www.guardian.co.uk/politics/2012/sep/24/vince-cable-small-business-bank1 [accessed 1st October 2012]

25   See example proposals for 'Green Quantitative Easing', retrievable from - http://www.greennewdealgroup.org/?p=175 and http://www.neweconomics.org/blog/2012/07/05/quantitative-easing-a-wasted-opportunity

26   Peston, R., (n. d.). How Credit Easing Works, *BBC News*, http://www.bbc.co.uk/news/business-17437484

27 Graeber, D., (2011). *Debt: The First 5000 years*, Melville House Publishing: Brooklyn, New York

28 Wray, R., (1998). *Understanding Modern Money: The Key to full-employment and price stability*, Cheltenham: Edward Elgar

29 Innes, A. M., (1913). What is Money, *Banking Law Journal* (May 1913): 377-08.

30 Carruthers, B. G. and Babb, S., (1996). The Colour of Money and the Nature of Value: Greenbacks and Gold in Postbellum America, *American Journal of Sociology*, 1010:1556-91

31 Davies, G., (2002). *A History of Money*. Cardiff: University of Wales Press, p. 27 and p. 663

32 Werner, R.A., (2005). *New Paradigm in Macro-economics*, Palgrave Macmillan: London, p. 258-59

33 Fisher, I., (1936). 100% Money and the Public Debt, *Economic Forum*, Spring Number, April-June 1936, pp. 406-20.;

34 Friedman, M., (1960). *A Program for Monetary Stability*, New York: Fordham University

35 Simons, Henry C., (1948). *Economic Policy for a Free Society*. University of Chicago Press: Chicago, Illinois, pp. 165–248

36 Tobin, J., (1985). Financial Innovation and Deregulation in Perspective, *Bank of Japan Monetary and Economic Studies*, 3, 19-29

37 Daly, H., (1999). *Ecological Economics and the Ecology of Economics*. Edward Elgar

38 Benes, J., and Kumhof, M., (2012). The Chicago Plan Revisited, IMF Working Paper 12/202. retrievable from http://www.imf.org/external/pubs/ft/wp/2012/wp12202.pdf.

39 Dyson, B., Greenham, T., Ryan-Collins, J. and Werner, R., A., (2010) *Towards a Twenty-First Century Banking and Monetary System: Submission to the Independent Commission on Banking*. London: **nef** retrievable from http://www.neweconomics.org/sites/neweconomics.org/files/Submission-ICB-Positive-Money-nef-Soton-Uni.pdf

40 Huber, J., and Robertson, J., (2000). *Creating New Money*. London: **nef**. Retrievable from http://www.neweconomics.org/publications/creating-new-money

41 Rochford, S., von Gunten, C., Mainelli, M. and Harris, I., (2012). *Capacity, Trade and Credit: Emerging Architecture for Commerce and Money*. London: Z/Yen Group

42 Fisher, I., (1933). *Stamp Scrip*, New York; Adelphi Company; Publishers; Copyright 1933, retrievable from http://userpage.fu-berlin.de/roehrigw/fisher/

43 Lietaer, B., Hallsmith, G., (2011). *Creating Wealth. Growing Local Economies with Local Currencies*, New Society Publishers, p. 117

44 Stodder, J., (2009). Complementary credit networks and macro-economic stability: Switzerland's Wirtschaftsring, *Journal of Economic Behaviour & Organisation*, 72 (2009), pp. 79–95

45 Lietaer, B., Arnsperger, C., Goerner, S. and Brunnhuber, S., (2012). *Money and sustainability: The Missing Link*, Triachy Press: Club of Rome, retrievable from http://www.clubofrome.org/?p=4478

46 Galbraith, J. K., (1975). *Money: Whence it came, where it went*. London: Penguin, pp. 18–19

THIS PAGE IS INTENTIONALLY LEFT BLANK

APPENDIX 1: THE CENTRAL BANK'S INTEREST RATE REGIME

A1.1.
Setting interest rates – demand-driven central bank money

The Bank of England's Monetary Policy Committee (MPC) meets once a month in order to set the interest rate which it judges will enable the inflation target to be met. However, this interest rate (known as the **policy rate**) is not the interest rate at which you or I would be able to borrow from high street banks. Instead, it aims to influence the interest rate at which banks lend to each other on the interbank market (known as Libor, see Section 4.3.1, Box 7), which in turn will influence the rates offered by banks to customers.

From 2006 up to 2009, the Bank of England (BoE) aimed to set the interest rate through a mechanism known as the **corridor system** (figure A1). Under this system, banks set their own reserve targets (the amount of central bank reserves they would plan to hold to enable all payments) every month, and borrowed these reserves from the central bank using sale and repurchase agreements (repos), see Section 4.7.[*]

If a bank found itself with reserves in excess of its target, then it could either lend them to other banks on the interbank market or deposit them at the Bank of England, and receive interest on them at a rate known as the **deposit rate**. If a bank needed additional reserves, it could borrow in the interbank market or overnight from the Bank of England, paying interest at the **lending rate**.

The deposit rate was set slightly below, and the lending rate slightly above, the policy rate (Figure A1). The interbank interest rate was unlikely to fall below the deposit rate, as, if so, it would be more profitable for a bank to simply deposit the reserves at the Bank of England rather than lend them to another bank. Equally, a bank would be unlikely to borrow from another bank at a rate higher than that which they could borrow from the Bank of England using the lending facility.[1] This created the aforementioned corridor around the policy rate (Figure A1).

As mentioned, the banks had to set reserve targets. They would only be paid interest on their reserves if the average balances over the month fell within a relatively narrow range around those targets. Outside this range, surplus reserves would not receive interest, and there were penalties for failing to meet their target, creating incentives for banks to manage their liquidity effectively[2].

---

[*] The 'repo rate' – the rate which the banks borrow reserves from the central bank, was set equal to the policy rate. This meant that as long as the banks hit their reserve targets, there was no cost to the banks of holding reserves, and no 'tax' on the banking system as a whole[3].

Figure A1: Corridor system of reserves[4]

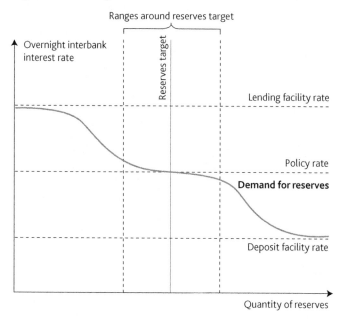

Students of economics might find this description of how the Bank of England sets interest rates rather confusing; most textbook models involve the central bank adjusting the quantity of reserves through open market operations (OMOs) and thereby changing the interest rate at which the supply of central bank reserves intersects with the demand for central bank reserves. However, as Paul Tucker, Deputy Governor of the Bank of England, states: 'Neither in the past nor in the current review have we even briefly entertained the notion that this is realistic.'[5]

He goes on to say that, under a reserves averaging scheme

> *Open market operations will not be used to inject a quantity of reserves according to a plan for the path of the monetary base. And they will not be used directly to adjust the quantity of base money to bring about the desired level of short-term interest rates. In other words, base money comprises neither a target nor an instrument of policy. Rather, the role of OMOs will be to satisfy the system's targeted level of reserves over the maintenance period as a whole.*[6]

A1.2.
Setting interest rates – supply-driven central bank money

The corridor system and reserve targeting was suspended in March 2009, following the financial crisis, switching to a **floor system**. This followed the decision of the MPC to embark upon the purchase of financial assets funded through the **creation of central bank money**, popularly known as **quantitative easing (QE)** (see section 4.7.3). At the time of writing, the bank has created £375 billion worth of central bank reserves, and used them predominantly to buy government securities.

So the banking system now holds central bank reserves far in excess of the reserve targets they previously set, and interest is paid on these reserves at the policy rate. Due to these excess reserves, the need for banks to borrow from each other on the interbank market has been greatly diminished, and thus the interbank rate closely matches the policy rate. Hence the UK has recently moved from a system of demand-driven central bank money (the reserves targeting scheme), to supply-driven central bank money (the floor scheme) (Figure A2).

Figure A2: The floor system of reserves[7]

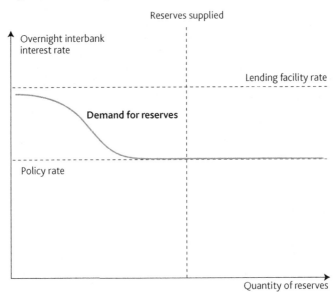

Under the floor system, banks have excess reserves; however, as mentioned in section 4.7, it is unclear whether this has had any impact on banks' lending to customers. Since the financial crisis, the banks' confidence has been severely diminished. Thus it appears to be banks' levels of confidence, rather than the level of reserves, which is dictating bank willingness to lend and create new money.

APPENDIX 2: GOVERNMENT BANK ACCOUNTS

Chapter 6 examined how the Government borrows, taxes and spends (fiscal policy). This appendix outlines in more detail how this process works, with a particular focus on the flows of funds between government bank accounts at the Bank of England (and the accounting relationships between them), private sector bank accounts and the money markets. The accounts the Government uses to intervene in foreign exchange markets will also be discussed.

A2.1.
The Consolidated Fund

Like any organisation that wishes both to receive and spend money, the Government has bank accounts. However, unlike most organisations, the Government's primary bank accounts are held at the Bank of England. The oldest of the accounts is the Consolidated Fund (CF) (Figure A3), which was established in 1787 as 'one fund into which shall flow every stream of public revenue and from which shall come the supply for every service.'[8] Administered by HM Treasury, the CF can essentially be thought of as the Government's current account. The taxes collected by HM Revenue and Customs (HMRC) are the primary inflows into the CF (Figure A3).[*] However, if the Government is running a deficit, then spending outflows exceed tax inflows. To make the account balance, the difference must be made up through government borrowing.

Figure A3: The Exchequer Pyramid – key bodies and relationships involved in government accounts[9]

---

[*] Other smaller inflows include Consolidated Fund Extra Receipts (CFERs) and any repayments from the Contingencies Fund. An example of Consolidated Fund Extra Receipts (CFERs) would be any fines levied which are not retained by the originating department. The Contingencies Fund is a fund used to provide any urgent expenditure or small payments which have not been approved by parliament.

A2.2.
The National Loans Fund

The National Loans Fund (NLF), in collaboration with the Debt Management Office, undertakes borrowing on behalf of the Consolidated Fund and forwards to the Consolidated Fund the funds needed to balance its account each day (Figure A3).

Established in 1968 in order to separate borrowing and lending activities from the Consolidated Fund, the NLF is run by HM Treasury and has its own bank account at the Bank of England. The NLF funds the deficit in various ways:

1. Savings deposited in National Savings and Investments (NS&I) accounts (which, excluding the ordinary account, are liabilities of the National Loans Fund).
2. Borrowing from the money markets through the issuing of sterling denominated government bonds, also known as gilt-edged securities or gilts and Treasury bills. These are sold to the Debt Management Account (DMA) and from there the Debt Management Office (DMO) sells them into the market (Figure A3).
3. Transferring any surplus unused balances from other government bank accounts.
4. The NLF also receives all the profits from the Issues Department of the Bank of England.[10] The Issues Department is responsible for supplying banknotes. This seigniorage revenue is, of course, a profitable activity, as the cost of producing a banknote is a small fraction of its face value (see Section 4.4, Box 8)

As well as making up any shortfall in the Consolidated Fund, the NLF provides finance to the DMA and the Exchange Equalisation Account (EEA) (Appendix 3). The NLF also makes loans to public sector bodies as well as providing finance to other government organisations which provide loans, such as the Public Works Loans Board that gives loans to local authorities.

Any national borrowing incurs interest charges that compound over time. Thus an important NLF outgoing is the paying of interest on gilts and on NS&I accounts. When the interest the NLF receives on its loans is less than the interest which it has to pay out (which is usually the case), proceeds from issuing government bonds usually make up the difference.

A2.3.
The Debt Management Account (DMA)

The DMA, administered by the Debt Management Office, is the final stage in the chain that links government spending to government borrowing. It lies at the top of the Exchequer Pyramid shown in Figure A3 and is, in effect, the key gateway between the Government and the wholesale financial markets (the 'money markets' in Figure A3). Established in 1998, its purpose is

> *...to carry out the Government's debt management policy of minimising financing costs over the longer term, taking account of risk, and to manage the aggregate cash needs of the Exchequer in the most cost-effective way.[11]*

Just as with the Consolidated Fund and the NLF, the DMA is an account at the Bank of England, although unlike the other two it is run by an executive agency of HM Treasury (the Debt Management Office) rather than the Treasury itself.

The Debt Management Office transacts with the markets using various instruments. The main instruments are gilts and Treasury bills (Box 3, Chapter 3), which are sold into the market from the DMA. Finally the Debt Management Office can also borrow from the market through sale and repurchase agreements (repos), and lend to the market through reverse sale and repurchase agreements (reverse repos) (Figure A3).

The Debt Management Office sells new gilts in what is known as the primary market, via an auction mechanism.[*] In 2011 and 2012, they sold a total of £277 billion of gilts (figure A4). These would have been sold almost exclusively to its 'primary dealers' – the gilt-edged market-makers (GEMMs; Box 10).[12] The money that is received for these gilts is transferred to the DMA and from there it is sent to the NLF, then to the Consolidated Fund, before finally being spent by the Government into the economy.

Box A1: Market-makers

A market-maker is a broker-dealer firm that accepts the risk of holding a certain number of shares of a particular security in order to facilitate trading in that security. Each market-maker competes for customer orders by displaying buy and sell quotations for a guaranteed number of shares. Once an order is received, the market-maker immediately sells from its own inventory or seeks an offsetting order. This process takes place in mere seconds. Market-makers profit from the difference between what they buy and sell their shares for.

In the UK, gilt-edged market makers (GEMMs) are licensed by the Government to deal in gilts (government bonds). There are currently 20 GEMMs in the UK and they are mainly larger investment banks – see http://www.dmo.gov.uk/index.aspx?page=Gilts/Gemms_idb http://www.dmo.gov.uk/index.aspx?page=Gilts/Gemms_idb for a full list. Market-makers play an important role in keeping the financial markets running efficiently because they are willing to quote both bid and offer prices for an asset.

---

[*] Conventional gilts are sold by 'multiple price auctions' and indexed gilts sold in 'uniform price auctions'. However, the DMO can and does sell gilts using other methods. For example, in 2010 / 2011 it planned to sell £29.2 billion gilts by appointing private banks to sell the bonds on the DMO's behalf (known as 'syndication') and £10 billion through 'mini tenders' which address emergency pockets of demand in various gilts. There are also many other types of auction which the DMO may use to sell or buy gilts, although none were planned for 2010-11[13].

Once a gilt has been sold to a GEMM on the primary market, it can be taken and resold on a secondary market. The secondary market is important because it makes a previously illiquid asset (a gilt with a fixed redemption date) liquid. Those who have bought gilts but wish to sell them before redemption can do so. This raises demand for bonds from the level they would have been at without a secondary market, and allows investors to hold liquid assets, whilst they still receive the benefits of having a fixed repayment date. Furthermore, the price of gilts in secondary markets is determined by genuine supply and demand rather than the primary market where GEMMS are required to both buy and sell gilts on demand at any time.[14] This price mechanism conveys important information to investors that will also affect the primary market.

As we have seen, government spending, via the Consolidated Fund, is usually financed by taxation and borrowing. In terms of intrabank payment, the process is no different from ordinary transfers, as described in Section 4.3. If a customer buys bonds or pays tax, the money moves from their commercial bank account to the Government's bank account at the Bank of England via transfers of central bank reserves.

At the end of each working day, any public funds in the Exchequer Pyramid (Figure A3) at the Bank of England are 'swept up' to the NLF, which itself is swept into the DMA. The Debt Management Office (DMO) has an agreement with the Bank of England to hold a certain cash balance every night to offset any late or unexpected outflows. If it exceeds the targeted balance, the DMO invests the surplus on the money markets until it is needed; if it is short of the target, it borrows the shortfall through the overnight or longer-term money markets. If public bodies do not minimise the balances in their own accounts with commercial banks and place funds in their Exchequer accounts, the amount of net government borrowing outstanding on any given day will be appreciably higher, adding to interest costs and making the fiscal position worse.[15]

In 2004, the Bank of England announced that by the end of 2009 it would stop providing retail banking services and focus on its core purpose of maintaining monetary and fiscal stability. The Government Banking Service was launched in May 2008. It incorporates the Office of HM Paymaster General and is the new banking shared service provider for the public sector. Contracts with the Royal Bank of Scotland (RBS) and Citibank have replaced the seven banking providers previously used by HMRC and NS&I. The banking services covered by the contracts include all transactions and account management functions, but the money itself remains with the Bank of England and therefore inside the Exchequer Pyramid (Figure A3). The new arrangements with the commercial banks also mean there is no need to re-tender for back-office services, with public bodies being able to interact directly with the banks online.[16]

Figure A4: The UK Debt Management Account, 2011-12

At 31 March 2012	2012 £m	2011 £m
Assets		
Cash and balances at the Bank of England	794	868
Loans and advances to banks	36,577	17,324
Securities held for trading	5,953	3,313
Derivative financial instruments	42	22
Investment securities classified as available-for-sale		
UK Government gilt-edged securities for use as collateral		
subject to sale and repurchase agreements	23,378	12,946
UK Government gilt-edged securities for use as collateral		
not pledged	76,334	64,957
	99,712	**77,903**
Other UK Government gilt-edged securities	49,454	49,241
Treasury bills	–	122,832
	149,166	**249,976**
Other assets	5,572	10
Total assets before deposit at National Loans Fund	**198,104**	**271,513**
Deposit at National Loans Fund	34,067	30,546
Total assets	**232,171**	**302,059**
Liabilities		
Deposits by banks	20,013	10,988
Due to government customers	47,194	51,040
Derivative financial instruments	38	53
Treasury bills in issue	75,937	63,574
Other liabilities	13	590
Total liabilities before funding by National Loans Fund	**143,195**	**126,245**
Advance from National Loans Fund	52,042	157,100
Revaluation reserve	18,982	5,779
Income and expenditure account	17,952	12,935
Total funding by National Loans Fund	**88,976**	**175,814**
Total liabilities	**232,171**	**302,059**

Source: United Kingdom Debt Management Office [17]

A2.4.
The Exchange Equalisation Account (EEA)

Historically, the UK has held foreign currency reserves so it could intervene in order to regulate the exchange value of sterling. However, there have been no government interventions to influence the sterling exchange rates since 1992, when the UK exited the Exchange Rate Mechanism (ERM), although there have been two interventions since then to support foreign currencies. The first of these occurred in September 2000 when the UK government and the other G7 countries intervened in order to prevent any further depreciation in the value of the Euro. The second occurred on 18 March 2011, when the UK government and the other G7 countries intervened in order to prevent any further appreciation of the yen following the earthquake that hit Japan on 11 March 2011. Both interventions were performed by the Bank of England, via the Exchange Equalisation Account (EEA).[18]

Other than intervening to support a currency, foreign exchange reserves are now held primarily for three reasons.
1. As a precautionary measure – in case of any future changes to exchange rate policy or unexpected shocks.
2. To provide foreign currency services to the Government.
3. To buy, sell and hold Special Drawing Rights (SDRs)*, as required by membership of the International Monetary Fund (IMF).[19]

Of course, foreign exchange reserves may also be held due to decisions made collectively by consumers and investors: if a country earns more foreign currency on its exports than it spends on imports, foreign exchange reserves will accumulate. Often, they are used by investors to fund overseas investments. However, this need not be the case. Norway, for instance, has found it impossible to maintain imports and capital outflows in line with foreign exchange accumulation due to oil exports. Consequently, foreign exchange reserves have accumulated. One issue with this is that foreign exchange earnings cannot be directly used for domestic spending – the money can only be spent abroad or on imports.

The government holds its foreign exchange reserves in the EEA and the National Loans Fund (NLF) (section A2.2). The EEA reserves consist of gold, foreign currency assets, and SDRs (see figure A5 for a table of the current balances).

The NLF reserves consist of the Reserve Tranche Position (RTP) at the IMF and bilateral loans to the IMF.[20] The EEA is funded by central government through the NLF, via a sterling account which the EEA maintains with the NLF. This allows the NLF to advance funds to the EEA and for the EEA to repay funds to the NLF.[21]

---

* Special drawing rights (SDRs) are supplementary foreign exchange reserve assets defined and maintained by the International Monetary Fund (IMF). Not a currency, SDRs instead represent a claim to currency held by IMF member countries for which they may be exchanged. See IMF factsheet on Special Drawing Rights, retrievable from http://www.imf.org/external/np/exr/facts/sdr.HTM

Figure A5: Assets and liabilities of the Exchange Equalisation Account 2011-12

	31 March 2012 £m	31 March 2011 £m
Assets		
Cash at central banks	1,496	1,512
Items in the course of collection from banks	884	672
Treasury bills	593	488
Debt securities	32,601	29,162
Derivative financial assets	923	782
Reverse repurchase agreements	3,710	2,102
Holdings of IMF Special Drawing Rights	9,266	9,202
Gold	10,374	8,954
Other financial assets	105	254
Total assets	**59,952**	**53,128**
Liabilities		
Deposits by banks	–	57
Items in the course of transmission to banks	864	597
Debt securities – short positions	1,212	889
Derivative financial liabilities	533	1,165
Repurchase agreements	3,904	3,223
Other financial liabilities	2	16
SDR allocation	9,822	10,024
Liability to the National Loans Fund	43,615	37,157
Total liabilities	**59,952**	**53,128**

Source: HM Treasury [22]

Unlike the other main government accounts, the EEA is managed by the Bank of England, not the Treasury. Furthermore, other than the gold coin and bullion, the EEA's foreign reserves are not held at the Bank of England, rather, the EEA is composed of five accounts held at four banks – two in dollars (held at the Federal Reserve Bank of New York and at JP Morgan Chase Bank); one in euro (held at Clearstream); and two in yen (held at the Bank of Japan and JP Morgan Chase Bank).[23]

As well as managing the reserves by investing in foreign currency assets,* the Bank also acts as the Treasury's agent for foreign currency liability management, which includes issuing debt (originating from the NLF) denominated in foreign currency in order to finance some of the reserves.[24]

---

* In the main these are bonds issued or guaranteed by the governments of the USA, euro area countries and Japan, gold, and SDRs, although other assets are also used. These include: securities issued by other national governments, supranational organisations and selected government and government-sponsored agencies; Pfandbriefe (a mostly triple-A-rated German bank bonds); foreign currency spot, forward and swap transactions; interest rate and currency swaps; bond, interest rate and swap futures; sale and repurchase agreements; forward rate agreements; deposits with the Bank; deposits with, and certificates of deposits issued by, highly rated banks; and corporate commercial paper and bonds[25].

A.2.5.
Bank of England Foreign Exchange Reserves

The Bank of England maintains its own separate, smaller pool of foreign exchange reserves, which it may use to intervene in foreign exchange markets in support of its monetary policy objectives.[26] Since December 2006, the Bank's reserves have been financed by issuing medium-term securities on an annual basis (March 2007, 2008, 2009 and 2010). The most recent (2011) issue is a $2 billion, three-year Eurobond, paying a coupon of 1.375 per cent, which matures on
7 March 2014. The Bank employs commercial banks as its agents to sell these bonds in the market.[27]

APPENDIX 3: FOREIGN EXCHANGE PAYMENT, TRADE AND SPECULATION

A3.1.
Trade and speculation

Businesses require foreign exchange services in order to buy, sell, and invest in different countries. An American car company (say General Motors) that owns a factory in the UK will need to convert dollars to pounds and vice versa. However, this creates a problem – if exchange rates can fluctuate, then it may be difficult for General Motors to know its costs (in dollars) when agreeing contracts.

General Motors can protect itself from currency risk through a process known as **hedging**. The two most common forms of hedging in the foreign exchange market are **forward contracts** and **options**. A forward contract allows General Motors to lock in the current exchange rate, so that whatever the exchange rate is at the end of the year, it can still exchange its pounds for dollars at the rate set in the contract (say £1 = $1.5). Options contracts are similar, but instead they give General Motors the right, but not the obligation, to exchange currencies at the exchange rate set in the contract. Although hedging can reduce the risk arising from exchange rate fluctuations, it is possible that General Motors might find itself in a worse position than if it hadn't made the forward contract. For example, if, when the time comes to exchange currencies, the exchange rate is £1 = $1, then General Motors could have paid its workers with just $10 million rather than the $15 million required when the exchange rate is £1 = $1.50 – a loss of $5 million.

Let us now consider with whom General Motors might be making forward contracts. One possibility could be a UK business that wishes to pay for something in dollars at the end of the year, and is also worried about currency risk. Another could be a speculator who wishes to bet on the outcome of exchange rate fluctuations. For instance, a speculator may enter into the contract with General Motors, agreeing to receive $15 million in exchange for £10 million next year, at an exchange rate of £1 = $1.50. If the exchange rate does not change, then the speculator neither gains nor loses from the exchange. However if, come the day of the exchange, the exchange rate stands at £1 = $1, the speculator can borrow £10 million at a UK bank, exchange it for $15 million with General Motors, then swap the $15 million back into pounds. At an exchange rate of £1 = $1 the speculator ends up with £15 million – a profit of £5 million. However, if the exchange rate went the other way then the speculator would suffer a loss.

Box A2. Foreign exchange instruments

Foreign exchange transactions can be broken down into their component parts, which are spot transactions and three different types of 'plain vanilla derivatives' (forwards, swaps, and options), as well as other foreign exchange (forex) products:

Spots: The spot transaction is the most widely known forex transaction. Spots are an exchange of two currencies at a rate agreed on the date of the contract, with the currency being delivered (electronically) within two business days. On average, spots accounted for $1,490 billion a day in 2010.

Forwards: Forwards are similar to spots; however, unlike in the spot market, the currency is delivered more than two business days after the contract is agreed. This allows participants to 'lock in' an exchange rate for a future transaction, thus eliminating uncertainty over fluctuations in the values of the currencies. On average, forwards accounted for $475 billion a day in 2010.

Currency swaps: Currency swaps allow for the exchange of two currencies on a specific date at a set exchange rate, and then a reversal of the swap on a future date, usually at a different exchange rate. Commonly, this is a combination of a spot trade with a forward trade of opposite direction (e.g. sell CHF 100,000 and buy EUR spot; buy CHF 100,000 and sell EUR 30 days forward). On average, currency swaps accounted for $1,765 billion a day in 2010.

Foreign interest rate swaps: Interest swaps allow counterparties to exchange streams of interest payments for a period of time, with the exchange of principle at a pre agreed exchange rate at maturity. On average, interest swaps accounted for $43 billion a day in 2010.

Options: Currency options give the holders the right (which they do not have to exercise) to acquire or sell foreign currency at a specified price for a certain period of time. On average, options and related forex products accounted for $207 billion a day in 2010.

A3.2.
The foreign exchange payment system

Only the very largest companies participate directly in forex markets. Generally their banks will facilitate any instruction to exchange one currency for another on their behalf. So how do banks convert one currency to another? Obviously they do not send bundles of cash around the world. Forex transactions are therefore settled electronically in one of six different ways:

1. Traditional correspondent banking
2. Bilateral netting
3. CLS Bank
4. On Us with settlement risk

5. On Us without settlement risk
6. Other payment vs. payment systems

The relative volumes of transactions under the different methods are shown in Figure A6 and we discuss them further below.

Figure A6: Amount of foreign currency settled per day by settlement method (2006)

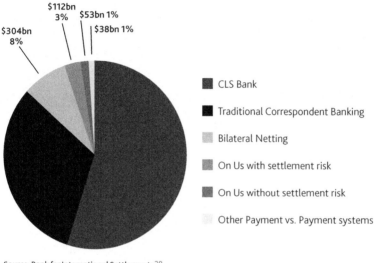

$112bn
3% $53bn 1%
$38bn 1%
$304bn
8%

- CLS Bank
- Traditional Correspondent Banking
- Bilateral Netting
- On Us with settlement risk
- On Us without settlement risk
- Other Payment vs. Payment systems

Source: Bank for International Settlements[28]

A3.2.1.
Traditional correspondent banking

Traditional correspondent banking is, as its name suggests, the traditional method for settling forex transactions. It is also known as gross non-payment versus payment settlement, or a non-PVP method. In 2006, it settled around 32 per cent of all forex transactions, or $1,224 billion a day (Figure A6). This is down from 87 per cent of all forex trades settled in 1997.[29] To understand why traditional correspondent banking has declined, we must first understand how it works.

Imagine Royal Bank of Scotland (RBS) engages in a spot trade with HSBC, in which it is selling yen for US dollars. Furthermore imagine that neither HSBC nor RBS have access to either the American or Japanese payment system, i.e. neither of them has an account with the US central bank, the Federal Reserve, or the Bank of Japan. However, HSBC has a bank account with a Japanese Bank that has access to the Japanese payment system, as well as an account with an American Bank that has

---

* A bank account that one bank holds for another bank is often called a 'nostro' account, and the bank holding the nostro account is often referred to as a nostro bank.

Figure A7: Foreign exchange using correspondent banking

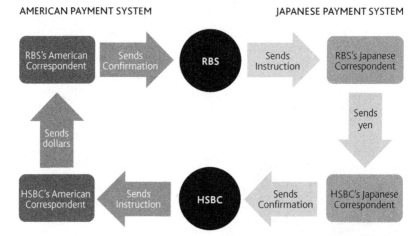

access to the American payment system. These are HSBC's 'correspondent banks'. RBS also has correspondent banks in both America and Japan (Figure A7).

After RBS and HSBC strike the trade, RBS sends an instruction to its correspondent in Japan, asking the latter to send the yen to HSBCs correspondent there. RBS's Japanese correspondent executes this instruction by debiting the account that RBS holds with it and sending the yen to HSBCs Japanese correspondent via the Japanese payment system. After HSBC's Japanese correspondent has received the funds, it credits them to HSBC's account and informs HSBC that they have arrived.

In parallel, HSBC settles its side of the trade by a similar process in which it instructs its correspondent in the United States (HSBC USA) to send US dollars to RBS's American correspondent.[30]

There are major risks involved in using traditional correspondent banking to settle forex transactions, one of which is 'Herstatt risk' (a form of settlement risk). Herstatt risk is the risk that one party to a forex trade pays out the currency it has sold, but does not receive the currency it has bought. Its name comes from the Herstatt Bank, which was forced into liquidation on 26 June 1974 by German regulators, because of a lack of income and capital to cover liabilities that were due. Before being closed, Herstatt Bank had received payments of Deutsche Marks which it had arranged to exchange for dollars (which were to be paid out by Herstatt's US correspondent bank) when the American payment system opened. However, the bank was closed before the American payment system opened, and thus the dollars were never sent. Therefore Herstatt risk occurs primarily due to problems in co-ordinating the timing of the payment of two currencies in different payment systems.

A3.2.2.
Bilateral netting

Bilateral netting is a variant on traditional correspondent banking and helps to limit settlement risk and credit risk. Rather than settle the gross value of all payments between two banks, netting arrangements permit banks to offset trades against each other so that only the net amount in each currency is paid or received by each institution. At the end of an agreed time period (usually a day), each counterparty will make a single payment to the other counterparty in each of the currencies in which it has a net debt and receive payment in each of the currencies in which it has a net credit. This is particularly useful when two counterparties transact or plan to transact forex regularly.[31]

A3.2.3.
Payment versus payment systems: the case of CLS Bank

The primary reason for the decline in traditional correspondent banking (non-PVP) is the advent of payment versus payment (PVP) systems such as Continuous Linked Settlement (CLS) Bank. PVP systems eliminate Herstatt risk by ensuring that both parties have paid into a third party account before either bank receives payment.

The CLS Bank was launched in 2002 by 70 of the world's leading financial service institutions. Since then it has become the largest forex settlement system with a 58 per cent market share of global forex trading activity by value in 2010 (up from 55 per cent in 2006). However, CLS Bank currently only settles in 17 currencies* – for these currencies their market share is 68 per cent.[32] The CLS Bank was created primarily to eliminate Herstatt risk. It does this by using a PVP system which settles both sides of a forex trade simultaneously.

CLS works in a similar way to traditional correspondent banking, but with an additional step[33,34]. For CLS to work each member of CLS has to have a single multi-currency account with CLS Bank, and CLS must maintain an account with each of the 17 central banks for which it provides currency settlement services. In the UK CLS bank is a member of CHAPS and therefore CLS Bank International has a settlement account within the Bank of England's RTGS system (see Section 4.6, Box 9).[35]

After RBS and HSBC strike the trade, RBS sends an instruction to its correspondent in Japan, asking the latter to send the yen to HSBC's CLS account. RBS's Japanese correspondent executes this instruction by debiting the account that RBS holds with it and sending the yen to HSBC's CLS account via the

---

* These are: US Dollar, Euro, UK Pound, Japanese Yen, Swiss Franc, Canadian Dollar, Australian Dollar, Swedish Krona, Danish Krone, Norwegian Krone, the Singapore Dollar, the Hong Kong Dollar, the New Zealand Dollar, the Korean Won, the South African Rand, the Israeli Shekel and the Mexican Peso.

Japanese payment system. In parallel, HSBC settles its side of the trade by a similar process in which it instructs its correspondent in the United States to send US dollars to RBS's CLS account.

Once CLS receives RBS's yen payment in its Japanese reserve account at the Bank of Japan and HSBC's dollar payment in its reserve account at the US Federal Reserve, it completes the transaction by sending dollars to RBS's American correspondent and yen to HSBC's American correspondent. Herstatt risk is eliminated as CLS waits till it receives both RBS's yen and HSBC's dollars of funds before paying out.

If either bank fails to pay the money into CLS, then CLS can simply return the money of the bank that did pay in. However, this may not be necessary, as CLS Bank also has committed standby lines of credit with major banks for each currency it settles. Therefore, in Figure A7, if RBS fails to pay in yen (e.g. due to a lack of liquidity), CLS can simply take HSBC's dollars, exchange them for yen with its standby bank in Japan, then give this yen to HSBC. In this way Herstatt risk is eliminated and liquidity risk has been reduced (although not eliminated as the standby banks credit lines are finite).[36]

This example is simplified. In reality, banks submit huge numbers of payment instructions each day, although crucially all the payment instructions must be received by CLS before 6:30am Central European Time (CET) (see Figure A8). By requiring banks to submit their payment instructions before they have to pay in, CLS can net these amounts against each other. For example, a bank may have arranged several forex transactions with various counterparties, and as a result submits pay instructions to CLS totalling £20 million. However, as a result of another set of forex trades it is scheduled to receive pay outs totalling £19 million. Thus, by determining the funding requirements of each bank on a 'multilaterally netted basis', the bank in question is required to pay in just £1 million. In reality the savings are much bigger. For every $1 trillion of value settled only $50 billion is required in liquidity – a 95 per cent reduction in funding requirements. In addition, netting also reduces the in-payments by 99.75 per cent, with an average of only 26 payments per day regardless of the value of the payments.[37]

A3.3.4.
On Us, with and without risk

On Us settlement refers to forex settlement where both legs of the forex trade are conducted on the books of a single institution. This requires a bank to be a member of both countries' payment systems for the currencies in which it is settling. As such it does not require any movement of money between banks, as the bank simply debits and credits the relevant accounts in each country. There are two forms of On Us:

1. Without settlement risk: Where the crediting of currency to the selling account is conditional on the debiting of currency from the buying account, for instance because both the buy and sell accounts are credited and debited simultaneously.

2. With settlement risk: Where the crediting of currency to the selling account is not conditional on the debiting of currency from the buying account. This could be due to the relevant RTGS systems not being open at the same time, forcing one party to the transaction to pay in first.[38]

A3.3.5.
Other payment versus payment settlement methods

CLS Bank is not the only PVP system. Hong Kong has local RTGS systems in Hong Kong Dollars (HKD), US dollars (USD) and Euros. In September 2000 the Hong Kong Dollar and US dollar RTGS systems were linked together. This was followed by linking the Euro RTGS system to the HKD and USD system in April 2003. Finally, in November 2006, this system was linked to Malaysia's Ringgit RTGS system.

The system works in the following way. The two parties to a forex transaction simply submit their payment instructions to the RTGS system, using a code to identify to the RTGS system that the payments are for PVP settlement. Once both instructions are matched against each other and the funds are available for settlement, the two RTGS systems will pay out each currency simultaneously, thus eliminating Herstatt risk.

Figure A8: CLS Bank operational timeline

Ongoing submission of instructions	Settlement cycle		Funding (Pay-In and Pay-Out processes)
up to 06:30 CET	07:00 – 09:00 CET		09:00 – 12:00 CET
	Funding and settlement takes place during a five-hour window when the opening times of the relevant RTGS systems overlap and are open to send and receive funds.		
Submit instructions	Funding and Settlement	Execution	Funding (Pay-In and Pay-Out processes)
Settlement Members submit instructions directly to the CLS system for matching. Instructions can be submitted up to 06:30 Central European Time (CET)* for each settlement date.\n\nAt 06:30 CET each Settlement Member receives its final net pay-in schedule for the day.	Settlement Members pay in net funds based on the 06:30 CET schedule to the CLS Bank account at the relevant central bank.\n\nCLS Bank settles each pair of matched payment instructions individually on a gross basis.\n\nFunding and settlement processing begins at 07:00 CET.	Between 07:00 and 09:00 CET, CLS Bank continuously receives funds from Settlement Members, settles instructions across its books and pays out funds to Settlement Members until settlement is complete. Instructions that cannot immediately settle remain in the queue and are continually revisited.\n\nSettlement is normally completed by 08:30 CET.	The funding and payout process continues until 10:00 CET for Asia-Pacific currencies and until 12:00 CET for European and North American currencies.\n\nBetween 09:00 and 12:00 CET the pay-ins and pay-outs are completed. All funds will have been disbursed back to eligible Settlement Members by 12:00 CET, ensuring the efficient use of liquidity.

The CLS operational timeline applies to CLS Settlement Members only. User Members and third parties settling in CLS may operate by a different funding timeline as agreed with their Settlement Member.

• The agreed best practice is to settle same day instructions outside CLS after 00:00 CET

Reproduced from CLS Bank. About us. Retrievable from: http://www.cls-group.com/Publications/CLS%20

References

1   Clews, R., Salmon, C, Weeken, O., (2010). The Bank's money market framework. *Bank of England Quaterly Bulletin*. Q4: 292–301, p. 293

2   Mac Gorain, S. (2005). Stabilising short-term interest rates, *Bank of England Quarterly Bulletin*, Q4: 2005

3   Fisher, P. (2011). *Recent developments in the sterling monetary framework*. London: Bank of England, p. 9. available online at http://www.bankofengland.co.uk/publications/Documents/speeches/2011/speech487.pdf

4   Chart reproduced from speech by: Fisher (2011). *op. cit.*

5   Tucker, P. (2004). Managing the central bank's balance sheet: where monetary policy meets financial stability. *Bank of England Quarterly Bulletin*, Q3: 2004 pp. 369-382.

6   *Ibid.* p.367.

7   Chart reproduced from speech by: Fisher (2011). *op. cit.*

8   HM Government, *Consolidated Fund Account 2009-10*, p. 2. Retrievable at http://www.official-documents.gov.uk/document/hc1011/hc04/0406/0406.pdf

9   Adapted from presentation by Riddington, T. (2007). *UK Government Accounts: The Exchequer Pyramid*. London: DMO.

10 HM Treasury. (2010). *National Loans Fund Account 2009-10*. London: The Stationery Office p. 2. available online at http://www.official-documents.gov.uk/document/hc1011/hc04/0409/0409.pdf

11 *Ibid.* p.2

12 DMO. (2004). *A guide to the roles of the Debt Management Office and Primary Dealers in the UK Government bond market*. London: DMO, p.26, para 124.

13 HM Treasury (2011), *Debt and Reserves Management Report 2010-2011*, p. 28. London: HM Treasury. available online at http://cdn.hm-treasury.gov.uk/2011budget_debtreserves.pdf

14 *Ibid.* p.22, para 108.

15 National Audit Office. (2009). *Government cash management*. Appendices 2–8. Retrievable from http://www.nao.org.uk/publications/0809/cash_management.aspx

16 *Ibid.* p.14.

17 United Kingdom Debt Management Office (2012), *Annual Report and Accounts 2011-2012 of the United Kingdom Debt Management Office and the Debt Management Account*, Debt Management Account Statement of financial position, p. 90. London: HM Treasury. available online at http://www.official-documents.gov.uk/document/hc1213/hc04/0458/0458.pdf

18 HM Treasury. (2011). *UK Official holdings of international reserves*. London: HM Treasury. Retrievable from http://www.hm-treasury.gov.uk/d/pn_37_11.pdf

19 HM Treasury. *Exchange Equalisation Account:* Report and Accounts 2009-10. London: HM Treasury, para 6.

20 *Ibid.*, para 1.

21 *Ibid.*, para 18.

22 HM Treasury (2012), *Exchange Equalisation Account: Report and Accounts 2011-12*, Statement of Financial Position, p. 24. London: HM Treasury. available online at http://www.hm-treasury.gov.uk/d/eea_accounts_201112.pdf

23 *Ibid.*, para 54.

24 *Ibid.*, paras 2 and 3.

25 HM Treasury (2010). *Exchange Equalisation Account: Report and Accounts 2009-10*, para 16. London: HM Treasury. available online http://www.hm-treasury.gov.uk/d/eea_accounts_200910.pdf

26 HM Treasury, Letter to the Governor on the new Monetary Policy Framework, retrievable from http://www.bankofengland.co.uk/monetarypolicy/Documents/pdf/chancellorletter970506.pdf [accessed 4th March 2013]

27 The Bank of England. (Market Notice). Retrieved from http://www.bankofengland.co.uk/markets/reserves/marketnotice110228.pdf

28 Bank for International Settlements. (2008). *Committee on Payment and Settlement Systems. Progress in reducing foreign exchange settlement risk.* BIS - Monetary and Economic Department, p.5.

29 Lindley, R. (2008). Reducing foreign exchange settlement risk. *BIS Quarterly Review September 2008* p.56.

30 Lindley, R. (2008). *op. cit.* p.55. .

31 Bank for International Settlements. (2000) *Supervisory Guidance for Managing Settlement Risk in Foreign Exchange Transactions.*, Basel: BIS - Monetary and Economic Department, p.11.

32 CLS. (2011). *CLS market share report.* February 2011 p.1.

33 Bank of England. (2003). *Strengthening financial infrastructure – Financial Stability Review: June 2003.* London: Bank of England, p. 81.

34 Bank of England. (2011). *Payment Systems Oversight Report 2010, March 2011.* London: Bank of England, p. 17.

35 Bank of England. (2009). *The Bank of England's oversight of interbank payment systems under the Banking Act 2009.* London: Bank of England, p. 8.

36 Lindley (2008). *op. cit.*

37 CLS Bank. (n.d.). *About us.* Retrieved from http://www.cls-group.com/Publications/CLS About Us.pdf

38 Bank for International Settlements. (2008). *Committee on Payment and Settlement Systems. Progress in reducing foreign exchange settlement risk.* Basel: BIS – Monetary and Economic Department, p.23.

BIBLIOGRAPHY

Alessandri, P., and Haldane, A. G. (2009). *Banking on the State*, presentation delivered to the Federal Reserve Bank of Chicago twelfth annual International Banking Conference

Bank for International Settlements (2003). *The role of central bank money in payments systems*, Basel: Bank for International Settlements. Retrievable from http://www.bis.org/publ/cpss55.pdf

Bank for International Settlements (2008). *BIS Quarterly Review*. Basel: BIS - Monetary and Economic Department

Bank for International Settlements (2008). *Committee on Payment and Settlement Systems. Progress in reducing foreign exchange settlement risk*. Basel: BIS - Monetary and Economic Department

Bank for International Settlements (2010). *Supervisory Guidance for Managing Settlement Risk in Foreign Exchange Transactions.*, Basel: BIS - Monetary and Economic Department

Bank for International Settlements (2010). *Triennial Central Bank Survey of Foreign Exchange and Over-The-Counter Interest Rate Derivatives Market Activity in April 2010*. Basel: BIS - Monetary and Economic Department

Bank of England (2003). *Strengthening financial infrastructure – Financial Stability Review: June 2003*. London: Bank of England. Retrievable from http://www.bankofengland.co.uk/publications/psor/index.htm

Bank of England (2009). The Bank of England's oversight of interbank payment systems under the Banking Act 2009. London: Bank of England

Bank of England (2011). *Market Notice 110228*. Retrievable from http://www.bankofengland.co.uk/markets/reserves/marketnotice110228.pdf

Bank of England (2011). *Payment Systems Oversight Report 2010*. London: Bank of England

Bank of England (2011). *Trends in Lending*. London: Bank of England. Retrievable from http://www.bankofengland.co.uk/publications/other/monetary/trendsinlending2011.htm

Barro, R. and Grossman, H., (1976). *Money, Employment and Inflation*. Cambridge: Cambridge University Press

Berry, S., Harrison, R., Thomas, R. and de Weymarn, I., (2007). Interpreting Movements in Broad Money. *Bank of England Quarterly Bulletin* 2007 Q3, p. 377. Retrievable from http://www.bankofengland.co.uk/publications/quarterlybulletin/qb070302.pdf

Blanchard, O. and Fischer, I., (1989). *Lectures on Macro-economics*, Cambridge, MA: MIT Press

Bundesbank (2009). *Geld und Geldpolitik*, as cited and translated by Werner, R.A. (2009). Topics in Monetary Economics, Lecture Slides for Master in Money and Finance. Frankfurt: Goethe University

Burgess, S. and Janssen, N., (2007). Proposals to modify the measurement of broad money in the United Kingdom: A user-consultation. *Bank of England Quarterly Bulletin* 2007 Q3, p. 402. Retrieved from http://www.bankofengland.co.uk/publications/quarterlybulletin/qb070304.pdf

Carruthers, B. G., (1996). *City of Capital*. Princeton: Princeton University Press

Carruthers, B. G., (2005). The Sociology of Money and Credit. In Smelser, N. J., Swedberg, R. (eds). *The Handbook of Economic Sociology*, 2nd Edition, Princeton: Russell Sage Foundation

Chen, Y. and Werner, R.A., (2010). *The Monetary Transmission Mechanism in China*. Centre for Banking, Finance and Sustainable Development Discussion Paper. Southampton: School of Management, University of Southampton

Choudhri, E. and Kochin, L.A., (1980). *The Exchange Rate and the International Transmission of Business Cycle Disturbances: Some Evidence from the Great Depression.* Journal of Money, Credit and Banking **12:** 565–574

Clews, R., Salmon, C. and Weeken, O., (2010). *The Bank's money market framework.* Bank of England Quarterly Bulletin Q4: 292–301

Clower, R, (1967). A reconsideration of the microfoundations of money. *Western Economics Journal.* Retrieved from http://www.carlostrub.ch/sites/default/files/Clower1967.pdf

CLS Bank (n.d.). *About us.* Retrievable from http://www.cls-group.com/Publications/CLS%20 About%20Us.pdf

CLS Bank (2011). *CLS market share report,* February 2011

Cobbett, W., (1828). *Paper Against Gold.* New York: John Doyle

Credit Suisse (2009). *Market Focus - Long Shadows: Collateral Money, Asset Bubbles and Inflation.* Fixed Income Research, **Market Focus,** May 5, 2009

Croome, D. R., Johnson and G. J. (eds), (1970). *Money in Britain 1959–69: The papers of the 'Radcliffe report – ten years after' conference at Hove, Sussex,* October 1969. London: Oxford University Press

Davies, G., (2002). *A History of Money.* Cardiff: University of Wales Press

Davies, R., Richardson, P., Katinatire, V. and Manning, M., (2010). Evolution of the UK Banking System. *Bank of England Quarterly Bulletin* **4:** 321–332. Retrievable from http://www.bankofengland. co.uk/publications/quarterlybulletin/qb1004.pdf

Debt Management Office (2004). *A Guide to the Roles of the Debt Management Office and Primary Dealers in the UK Government bond market.* London: DMO

Dodd, N., (1994). *The Sociology of Money,* Cambridge: Polity Press

Eichengreen, B.J., (2008). *Globalizing capital: a history of the international monetary system.* Princeton University Press; 2nd edition

Eichengreen, B. and Sachs, J., (1985). Exchange Rates and Economic Recovery in the 1930s. *Journal of Economic History* **45:** 925–946

El Diwany, T. (2003). *The Problem with Interest,* 2nd Edition. London: Kerotac

ESCP Europe / Cobden Centre, (June 2010). *Public attitudes to banking.* Retrievable from www. cobdencentre.org

Febrero Eladio (2009). Three difficulties with neo-chartalism. *Journal of Post Keynesian Economics.* N York: M.E. Sharpe, Inc. **31(3):** 523–541

Ferguson, N., (2008). *The Ascent of Money: A Financial History of the World.* London: Penguin

Financial Times (5 August 2011). *Market Unimpressed by ECB action.* Retrievable from http://www. ft.com/cms/s/0/fc04a956-bf71-11e0-898c-00144feabdc0.html#ixzz1ULKrwIT9 [accessed 6 August 2011]

Financial Times. (15 February 2011). *Liquidity gap yawns at new reserves clause.* Retrievable from http://www.ft.com/cms/s/0/a75dbab2-385a-11e0-959c-00144feabdc0.html#axzz1MM2xlhBr [accessed 14 May 2011]

Friedman, M., (1963). *Inflation: Causes and Consequences.* New York: Asia Publishing House

BIBLIOGRAPHY

Galbraith, J. K., (1975). *Money: Whence it came, Where it Went.* London: Penguin

Geithner, T. F., (June 2008). *Reducing systemic risk in a dynamic financial system.* Remarks at the Economic Club of New York, New York

Goodhart, C.A.E., (1975). *Monetary Relationships: A View from Threadneedle Street.* Papers in Monetary Economics. Syndey: Reserve Bank of Australia

Goodhart, C.A.E., (1989). Has Moore become too horizontal? *Journal of Post-Keynesian Economics* **14:** 134–136

Gorton, G. and Metrick, A., (2010). *Regulating the shadow banking system.* London: Social Science Research Network

Graeber, D., (2011). *Debt: The First 5000 years.* New York: Melville House Publishing

Grierson, P., (1977). *The Origins of Money.* London: Athlone Press

Hahn, F. and Brechling, F.P.R. (eds), (1965). *Theory of Interest Rates: proceedings of a conference held by the International Economic Association.* London: Macmillan

Harvey, D., (2006/1982). *The Limits of Capital.* London: Verso

Hayek, F., (2008/1931). *Prices and Production.* Auburn, Alabama: Ludwig von Mises Institute, p. 289. Retrievable from http://mises.org/books/hayekcollection.pdf [accessed 6 June 2011].

HM Government (2010). *Consolidated Fund Account 2009-10.* Retrievable from www.official-documents.gov.uk/document/hc1011/hc04/0406/0406.pdf

HM Treasury (2011). *UK Official holdings of international reserves.* London: HM Treasury. Retrievable from http://www.hm-treasury.gov.uk/d/pn_37_11.pdf

HM Treasury (2010). *Exchange Equalisation Account: Report and Accounts 2009-10.* London: HM Treasury

Huber, J. and Robertson, J., (2000). *Creating New Money: A Monetary reform for the information age.* London: **nef** (the new economics foundation)

Huerta de Soto (2006/1998). *Money, Credit and Economic Cycles*, 2nd English edition, Auburn, Alabama: Ludwig von Mises Institute

Independent Commission on Banking (2010). *Interim paper: Consultation on reform options*, p.16, paragraph 8. Retrievable from http://s3-eu-west-1.amazonaws.com/htcdn/Interim-Report-110411.pdf [accessed 22 August 2011]

Independent Commission on Banking (2010). *Issues Paper: Call for Evidence*, pp.144–5. Retrievable from http://bankingcommission.independent.gov.uk/wp-content/uploads/2010/07/Issues-Paper-24-September-2010.pdf [accessed 22 August 2011]

Ingham, G., (2004). *The Nature of Money.* Cambridge: Polity Press

Ingham, G., (2008). *Capitalism.* Cambridge: Polity Press

Innes, A.M., (1913). What is Money? *Banking Law and Journal.* **May:** 377–408.

Jenkinson, N., (2008). *Strengthening Regimes for Controlling Liquidity Risk: Some Lessons from the Recent Turmoil.* Speech given at the Euromoney Conference on Liquidity and Funding Risk Management. Hyatt Regency. London, 24 April 2008

BIBLIOGRAPHY

Jevons, W. S., (1896/75). *Money and the Mechanism of Exchange*. New York: Appleton and Company

Keynes, J. M., (1930). *A Treatise on Money: Vol 1, A Pure Theory of Money*

Keynes, J. M., (2008/1936). *The General Theory of Employment, Interest and Money*. BN Publishing

King, M., (1994). The transition mechanism of monetary policy. *Bank of England Quarterly Bulletin*, August 1994, p. 264. Retrieved from http://www.bankofengland.co.uk/publications/quarterlybulletin/qb940301.pdf

Knapp, G. F., (1905). *The State Theory of Money*. London: Macmillan

Lapavitsas, C., (2005). The emergence of money in commodity exchange, or money as monopolist of the ability to buy. *Review of Political Economy* **17(4):** 549–569

Leyshon, A., Thrift, N., (1997). *Money / Space: Geographies of Monetary Transformation*. Routledge: London

Lindley, R., (2008). *Reducing foreign exchange settlement risk*. BIS Quarterly Review, p. 56

Lyonnet, V., and Werner, R. A., (2012). Lessons from the Bank of England on 'quantitative easing' and other 'unconventional' monetary policies. *International Review of Financial Analysis*, Volume 25, December 2012, pp. 94-105

MacGorain, S., (2005). Stabilising short-term interest rates, *Bank of England Quarterly Bulletin*, Q4: 2005

Malinvaud, E., (1977). *The Theory of Unemployment Reconsidered*. Oxford: Basil Blackwell

Marshall, A., (1996/1899). Evidence to the Indian Currency Committee in Marshall, A. (n.d.). *Correspondence of Alfred Marshall, Economist. Vol: II, 1891–1902 at the Summit*. Cambridge: Cambridge University Press

Marx, K., (1894). *Capital. Volume III*, part V, Chapter 29. Harmondsworth: Penguin. Retrievable from http://www.marxists.org/archive/marx/works/1894-c3/ch29.htm

Marx, K., (1976/1867). *Capital. Volume. I*. Harmondsworth: Penguin

McKenna, R., (1928). *Post-war Banking Policy*. p. 93

Mellor, M., (2010). *The Future of Money: From Financial Crisis to Public Resource*. London: Pluto Press

Menger, C., (1892). On the Origins of Money. *Economic Journal* **2:** 239–255

Mill, J. S., (1871/48). *Principles of Political Economy*. London; Longmans, Green and Co

Minsky, H.P., (2008/1986). *Stabilizing an Unstable Economy*. Yale: McGrawhill

Monetary Policy Committee and Bank of England (1999). *The Transmission mechanism of monetary policy*. London: Bank of England. Retrievable from http://www.bankofengland.co.uk/publications/Documents/other/monetary/montrans.pdf

Mosler, W., (2010). *Seven Deadly Innocent Frauds of Economic Policy*. US Virgin Islands: Valance Co.

Mullbauer, J. and Portes, R., (1978). Macro-economic models with quantity rationing. *Economic Journal* **88:** 788–821

National Audit Office, (2009). *Government cash management*. Appendices 2–8. Retrievable from http://www.nao.org.uk/publications/0809/cash_management.aspx [accessed 3 August 2011]

Nichols, D. M., (1992/1961). *Modern Money Mechanics: A workbook on Bank Reserves and Deposit Expansion*. Chicago: Federal Reserve Bank of Chicago. Retrieved from http://www.archive.org/stream/ModernMoneyMechanics/MMM#page/n1/mode/2up [accessed 29 April 2011].

Office of Fair Trading, (2008). *Personal Current Accounts in the UK*, p. 17. Retrievable from http://www.oft.gov.uk/shared_oft/reports/financial_products/OFT1005.pdf

Pettifor, A., (2006). *The Coming First Wold Debt Crisis*. London: Palgrave Macmillan

Pigou, A. C., (1949). *The Veil of Money*. London: Macmillan

Pressnell, L.S., (1956). *Country Banking in the Industrial Revolution*. Oxford: University Press / Clarendon Press

Radford, R. A., (1945). The Economic Organisation of a POW Camp. *Econometrica*, Volume 12

Reinhart, C. M., Rogoff, K, S., (2009). *This Time is Different: Eight Centuries of Financial Folly*. Princeton: Woodstock

Riddington, T., (2007). *UK Government Accounts: The Exchequer Pyramid*. London: DMO

Rothbard, M., (1974). *The Case for a 100 Percent Gold Dollar*. Washington, DC: Libertarian Review Press

Rowbotham, M., (1998). *The Grip of Death*. Oxford: John Carpenter Publishing

Schumpeter, J., (1994/1954). *History of Economic Analysis*, New York: Oxford University Press

Sidrauski, M., (1967). Rational choice and patterns of growth in a monetary economy. *American Economic Review* **57**(2): 534–544

Simmel, G., (2004/1907). *The Philosophy of Money*, 3rd Edition. London: Routledge

Singh, M., Aitken, J., (2010). *The (sizable) role of re-hypothecation in the shadow banking system*. IMF working paper, WP/10/172. Washington: IMF

Stigler, G., (1967). Imperfections in the Capital Market. *Journal of Political Economy*. June 1967, 85: 287-92

Stiglitz, J., Weiss, A., (1981). Credit rationing in markets with imperfect information. *American Economic Review* 71: 393–410

Thiel, V., (2009). *Doorstep Robbery*. London: **nef**

Tucker, P. (2004). Managing the central bank's balance sheet: where monetary policy meets financial stability. *Bank of England Quarterly Bulletin* Q3: 364

Tucker, P., (2008). Money and Credit: Banking and the macro-economy. Speech given at the monetary policy and markets conference, 13 December 2007 *Bank of England Quarterly Bulletin* 2008, Q1: 96–106. Retrieved from http://www.bankofengland.co.uk/publications/speeches/2007/speech331.pdf

Turner, A., (2011). *Reforming finance: are we being radical enough?* Clare Distinguished Lecture in Economics and Public Policy, 18 February 2011 Clare College: Cambridge

Voutsinas, K., Werner, R.A., (2011a). *New Evidence on the Effectiveness of Quantitative Easing in Japan*. Centre for Banking, Finance and Sustainable Development Discussion Paper. Southamption: University of Southampton, School of Management

Walker D., (ed.) *Money and Markets*, Cambridge: Cambridge University Press

Walras, L., (1954/1874). *Elements of Pure Economics*. London: Allen & Unwin

Werner, R. A., (1995a). *Liquidity Watch report*, Tokyo: Jardine Fleming Securities

Werner, R. A., (1995b). *Keiki kaifuku, ryōteki kinyū kanwa kara, (How to Create a Recovery through 'Quantitative Monetary Easing')*, The Nihon Keizai Shinbun (Nikkei), 'Keizai Kyōshitsu' ('Economics Classroom'). 2 September 1995 (morning edition), p. 26; English translation by T. John Cooke (November 2011). Retrievable from http://eprints.soton.ac.uk/340476/

Werner, R. A., (1998). *Bank of Japan window guidance and the creation of the bubble*, in Rodao, F. and A. Lopez Santos (eds.), *El Japon Contemporaneo*. Salamanca: University of Salamanca Press

Werner, R. A., (1997). Towards a new monetary paradigm: A quantity theorem of disaggregated credit, with evidence from Japan. *Kredit und Kapital* Vol: 276–239. Retrievable from http://eprints.soton.ac.uk/36569/

Werner, R. A., (2003). *Princes of the Yen, Japan's Central Bankers and the Transformation of the Economy*. New York: M. E. Sharpe

Werner, R. A., (2002). Monetary Policy Implementation in Japan: What They Say vs. What they Do. *Asian Economic Journal*. Volume 16, no.2. Oxford: Blackwell, pp. 111-151

Werner, R. A., (2005). *New Paradigm in Macro-economics*. Basingstoke: Palgrave Macmillan

Werner, R. A., (2009). *Can credit unions create credit? An analytical evaluation of a potential obstacle to the growth of credit unions*. Discussion Paper Series, No. 2/09. Southampton: Centre for Banking, Finance and Sustainable Development, University of Southampton

Werner, R. A., (2010). *Comment: Range of Methodologies for Risk and Performance Alignment of Remuneration*. Submission to the Basel Committee on Banking Supervision, 31 December 2010. Retrievable from http://www.bis.org/publ/bcbs178/richardwerner.pdf

Werner, R. A., (2010a). *Comment: Strengthening the Resilience of the Banking Sector*. Submission to the Basel Committee on Bank Supervision, April 2010. Retrievable from http://www.bis.org/publ/bcbs165/universityofsou.pdf

Werner, R. A., (2010b). Comment: A simple rule is needed to prevent future banking crises. Letter to the Editor, *Financial Times*, 17 November 2010

Werner, R. A., (2011). Economics as if Banks Mattered – A Contribution Based on the Inductive Methodology. *Manchester School*, Volume 79. September, pp. 25–35. doi: 10.1111/j.1467-9957.2011.02265_5.x

Werner, R. A., (2012), Towards a New Research Programme on 'Banking and the Economy' – Implications of the Quantity Theory of Credit for the Prevention and Resolution of Banking and Debt. *International Review of Financial Analysis (In Press)*.

Withers, H., (1909). *The Meaning of Money*. London: Smith and Elder

World Bank, (1993). *The East Asian Miracle, Economic Growth and Public Policy*. Oxford: Oxford University Press

Wray, L. R., (1998). *Understanding Modern Money: The Key to Full Employment and Price Stability*. Cheltenham: Edward Elgar

THIS PAGE IS INTENTIONALLY LEFT BLANK

ABOUT THE AUTHORS

Josh Ryan-Collins is a Senior Researcher at **nef** (the new economics foundation) where he is leading a programme of research on the history and practice of monetary systems. He is studying for a PhD in finance at the University of Southampton.

Tony Greenham is Head of Finance and Business at **nef**. He is a former investment banker, a Chartered Accountant and regular writer and media commentator on banking reform.

Professor Richard Werner is Director of the Centre for Banking, Finance and Sustainable Development at the University of Southampton and author of two best-selling books on banking and economics. He is credited with popularising the term 'quantitative easing' in 1994 whilst Chief Economist at Jardine Fleming Securities (Asia), following a spell as visiting research fellow at the Japanese Central Bank.

Andrew Jackson contributed to this book after graduating from the University of Sussex with an MSc in Development Economics. He is currently studying for a PhD in finance at the University of Southampton.

Printed in Great Britain
by Amazon

47666937R00106